The Call of Heaven:
Bro. Gino, Stigmatist

Rev. Robert J. Fox

CHRISTENDOM PUBLICATIONS
Crossroads Books
Route 3, Box 87
Front Royal, Virginia 22630

ISBN: 0-931888-06-9

LC Cat. Card No.: BX 4705.B957F7

NIHIL OBSTAT:
  Rev. Edward J. Berbusse, S.J., *Censor Deputatus*
  December 21, 1981

IMPRIMATUR:
  †Most Rev. Thomas J. Welsh
  Bishop of Arlington
  December 21, 1981

DEDICATION

The author dedicates this book to the Immaculate Heart of Mary, in thanksgiving for 25 years in the priesthood of Her Son, Our Lord and Savior, Jesus Christ.

I am all Yours and all that I have is Yours, O Most Loving, Jesus, through Mary, Your Holy Mother.

Cover illustration by Patrick Diemer.

Contents

"As the Father has loved me, so I have loved you. Live on in my love. You will live in my love if you keep my commandments, even as I have kept my Father's commandments and live in his love. All this I tell you that my joy may be yours and your joy may be complete." (John 15:9-11)

Author's Preface

The Call of Heaven contains the life and mission of Brother Gino Burresi, O.V.M., the Stigmatist of San Vittorino in Italy. The title, however, embraces more than the call which Heaven has given this Brother, who is a deacon of the Church. It embraces the call that heaven gave to the entire world, through three children at Fatima in 1917 when God's Mother announced: "God wishes to establish in the world devotion to my Immaculate Heart." The *Call of Heaven* then, is the call of God, the call of the Immaculate Heart of Mary, calling all of us back to her Son, back to the Gospels.

This volume represents the first extensive account of the stigmatist of San Vittorino. There has been a concentrated effort to avoid the sensational. At times the facts themselves are arresting, and while there have been no efforts to conceal the unusual, there has been a desire to relate the facts as objectively as possible.

When it was first suggested that a life of Brother Gino should be written, the question that needed to be answered was "Why?" The second question was "How will you develop it?"

"Why?" I answered that God does nothing for nothing. If the charisms of Brother Gino are authentic, then they are not for himself, and if his life and apostolate are so intimately wrapped up in the message of Fatima, and Fatima is for the world, then the facts ought not be hidden under a bushel basket. "No one lights a lamp to put it under a tub; they put it on the lamp-stand where it shines for everyone in the house. In the same way your light must shine in the sight of men, so that, seeing your good works, they may give the praise to your Father in heaven." (Matthew 5:15-16).

I was not certain my explanation sufficed so I continued by noting that the world today is lacking in faith. There is so much indifference, even complete lack of faith. Brother Gino is a sign of faith. Youth especially have been disillusioned. Youth need men of faith and love of God and fellow men to whom they can look. Youth, all men in fact, need a sign that says, "Look, this Catholic faith is for real. It is true. It is holy and apostolic. Besides, Brother Gino points not only to Jesus in the Holy Eucharist, and to the Madonna of Fatima, he points to the Holy Father, the Pope, and says, "Listen to him. Obey him. He speaks for Jesus."

"How will you develop his life?" The facts, of course. But more important must be the message behind the facts of his life: that God has chosen him for a particular apostolate. To simply write historical facts of the life of the stigmatist of San Vittorino, and to present them in a style of sensationalism, may well capture the interest of men for a time. But that would not be my purpose. Here is a man who seems to have grasped the message of Fatima as a reaffirmation of the Gospels. He appears to be living the consecration to Mary's Immaculate Heart. I should like to demonstrate for readers what can happen in their lives, too, if they consecrate themselves well to the Immaculate Heart of Mary and live that consecration.

Finally permission was granted to begin the work, and so I went to San Vittorino and was able to mix informally with the stigmatist in the shadows of the Sanctuary of Our Lady of Fatima which presently draws pilgrims from throughout the world and where miracles of grace take place in the conversion of souls, and where sometimes people are physically healed in a way that baffles science.

The wounds, the perfume, the passion of Holy Week: all are to be found in this book. Found too is the fact that those who have been influenced by Brother Gino no longer hang on to the mere facts of the wounds, the perfume, the unusual in his life. In fact, seminarians and priests who have lived with Brother Gino and have met him frequently over the years, sometimes find it difficult to understand the curious probings and seemingly excessive interest at times in the stigmata. "Is is not more important what he is in his efforts to do the will of God, to inspire others to conversion from sin, to prayer and sacrifice so as to become holy? Is it not more important that we ourselves become consecrated to the Immaculate Heart of Mary, living that consecration so as to live in the grace and holiness of God?"

I must answer "yes" to the above questions. When I first wrote on Brother Gino in the national Catholic press in the United States the interest among thousands was immediate. Some wanted to know every detail, almost as if there were some obligation requiring the revelation of every intimacy of his soul and person. Some form concepts about persons who have charisms almost as if they are God Himself and can dictate to God exactly what He should do on their behalf. Others would imagine that almost any question about events which only God could know, would bring an immediate infallible answer from one bearing the wound marks of Jesus Christ. Such fanatical reactions can arise among certain individuals who lose their perspective. Similarly, a stigmatist's every word may erroneously be embraced as if Scripture itself, and even these very words are often exaggerated or distorted, with legends developing which do not represent the true consecrated person of God who is simply trying to cooperate with God's graces.

The very persons who would demand every moment and detail of the life of a person God uses in a special way, would doubtlessly be shocked if intimate details of their own lives were requested. What needs to be remembered is that while a charism is not for oneself alone but for the sanctification of others, this does not mean the charism is merely to satisfy the curiosity of others; rather, it is to lead them to think, behave, change according to the mind of Jesus Christ. "After all, the depths of a man can only be known by his own spirit, not by any other man, and in the same way the depths of God can only be known by the Spirit of God....As scripture says:*Who can know the mind of the Lord, so who can teach him?* But we are those who have the mind of Christ." (I Cor. 2:11-12). "You must give up your old way of life; you must put aside your old self, which gets corrupted by following illusory desires. Your mind must be renewed by a spiritual revolution so that you can put on the new self that has been created in God's way, in the goodness and holiness of the truth " (Eph. 4:23-24). "In your minds you must be the same as Christ Jesus" (Phil. 2:5).

Holiness in each one of us does not consist then in simply running after reported apparitions or trying to convince others that miracles are taking place. Holiness is discovering and doing the will of God. "It is not those who say to me, 'Lord, Lord', who will enter the kingdom of heaven, but the person who does the will of my Father in heaven" (Mt. 7:21). It is little wonder that some thought to be close to God who have used their charisms for the sanctification of others, even reminding certain persons that they must change, throw off the old ways, put on the mind of Jesus Christ and become Christ-like, have been rejected by the same persons who sought their attentions. Not everyone who brushed close to Jesus became holy. Some had to face a more severe judgement because of it. "If I had not come, if I had not spoken to them, they would have been blameless; but as it is they have no excuse for their sin. Anyone who hates me hates my Father. If I had not performed such works among them as no one else has ever done, they would be blameless; but as it is, they have seen all this, and still they hate both me and my Father" (John 15:22-24).

Jesus spoke frankly, abruptly, to those who were self-righteous, unwilling to change.

> If God were your father, you would love me, since I have come here from God; yes, I have come from him; not that I came because I chose, no, I was sent, and by him. Do you know why you cannot take in what I say? It is because you are unable to understand my language. The devil is your father, and you prefer to do what your father wants. He was a murderer from the start; he was never grounded in the truth; there is no truth in him at all. (John 8:42-46)

Those then who come into contact with anyone obviously gifted with charism ought be willing to take the consequences since the purpose for which the gifts were given was to call others to sanctification, which may often require trimming and pruning, which can be painful as the truth can be painful to one's pride. Those who have come to San Vittorino and met Brother Gino with unwillingness to repent, or who have attempted to kiss the Brother's hand with decorated lips, or religious not identified with religious garb—these have often had to deal with a moment of truth.

At the same time, I have had to remind the Oblates of the Virgin Mary, the religious congregation to which Brother Gino belongs, that it appears God has given the stigmata, the perfume, the events of Holy Week as a sign of faith. There are thousands in the secular world living in paganism, atheism, and compromised Christianity who know neither Jesus Christ nor the dogmas of our Catholic faith and who have become confused in these modern times. Readers may not need the signs of the unusual in Brother Gino (and he certainly does not need them himself—he would prefer to live a normal life of holiness without the eyes of the world upon him) but even souls with devout faith often do not understand what consecration to the Immaculate Heart of Mary means. Hopefully this book, this life, will help eliminate that deficiency, and many more souls will discover the Secret of Her Heart.

No one is required by *divine* faith to accept the unusual happenings in the life of Brother Gino. Even when the Church has given its approbation to private revelations, such as Guadalupe, Lourdes or Fatima, no Catholic is bound to accept them on *divine* faith. However, for one who studies such approved apparitions from authentic sources and documents, it would be foolish not to place *human* faith in such authenticated apparitions. But I wish to stress that the Church—even local Church authority—has made no definitive pronouncement on the Sanctuary of San Vittorino, even as regards *human* faith.

Pope Benedict XIV once wrote of private revelations saying: "We have already said that those revelations, although approved of, ought not and cannot, receive from us any assent as embracing Catholic faith, but only human credence, in keeping with the rules of prudence, according to which the aforesaid revelations are probable and may be piously believed." The Pope was speaking of private revelations of holy persons, such as St. Bridget and St. Catherine of Siena.

The present book in itself should satisfactorily explain the difference between what we must hold through *divine* faith, and what we may piously accept with *human* faith. For those who find in the present volume inspiration, instruction, and perhaps a review of the faith, it is my prayer that their divine faith in the Most Blessed Trinity and in God the Son made flesh under the Heart of Mary by the overshadowing of the Holy Spirit will be enhanced.

Finally, in obedience to the decree of Pope Urban VIII, I declare that the graces and other seeming supernatural facts related in this book, rest on human interpretation alone, and I submit myself without reserve to the decisions of the Apostolic See.

*****

A note should be added. It was *not* the Oblates of the Virgin Mary that requested this book. I myself desired to make its contents widely known because, from response to the little I have written previously about Brother Gino, I have learned that people find his life deeply edifying, and I wish more souls to be helped in similar manner.

In view of this purpose and desire on my part, there was a certain necessity to project myself into the book, in order to protect Brother Gino and the Oblates of the Virgin Mary from difficulties owing to faulty reporting. We were dealing with matters of *human* faith about a *living* man, and I had an obligation to assume responsibility by reporting events specifically as I myself perceived them. On the other hand, to protect the reader, I have attempted to report nothing which cannot be documented from sources beyond my own perceptions.

Where more could have been said, such as regards bilocation, I have declined to do more than to assist the apostolate of Fatima, and not merely satisfy curiosity.

D. Alberto Cosme do Amaral, Bishop of Leiria-Fatima has summarized well the motivation for this book: "Lent and the Fatima message are identified in the same appeal to interior conversion, to change our lives, to return to the ways of love, with a love ever greater, a contemplative and crucified love." Brother Gino, in the author's opinion, lives a continuous Lent with a "crucified love".

The same Bishop of Leiria-Fatima said in a homily, at the same time while I was preparing this volume: "The lives of the Servants of God, Francisco and Jacinta, are unmistakably theocentric, like that of Francis of Assisi who roused the people of Umbria, its hills and valleys, with his cries: 'My God and my All! Love is not loved!'".

He continued: "Why are our souls not filled with the fervour of love like these children of the Serra de Aire? Why are we so half-hearted and calculating in our giving of ourselves? Why do we continue to keep aloof in our living the radical demands of the Gospel? If we do not do as they did, we shall not become citizens of the Kingdom of Heaven.

The Lenten and Fatima message are identified in the same appeal for penance and mortification, which means renunciation, privation, fasting, almsgiving, imitation of the suffering Jesus, in order to convert sinners and to help the needy.

"We can see," he said, "that the spirituality of the Servants of God, Francisco and Jacinta, is profoundly Trinitarian, rooted in the mystery of all mysteries, the Mystery of the Most Holy Trinity, revealed by the Angel in 1916. It is, at the same time,

Christological. For them, as for Christians of all time, Mary is the way which leads to Jesus, in the most direct and efficacious manner. In their love of Our Lady they learned to love Christ in the mystery of His Redemption and in the mystery of His Eucharistic presence. The Christ of the Cross, the Christ of the Host, polarized their hearts, their whole capacity for loving. Their spirituality is ecclesiological. The seers prayed and mortified themselves for the Holy Father. Jacinta never forgot that vision of the Vicar of Christ, in a very big house, kneeling by a table, with his head buried in his hands, weeping. Outside the house, there were many people, throwing stones, cursing him and using bad language....

"The spirituality of the seers", said Bishop Alberto Cosme do Amaral, "bears the mark and signs of authenticity; it is Trinitarian, Christological, contemplative and apostolic. In it are admirably expressed the mystery of Christ, the mystery of the Church, the mystery of Mary, illumined by the mystery of the Trinity, the source of all mysteries. It carries out, in favour of humanity, the trajectory of the Church, the community of salvation—from God to God, bearing with it the universe redeemed by the Blood of the Lord."

That spirituality I discovered in the life and mission of Brother Gino of San Vittorino. I now present it to my readers.

"I, the prisoner in the Lord, implore you therefore to lead a life worthy of your vocation...There is one Body, one Spirit, just as you were called into one and the same hope when you were called." (Ephesians 4:1-5)

Introduction

I first met Brother Gino Burresi, O.V.M., in October of the Holy Year 1975. The meeting was brief. The effect in my mind and others was indelible. As a matter of fact, pictures which I have seen of this reported stigmatist with a long black cape had not impressed me. He seemed aloof. Or was it a prejudice of mind carried over from seminary days when certain seminarians who wore those special long black capes seemed apart from the rest of the young men?

Brother Gino that early October morning was scheduled to depart for an annual vacation to his parents' home in Toscana about 300 kilometers from Rome. I was told this reported stigmatist would wait until I arrived around 9:00 in the morning. Young men studying for the holy priesthood at San Vittorino knew of me through the Catholic press and Brother Gino agreed to await our group before departing.

That Brother Gino would wait for us I found humbling. Most of my pilgrim group of 121 which had traveled to Fatima, Lourdes, Ars, Paray-le-Monial and finally to Rome that year did not express interest in the special side trip to San Vittorino. I was later told that some had heard this man could read souls and were afraid to go. "How foolish," I thought. "If this man is authentic, he will surely be Christ-like and should he find the need to tell me or others that the state of our souls leaves much to be desired it will be in the manner of the all-loving Christ. But concern had crossed my mind too..."

The moment arrived for Brother Gino to meet our group, hardly a fourth of the original group of pilgrims. We were told that under the circumstances only I was to speak to Brother Gino. He is an unusual man in the sense that he suffers much. The wounds are not a show-piece for the curious. If real, they are the signs of a man, it would seem, closely identified with Christ and Him crucified. "...The marks on my body are those of Jesus." (Gal. 6:17).

Brother Gino walked directly up to me. I bowed to kiss his hand and experienced the sweetest perfume, quite indescribable, a perfume that seems to penetrate the lungs and refresh the soul. This lay Brother, tall and straight, bent low in return, immediately and profoundly, to kiss my hand. I could sense he had a profound respect for the priesthood of Jesus Christ, even as found in this weak vessel of clay.

I told Brother Gino of my plans to organize a Fatima Youth Apostolate, the Cadets of Our Lady of Fatima. Our goal would be to use Fatima as a vehicle to reaffirm the Gospels, to teach and form youth in the fullness of Catholic faith, and a guideline would be undivided loyalty to our Holy Father, the Pope. Brother Gino whose gaze penetrated my eyes, searching, reaching, it seemed, into the depths of my soul, replied, "Do it and do it quickly. It is already almost too late." My former impression of this reported stigmatist now melted into a reverential respect in the face of humility and sanctity. I asked him regarding writing for the Catholic press, "Any advice for me?" He spoke softly, so softly one had to listen well to hear him speak. "Stick to the basics," was all he said.

Brother Gino is a man of few words. If he could, he would escape from the attention of the world to be alone with his Lord and the Madonna. But God has given him more than one charism and the will of God has been clearly expressed to him and with this he will not argue, be it to his liking or not. "Nevertheless, let your will be done, not mine" (Luke 22:42).

"Brother Gino, do you have any personal word for me?" The answer came swiftly, softly, unhesitatingly, "Be holy." It is the call he gives to all priests. His advice to me was to be no different. We need holy priests.

Constantly he reaches out to young men in whom he sees the potential of a priestly vocation. With these he is loving but firm. The weaknesses of contamination with the world must be trimmed away. In the raw material of the young man, and some not so young, there must take place the process of pruning, dying to all of self that is not Christ so as to form them into the Heart and Model of the Mother.

"My lover speaks; he says to me, 'Arise, my beloved, my beautiful one, and come! For see, the winter is past, the rains are over and gone. The flowers appear on the earth, the time of pruning the vines has come'..." (Song of Songs, 2:10-12). "I tell you, most solemnly, unless a wheat grain falls on the ground and dies, it remains only a single grain; but if it dies, it yields a rich harvest. Anyone who loves his life loses it; anyone who hates his life in this world will keep it for the eternal life. If a man serves me, he must follow me; wherever I am, my servant will be there, too" (John 12:24-26).

When, however painfully, there is finally formed a man of God, not worthy, but at least fit for ordination and to be a vessel of clay, pliable, bending to the will of God, and in whom the priesthood of Jesus Christ can touch souls, transform them, preach the Word of God, only then will men again see God's Word made flesh in holy priests of today.

"Be holy." His final words lingered in my mind as we followed this man with the wounds of Jesus in his body to the car which would take him the many kilometers away for a much needed rest and vacation. Our pilgrimage group gathered around the car. I decided secretly to give Brother Gino the priestly blessing. Immediately his right hand, covered with the black mittens which expose the fingers, rose to sign himself with the Sign of the Cross. The Rosary in the same hand with which he blessed himself could be seen. It was some minutes before the car departed. And I plead guilty to being the one to start the applause of our American pilgrims. Such attention directed to himself is not what Brother Gino desires. The spirit reminds me of one who went to Fatima expecting God's Mother Mary to say, "Here I am," but instead heard her say, pointing to the Eucharistic Jesus, "There *He* is."

Standing in the midst of the courtyard, looking toward the impoverished crypt Church and uncompleted Sanctuary that could not progress for lack of funds, I raised my hand to my face. The perfume of Brother Gino's wounds had transposed itself to my hand. Just then a lady came up very excited. "Father, I kissed his hand but I experienced no perfume." Another said, "Nor I". This, I was to learn later, invariably takes place with at least a few pilgrims in each group.

"Oh!, here, smell my hand and be satisfied." It still emitted the perfume of his hands. The first lady took my hand and shouted, "Now I smell it. Yes it is beautiful." The next lady who had failed to experience the perfume, "I too." I became engrossed in conversation, ignoring the pilgrims who had formed a line and one by one were smelling the perfume of Brother Gino that still lingered upon my hand. Suddenly I realized what was happening. Abruptly I pulled my hand back. What would the Oblate Fathers and seminarians who might be looking out the windows think? Surely it would seem that I was ridiculing Brother Gino. God forbid. Stepping onto the bus—more requests to smell the perfume. Not on your life. Yet I secretly experimented myself. It was still there and remained for some hours. Moreover, the rest of that October day, about every hour, but never when my mind was on Brother Gino, suddenly, although far removed from the lay brother, I would experience unmistakably the perfume of his wounds, penetrating to the lungs. Then it would be gone again, only to return when least expected.

About 2:00 p.m. that same afternoon, I was in front of the entrance to the Sistine Chapel at the Vatican. By now Brother Gino must surely have reached his destination, or be approaching his goal miles away. My mind was far from him. Approaching the entrance area, I was greeted by some of the pilgrims who had accompanied me to Fatima, through Spain, France and down through Italy by bus until we reached Rome for the Jubilee Indulgence of the Holy Year and for a general audience with Pope Paul VI. There I did something I had never done before.

"Father, here is a young man who has never heard of Our Lady of Fatima." The handsome young man looked up at me with innocent eyes that sought more information. "How old are you?" I asked. "Twenty." Without forethought, I extended my hands like a bishop at an ordination ceremony. Holding them over and upon his head, with witnesses gathered, I said, "Young man, some day you will be a priest."

At the moment of the imposition and words I again experienced unmistakably the perfume of Brother Gino. I said nothing about the perfume. The young man stammered and admitted, "Maybe. I have good Catholic parents..." As we turned to enter the Sistine Chapel, leaving the young man from the United States behind, pilgrims turned to me to say, "Father, when you did that we smelled the perfume of Brother Gino." At the general papal audience later that same afternoon, again and again the perfume returned. It also issued periodically from my copies of the holy cards of the Madonna of Fatima, with the consecration to her Immaculate Heart, which Brother Gino gives to each pilgrim who approaches him.

After that October day in 1975, I was not to experience the perfume again until I returned to San Vittorino July 25, 1979, to spend a week of interviews with Brother Gino, ordained a deacon on Sunday, May 21, 1978. Again the perfume, "the odor of ctity," was evident.

This time I was able to interview Brother Gino again and again at length. I discovered his human side, worn out by the constant flow of pilgrims, each one wanting special attention, and many not able to understand why he could not listen or talk at length to each one. Fortunately, I was able to drive in a car with Brother Gino to his favorite spring for mineral water and spend a day with him in the Oblate novitiate, high on a mountain which I called an "eagle's nest." There, while gazing in the distance at other mountains, one senses in the haze the mystery of the Divine. I observed Brother Gino with many young men, novices, and it seemd that the stigmatist was having some of his happiest moments as he teased them with his unique sense of humor and gave them deep spiritual food for thought and contemplation.

Father Joseph G. Breault, O.V.M. teased Brother Gino that day of relaxation, a Friday when Brother Gino has his one day of the week when he does not meet pilgrims. The priest told Br. Gino that he had good news. "Father Fox has decided to become an Oblate of the Virgin Mary." With a twinkle in his eye Brother Gino looked at me and replied: "In that case I'll get no more rest—with all his questions!" Later Brother Gino was to make a play on words with my last name, "Fox." He said in Italian, "Like a fox who goes to the chicken coop, you take not the thin or lean chickens, with your questions, you snatch only the fat ones."

I did not have the heart that day on the mountain top to push for another interview. I sensed the relaxation at the Novitiate and found joy and satisfaction simply witnessing the Stigmatist in spiritual conversation with those young men aspiring to the holy priesthood. For that is what Brother Gino constantly calls for, "holy priests".

As we got into the car at 9:00 p.m. that evening to return to San Vittorino, Brother Gino's first words were, "When will I be able to spend another day like this?" (July 27, 1979). Thinking of all who press upon him constantly, he added, "I am not a machine. I am a man." Another day, at the dinner table, when Brother Gino was cooperating with me under obedience, expressed fear concerning this book. I answered, "When they read this book they will know you are a man and not a machine."

That July day had begun beautifully as I had celebrated the Holy Sacrifice of the Mass at the new convent for the Sisters which Brother Gino had founded with the permission of the Bishop of Tivoli. The title of the Sisters is *Pia Unione delle Suore*

Oblate di Maria Vergine di Fatima (Oblate Sisters of the Virgin Mary of Fatima).

At the Holy Mass Brother Gino had requested to participate in the capacity of deacon. This I considered a great honor. But what does one preach in the presence of a holy deacon who in his own preaching relies not on self but totally on the Holy Spirit?

On one occasion Brother Gino himself was invited to preach to a gathering of priests with the Bishop present. He told the Bishop he had not prepared anything in particular but must rely upon the Holy Spirit. Two young priests were seen snickering at the prospect of this Brother (newly ordained deacon), preaching before their Bishop and all these priests. Brother Gino began and before long more than one priest was seen in tears. The two young priests paid close attention, amazed at the message. Later they approached Brother Gino to congratulate him on the message saying, "You meant us. That was for us." Brother Gino had preached on the necessity of respect and obedience to the office of Bishop. The priests were reminded that the source of their priesthood from Jesus Christ had come through the bishop.

Fr. Joseph G. Breault, O.V.M. translated my homily the day Brother Gino acted as deacon at the Mass which I offered at the Sisters' convent, which is near the Sanctuary of Our Lady of Fatima at San Vittorino. I spoke to the Sisters of how edified I had been when I visited their convent the day before. "As soon as I entered, I noted the spirit of joy, love and unity among you. This is of God. Beware of the devil. He is the father of liars (John 8:44) and of division. He will attempt to divide you." I continued: "You will be tempted with thoughts that you are not worthy of this great calling in this religious Order of the Oblate Sisters of the Virgin Mary of Fatima. Do not fear such thoughts of unworthiness. Fear rather when you begin to think yourselves worthy."

Making reference to the many young men flocking to San Vittorino, young men from throughout the world and especially from the U.S.A., to an order not many years before thought to be dying, but now doubled in population in a short time, and with young women flocking to San Vittorino to become sisters, again a large proportion at least initially from the U.S.A., having in mind too the Sanctuary rising in the wilderness and the conversions and healings taking place here, I assured them: "This is not natural. This is supernatural. What is happening at San Vittorino is of God."

When it came to the consecration of the bread and wine into the Body, Blood, Soul and Divinity of Our Lord and Saviour Jesus

Christ, Brother Gino standing beside me at the altar began to tremble, tilting his shoulders. This happens at every holy Sacrifice of the Mass at the two-fold consecration at which Brother Gino is present. He tries to control this as best he can. It appears that at the consecration the Brother experiences in a special way the sufferings of Jesus Christ crucified.

Our Catholic Doctrine states that at every holy Mass, the Sacrifice of the Lord's Body and Blood is perpetuated. The Vatican's *General Catechetical Directory*, under "The Eucharist, Center of the Entire Sacramental Life," states it this way: "This sacrifice is not merely a rite commemorating a past sacrifice. For in it Christ, by the ministry of the priests, perpetuates the sacrifice of the Cross in an unbloody manner through the course of the centuries. In it too He nourishes the faithful with Himself, the Bread of Life, in order that, filled with love of God and neighbor, they may become more and more a people acceptable to God." (58)

To participate then at the holy Mass is the same as being present at the foot of the Cross on Calvary. Only the manner of offering differs. The true living Body and Blood of Jesus Christ, the Son of God made man is present in the transubstantiation of bread into the sacred Body and wine into the precious Blood of Jesus Christ. The Sacrifice of the Cross is re-enacted. Brother Gino's physical reactions are a sign, it seems, of the Sacrifice of the Cross perpetuated today.

At the coffee after the Mass, the Oblate Sisters of the Virgin Mary of Fatima gathered around Brother Gino and myself. On this occasion too, the Brother's human touch came forth. This man has often stood alone watching the Sisters at recreation through the window. He tells them: "Oh! to be a novice again. It is the happiest time of one's life." But at coffee that morning Brother Gino had a sterner lesson: he warned those approaching profession how the devil would tempt them away to apparent greener pastures.

In this as in all else, Brother Gino is a man of charity, and of obedience. It was obvious that his cooperation with me to obtain details for this book was in obedience to superiors and in the realization that his own mission given him by God is not for himself but for others. He would escape any personal attention, were that possible and yet he must in God's will remain at the disposal of others if it will bring them closer to God through the love of the Mother's Heart. In this connection, I teased Brother Gino about the scar on his face. "It is completely gone now.

What has happened to it?" He replied, "The Madonna plays games with me. When I need it for humility, it returns." I asked in jest, "When you are bad, it returns?" He answered, "Yes", and added, "When I need humility."

At various times during the interviews when I apparently drew very close to supernatural experiences which have guided Brother Gino, such as the inspiration to build the Sanctuary of Our Lady of Fatima at San Vittorino and the inspiration to found the religious Order of the Oblate Sisters, I found him evasive. Never did he present himself as one of supernatural powers. At least twice, the answer to my questions were an Italian expression which translates into English, "I would like to jump over the ditch." It was a polite way of indicating he did not wish to answer the question.

But more than this, the directness, the simplicity of his faith-filled answers came through to me again and again. Always there was charity. Where there was some evasion, it was due to prudence, I concluded. There are things of a man's heart that are so intimate that they are best reserved for relationships between the soul and God alone. At times, however, I felt that by not answering my questions, he had answered them.

At one point during the interviews Brother Gino told me that I was always thinking that I wanted this to be a good book, and had completely forgotten all else, all my worries. It was true. This book must touch the heavens. This book must reveal the Finger of God at Fatima, which is for the world, extending across space and time and letting drop down the dew of heaven (Isa. 45:8) to refresh hungered and thirsty souls. Could I be competent for such a task? Could I prove worthy? Hardly.

I returned to Fatima after my stay in Rome and the interviews at San Vittorino. The first chapter of this book had to be written in the Cova da Iria, at the Capelinha itself, before the little open-air Chapel of Fatima which shelters the very spot of the former little holm oak tree on which the Mother of God gave a message for the world, calling us all back to the Gospels. Then I placed this first chapter upon the pillar of apparitions in the Capelinha, laying my hands there as I had the very first time I came to Fatima, and renewed my personal consecration which I had made to the Mother of God as a seminarian. "O Lady! Take these hands. Accept this heart with all its imperfections. Transform it as you once did Jacinta, Francisco and Lucia."

At that first pilgrimage to Fatima I had asked Our Lady, as Lucia did in her first words each time God's Mother appeared:

"What do you want of me?" Little did I dream she would ask me to be an instrument of the Fatima Youth Apostolate in teaching and forming youth in the fullness of Catholic faith, an Apostolate for which Brother Gino would become a spiritual Father in prayer and suffering, and for which he would agree even, under the direction of his superiors, to accompany me to Fatima for a boy's pilgrimage. Nor did I dream that sisters of the Order he was later to found would help serve as counselors for the girls' pilgrimage.

It is worth mentioning here that Brother Gino does not appreciate being called the founder of these Oblate Sisters. "The Madonna" is the one who always seems to get the credit for any success to his work. The power of her intercession cannot be measured; he honors her at every turn.

An example was the marvelous painting of "Our Mother of Sweetness" which Brother Gino presented to me. One day we were in the seminary chapel at San Vittorino. Brother Gino was leading Father Breault and me along the Way of the Cross, the images for which he had painted. It was then I asked, "Would you paint me a picture?" The answer, "It is already painted." He left for his room and returned with "Our Mother of Sweetness". Brother Gino has had no professional training in painting, but he explained that this, like each of his paintings, conveys a message. "Why Brother Gino did you decide to paint this particular picture for me?" He answered: "So that you will convey to youth the sweetness of Our Mother's Heart."

If Brother Gino honors Our Lady fully, it is Jesus in the Holy Eucharist around which his life gravitates. He is most sensitive to the Real Presence of Our Lord and Savior Jesus Christ in this most august Sacrament of the Altar. At least on one occasion vividly described to me, Brother Gino detected that a priest walking by was secretly carrying Our Lord in the Holy Eucharist. Upon investigation, it proved to be true. But just as Brother Gino is most sensitive to the Real Presence of Jesus Christ in the Holy Eucharist, so he has had encounters with the evil one. On one occasion the devil showed him two platters upon which were representations of sins against purity by which Satan captures souls and rules the world.

As the pilgrims coming to San Vittorino have grown in numbers, Brother Gino is no longer able to give frequent long interviews in his office or reception room as was formerly his custom. Now it is difficult to give even brief attention to the many who approach him to kiss his hand and ask for his prayers. His patience is likewise tested with those who return again and again, standing around in curiosity with no significant problem. It is severely tested with those who return but are not truly interested in changing themselves as would be necessary to solve their problems.

It is to youth that Brother Gino is attracted first after Our Lord in the Holy Eucharist and the Madonna. Always, in some way, the Madonna is involved whenever he speaks more than a few spiritual words. Young men especially find Brother Gino receptive to their needs and requests, but young ladies too will receive his special help when hearts are open and receptive to God's grace. To more than one youth he has advised, "Go to confession." Usually the youth will come away from Brother Gino changed, immediately asking where a priest may be found. By the same token, it has not been unknown that this Brother of San Vittorino has refused to permit a young man to kiss his wounded hand. A repentant, sincere confession will later find the youth graciously received with all the privileges of others.

The room of Brother Gino at San Vittorino is not austere. There is a beautiful statue of Our Lady of Fatima in his private quarters, one, too, of the Sacred Heart of Jesus. It is a beautiful room in general which includes a Crucifix known at times to issue a perfumed oily fluid. Brother Gino makes no comments about such matters. He does comment, however, on the proper use of externals in the spiritual life.

One who externalizes his religion excessively or in an emotional manner, such as by excessive external images, will not gain the Brother's sympathy. The Rosary, the Cross and the Scapular: these are sufficient for one to carry or wear. Similarly on at least one occasion a lady excessively inclined toward a pentecostal piety was putting on external emotional demonstrations in the Communion line waiting her turn. The Brother did not hesitate to tell her to stop the nonsense and show proper reverence for Jesus Christ in the Most Blessed Sacrament. Again, if a youth comes who loads himself down with external religious symbols, Brother Gino, who speaks in harmony with the directives of the Superior of the boys, cautions the young man. He will say, "The Cross and the Scapular suffice. In the Cross you have the Son. In the Scapular you have the Mother. With these you have everything. The others must be reflected in your life."

Brother Gino seeks silence and solitariness in union with God. At the same time he enjoys a good joke, or better yet, he enjoys telling amusing stories to make others laugh, some of which he shared with me and I shall share with readers. This was obvious to me the day I spent with him at the novitiate where there was much laughter, some of it rather noisy as is typical among American youth. His response to this was: "When they are playing, they are not sinning." Indeed, youths arriving at San Vittorino to study for the holy priesthood may be uncomfortable at first in the presence of those penetrating eyes of the stigmatist, especially having heard stories, sometimes distorted. But as time passes these very youths become very close to Brother Gino and receive his manly and fatherly affection. The boys become as his sons.

It is not surprising that Brother Gino who suffers much himself should state that he was particularly happy to learn about the new branch of Suffering Cadets who are willing to accept and offer their sufferings for the conversion of America and youth throughout the world. He was referring to that branch of the Fatima Youth Apostolate, the Blue Army Cadets of Our Lady of Fatima. He sent the Suffering youth a poem, saying, "May the Mother of Christ, whose Heart was pierced by the sword, obtain the blessings of her Son upon your offering." The poem, while an edification for those who suffer, in a special way also reveals something about the Brother's spiritual life and how he accepts the sufferings he himself has in union with those of Jesus Christ.

My suffering is a little key of gold,
Small, but with a great treasure in its hold.

It is a cross, but it is the cross of Jesus,
Once embraced, it ceases to displease us.

I have not counted the troubled days which life for me affords;
I know that Jesus all of them within His heart records.

He has told me that, seen from future life,
A moment will appear the length of present strife.

Life, vigil of the feast, now wanes,
Death dies, and only Paradise remains.

Yet still a few more tears of this my bitter pain,
Then an endless song of joy in His eternal reign.

The spiritual child-like qualities of Brother Gino are revealed in an incident that took place one morning. He came from his night's rest smiling and radiating joy. "I have a treasure", he joyfully announced. Clutching his heart, as if holding something very valuable, the Brother kept repeating that he held a priceless treasure. "I have a treasure....I have a treasure..."

"Let me see it," said one of the seminarians. The joy of the Stigmatist was contagious as he continued to grasp at his heart. "I have a treasure..." The seminarian asked if the Brother held some valuable object. Finally it was revealed that the Brother had had an unpleasant dream. "But the devil did not take my treasure from me. I still have God in my soul."

The Brother then explained that if one lives a consecration to Mary, then even in sleep, in dreams the devil cannot get at one to steal the priceless treasure of sanctifying grace. Obviously then, the Brother, being a Mystic, is never really alone in his desire for privacy for prayer, something the pilgrims seem too unwilling to afford him. He is very much aware of the Sweet Guests of his soul, the Most Blessed Trinity that dwell in every soul in the state of grace, as in a temple. "Your body, you know, is the temple of the Holy Spirit, who is in you since you received him from God" (1 Cor. 6:19). "The temple of God has no common ground with idols, and that is what we are—the temple of the living God. We have God's word for it: I will make my home among them and live with them; I will be their God and they will be my people" (2 Cor. 6:16). "If anyone loves me he will keep my word, and my Father will love him, and we shall come to him and make our home with him" (John 14:23).

Some young men who have come to San Vittorino have been referred to by the Brother as Magdalen. "For this reason I tell you that her sins, her many sins, have been forgiven her, because she has shown such great love." (Luke 78:47). The Brother obviously is making reference to a converted sinner who now loves the Lord, thus giving hope to all youth who may in shame of past remembrances fear acceptance, but are reminded of the great love of St. Mary Magdalen that followed her conversion and won the praise of the Lord.

But then he has special titles and nick-names for those young men who obviously have always preserved their baptismal innocence. Having known some of these young men through the "Youth For Fatima" pilgrimages before they found their way to the Seminary and San Vittorino, I could well appreciate what the Brother means. In this modern sinful world there are still beautiful souls, who have safeguarded their purity and have lived constantly in a state of grace, sharing God's life, since the moment of their baptism. They are ignorant of the world. They are simply "in the world, but not of the world" (John 17:14-15). Their baptismal innocence is intact.

Brother Gino loves them all and often sees to the depths of their souls. While it is not always the case, and no one claims infallible judgement of discernment, yet the Stigmatist of San Vittorino has been known to tell a young man a past event the youth would rather have forgotten and even had forgotten. The details, even the room furnishings described, were too much to be merely coincidental.

Where does one begin and where does one end in telling the story of this consecrated life? Even the death of Brother Gino will not end what God is doing and His Mother is accomplishing in this soul who already as a small child was fond of gathering flowers for the Madonna. His life and his example will go on gathering flowers for the Madonna in the multiple souls that will be touched and the glory given God and honor given His Mother.

That Sunday, May 21, 1978, Solemnity of the Holy Trinity, when the powers of the diaconate, the first of the Sacrament of Holy Orders, were conferred upon Brother Gino, marked a new phase in his life and a deeper opening to the Holy Spirit. He prepared well in humility and feared the day. "My soul proclaims the greatness of the Lord and my spirit exults in God my saviour; because He has looked upon His lowly handmaid..." (Luke 1:46). "The fear of the Lord is the beginning of wisdom" (Ps. 111:10).

Perfume filled the Sanctuario Nostra Signora di Fatima that day in May in a manner usually experienced only by those very close to Brother Gino. Thereafter Brother Gino admitted quietly to trusted friends that he experienced a deeper wisdom of the Holy Spirit in giving advice to souls. He found himself able now to advise souls in a way unknown before his ordination. Others closely acquainted with the Stigmatist admitted that they too noticed a change.

In visiting Brother Gino I sought his opinion about certain Modernistic theologians and educators who held that Jesus Christ did not always know who He was. I voiced their expressed statements that Jesus Christ only gradually discovered who He was. Only gradually did Jesus come to realize that He was the Son of God made man who had a divine mission from God the Father as Redeemer of the world. The Brother answered briefly and directly, as is his style. "They do not know Jesus Christ."

The life of Brother Gino which follows can help us all know Jesus better.

"Think of God's mercy, my brothers, and worship him, I beg you, in a way that is worthy of thinking beings, by offering your living bodies as a holy sacrifice, truly pleasing to God. Do not model yourselves on the behavior of the world around you, but let your behavior change, modelled by your new mind. This is the only way to discover the will of God and know what is good, what it is that God wants, what is the thing to do." (Romans 12:1-2)

I. The Oblates of the Virgin Mary

Brother Gino should be studied in the context of his religious vocation, which is that of an Oblate of the Virgin Mary. It is the life of Christ as presented by Father Pio Bruno Lanteri, founder of the Oblates, that Brother Gino strives to imitate. Understanding the Oblates and its founder we will learn much about Brother Gino's spirituality.

Father Lanteri was a humble Italian priest who lived during the troubled period during and after the French Revolution. He was born in Cuneo, Piedmont, in Northern Italy. Even though his health was poor, he managed with God's help to establish and extend the work of several associations for religious and laity. Pope Pius XI, impressed with his work, named him, "the Precursor of Catholic Action."

Dr. Pietro Lanteri and Margherita Fenoglio, charitable toward the poor and suffering, were the parents of Pio Bruno Lanteri, born on May 12th, 1759. He was baptized into Christ that very same day at the Church of Santa Maria.

Bruno had just turned four years of age when his mother died in childbirth. Dr. Pietro Lanteri, alone with a very young family, did something then which the young Bruno was never to forget. His father took him to the parish Church, and there before the altar of Our Lady he spoke to Bruno: "You no longer have a mother here on earth. From now on, the Blessed Virgin will be your mother. Love her as your true Mother." This was doubtlessly the beginning of the Lanterian spirituality that characterizes the Oblates of the Virgin Mary.

Dr. Lanteri guided Bruno through all the stages of normal

development and tended assiduously to his sacramental preparations and general spirituality. His father had hopes of Bruno becoming a university professor, since the young man was attracted to studies. However, his father was grieved when at the age of seventeen Bruno announced he wanted to become a Carthusian. A man of strong Christian principles, Dr. Lanteri offered no opposition but rather accompanied Bruno to the Carthusian monastery of Chiusa Pesio just a few miles from the home city of Cuneo. Because of poor health Bruno had to discontinue preparations for the austere, penitential life of the Carthusians. Still, his desire for the holy priesthood mounted.

When on September 17, 1777 the young Bruno put on the clerical habit and went to Turin for theological studies, almost everywhere there were influences of the heresies of Jansenism. Jansenism was the name given to the heretical doctrines of Cornelius Jansen (1585-1638), Bishop of Ypres, Belgium, who taught predestination, loss of free will and the irresistibility of grace. He taught that human nature was completely corrupted by original sin and that Christ did not die for all men. His false doctrines resulted in heated controversies in theological circles giving birth to a rigoristic and severe type of morality and asceticism which paralysed souls. Rather than drawing souls to the love and mercy of God, Jansenism removed them from such confidence in the all-good and holy God.

Both professors and fellow students were affected by the spirit of Jansenism and Bruno too experienced spiritual turmoil. Bruno's continued acceptance of God's Mother as his own produced prayers that were answered. He fell under the guidance of Father De Diessbach, a Jesuit priest who had converted from Calvinism to Catholicism. Under his direction, Bruno was initiated into an apostolate that included work among the poor and abandoned peoples of Turin. With Fr. Diessbach to guide him, Bruno Lanteri engrossed himself in studies and apostolic works and advanced peacefully toward the cherished goal of participating in Christ's holy priesthood.

Bruno Lanteri consecrated himself in a special way into the hands of the Blessed Virgin Mary, just before receiving the diaconate. On August 15, 1781 he drew up an offering of himself to Mary very similar to the Treatise on True Devotion of St. Louis de Montfort (1842). He wrote:

Let all those into whose hands this writing may fall know that I, the undersigned, give myself as a perpetual slave to the Blessed

Virgin Mary, with a pure, perfect, and free donation of myself
with all my possessions in order that she, as my true and absolute
Mistress, may dispose of them according to her good pleasure. In
conformity with which, I undersign myself: Pio Bruno Lanteri.

This consecration to Mary was a "pure, perfect, and free
donation of himself and his possessions, which, as his true and
absolute Mistress, she was free to dispose of according to her
good pleasure."

On May 25, 1782 Bruno Lanteri was ordained a priest of God
at Turin in the Church of Mary Immaculate. Father Lanteri
worked hard to open all areas of society to an authentic
Christianity through true interior formation. The Spiritual
Exercises of St. Ignatius he held in high regard to achieve this
purpose. He opened a "La Grange" country-house about twenty
miles from Turin for the purpose of receiving groups of priests
and laymen desiring to make the Exercises. In 1807 he reopened
a house of Ignatian exercises located in the Val di Lanzo.

Fr. Lanteri was suspected of secret plottings against the
government. A man was sent to take the Exercises so as to report
back all the proceedings. As a result of Fr. Lanteri's excellent
expositions of the beauty of the Faith, the man was converted to
a life of piety.

"I wish to be a copy of Christ," Fr. Lanteri wrote as a newly
ordained priest. "There is nothing else in the world that is more
secure, more noble, and more genuine." He sought to become
all things to all men, so that all might discover salvation of Jesus
Christ. "Away with all useless thoughts: all must serve to
capture souls from the world and bring them to God. Always
think, speak and labor as a Saint. Without an interior spirit, one
will never accomplish anything: one needs fire, fire, fire: an
intense and heroic love for God. But the spirit of God is orderly
and calm."

A noted feature of Brother Gino is that he constantly
recommends undivided loyalty to the Pope as the chief Vicar of
Jesus Christ upon earth, as the visible head of the Church. Fr.
Lanteri looked upon the Holy Father as the central figure in the
Church. He compared the pope to the director of a spiritual
orchestra, as the prism through which is shed the light of the
Christian truth.

Whether he was writing letters, giving conferences or
sermons, writing educational materials or just engaged in
conversation, Fr. Lanteri's words were constantly nourished by

loyalty and love for the Holy Father. If anyone spoke even a slight irreverence toward the Vicar of Christ in the presence of Fr. Lanteri, immediately his disposition changed. Instead of being mild and gentle as was his usual manner, he would become inflamed with a fiery aggresive manner, and with eyes glowing, he would become eloquent with indignation in his defense of the papacy. While Fr. Lanteri could find excuses to pardon the mistakes of individuals or remain silent on other matters, when the subject was the Pope, he could not remain silent and manifest reserve. As he repeatedly said, "It is a question of the unity, of the center, of the foundation of the faith. One cannot and one must not remain silent." To attack the Pope was the same, in his mind, as attacking Jesus Christ.

Fr. Lanteri was deeply grieved when Pope Pius VII was forcefully taken from his Roman seat during the Napoleonic era and made a prisoner at Savona (1809-1812), then at Fontainebleau in the hope that the Pope might give in to the Emperor who wanted control over Pope and bishops. It was Fr. Lanteri who during these years managed to get secret documents into the hands of the Pope which His Holiness in turn used to bring a death blow to the pretensions of Napoleon.

The Emperor was infuriated, imprisoned several Cardinals and commanded a strict watch over suspect persons. Fr. Lanteri was a prime suspect, although repeated searches uncovered nothing. At one time the police in Paris ordered Fr. Lanteri (who, they said, had been "involved in the intrigues which took place concerning the secret correspondence with Savona") to cease all priestly functions. He was removed to his country residence about twenty miles from Turin where he spent the next three years writing, studying, praying, until the decline of Napoleon enabled him to return to Turin and continue his many apostolates, which included contacts with friends from Florence to Milan, Vienna, Germany, and the southeast of France.

Father Lanteri was devoted to spreading the Word of God through the written word. Upon entering Catholic bookshops to purchase books, priests would often find a packet of selected books waiting for them, secretly paid for by Fr. Lanteri. During missions people would discover that their missioners had freely sent to them thousands of catechisms, copies of the Eternal Maxims of St. Alphonsus Ligouri, and books of devotion.

If newspapers reported events of importance for Catholics, such as the imprisonment of a Cardinal or a Bishop, interferences with churches or convents, the publication of erroneous catechisms, without fail there would soon be made available leaflets and pamphlets to alert the faithful, clarify the issues and give encouragement. Fr. Lanteri managed to find women, young seminarians, elderly priests, to bring comfort and whatever aid was necessary to invalids, the sick, the poor, those imprisoned. From the school of Fr. Lanteri came forth leaders and saints such as St. Joseph Cafasso, St. John Bosco and St. Joseph Cottolengo.

In the 17th and 18th centuries in various European cities there arose several secret Catholic societies which, although secret, subjected themselves to ecclesiastical authority. Among their purposes was to gather together in every large city a small group of men and women to be centers of an apostolate to check movements away from faith and morality by the distribution of good literature. Bruno Lanteri's Fr. Diessbach put this idea into action in 1776 by forming the Association of Italian Catholics to print and distribute sound books to defend Catholic dogma and morality. From this movement there developed an Apostolic Society, which over and above the diffusion of good books, sought the direct sanctification of its members. The new society, "Amicizia Cristiana" originated in Turin and in less than twenty years it had spread throughout Italy, and extended itself to Switzerland, Austria, Bavaria and France.

Fr. Lanteri, as a disciple of Fr. Diessbach, was a most diligent collaborator in all this and by 1805 he found himself alone at the head of the entire work and organization. It was under his direction that the "Amicizia Cristiana" passed successfully through the Revolutionary and Napoleonic periods and then was born openly and publicly as "Amicizia Cattolica".

Fr. Lanteri said: "The aim of our 'Amicizia Cristiana' is twofold: in the first place, our own advancement, and in the second the sanctification of others." Fr. Lanteri proposed then, not simply the propagation of good literature to bring about the social reign of Jesus Christ, but a zealous personal dedication and self-sanctification with a concern to inspire other souls to sanctification. There grew from the various "Amicizie" of Fr. Lanteri a crowning achievement in the later foundation of the Congregation of the Oblates of the Virgin Mary. Among other tasks, the Oblates were to pursue the formation and sanctification of the clergy. For this, Fr. Lanteri directed a traditional spirituality, a great love of God, zeal for souls, sincere imitation of the virtues of Christ, a spirit of good will and of immense mercy toward sinners, a filial devotion to the Blessed

Virgin Mary, and an unbending loyalty to the teaching and directives of the Magisterium of the Church.

Readers will be mindful that the present book dedicated to making known the life of Brother Gino of San Vittorino, a member of the Oblates of the Virgin Mary, founded by Fr. Pio Bruno Lanteri, has for a chief purpose to illustrate the effects of this Stigmatist's personal consecration to the Immaculate Heart of Mary, so strongly requested at Fatima. The effects, of course, are to be found not simply in his personal life, but in the sanctification of others.

Fr. Lanteri's love for the Blessed Virgin Mary was zealous in infusing into all men the love of Mary whom he called "his Paradise". On his desk there was always an image of Mary which he often kissed with great reverence. Each hour of the day he would greet his Mother, he visited daily some church dedicated to her and he would prepare himself for her feasts with special prayers and strict penances.

It was a logical conclusion, flowing from his personal Marian spirituality, that when he enlarged his apostolate to a religious Institute, it would be dedicated to Our Lady. For his spiritual sons he chose the name, "Oblates of the Virgin Mary". His idea was to have souls totally consecrated to God through the hands of Mary. He would say: "I am not the Founder. The Founder is Our Lady." We see an echo of this attitude in Brother Gino who does not want to consider himself, but Our Lady, as the Founder of his pious union of nuns, the Oblate Sisters of the Virgin Mary of Fatima.

As for Fr. Lanteri, his Oblates must be more than sons of Mary. They must be apostles of Mary as well. "In order to bring souls to God it is necessary to make them pass through the hands of Mary." In giving the Spiritual Exercises and in conducting missions, Fr. Lanteri desired that his Oblates never fail to deliver at least one sermon on the Blessed Mother. He said: "That which, at times, all our exhortations and meditations are unable to do, Our Lady will accomplish."

The Congregation of the Oblates of the Virgin Mary was canonically erected at Carignano in 1816. Fr. Lanteri endured ten years of sorrow and struggle to bring this about. On July 7, 1827 the Founder, together with his Oblates, entered the house of St. Clare in Pinerolo where they were welcomed by the Bishop. Fr. Lanteri had gone to Rome and received Pontifical approval and had the joy of pronouncing his religious vows at the feet of the Holy Father.

By the early months of 1830 it was obvious that the health of Fr. Lanteri would limit the time he would remain upon earth. During his last night a lay brother asked Fr. Lanteri if he needed anything. "Nothing," was the reply, "but I see a beautiful Lady with a Child. She is placing Him in my arms." The brother answered, "It must be the Blessed Mother come to visit you." Fr. Lanteri did not reply but, smiling, remained entirely enrapt in that heavenly vision.

The lay brother then summoned the entire community. Fr. Lanteri blessed all his Oblates who had gathered around his bed and left them a last testament: "Love one another, love one another intensely: be always united in heart at the cost of any sacrifice whatsoever." With these words, he died. It was August 5th, 1830, the feast of Our Lady of the Snow.

It took 40 years, 1870, before the first life of Fr. Lanteri was published by Fr. Gastaldi. Pressing duties and persecutions of the Congregation prevented their making known to the Church his heroic sanctity. In 1930 the diocesan process was initiated in Pinerolo. In May 1952 the Cause for beatification was officially introduced, entering its final stage. The Decree concerning the heroic virtue of Fr. Lanteri was issued on November 23, 1965; he was pronounced venerable.

Brother Gino Burresi, O.V.M., together with his fellow Oblates, frequently urges people to manifest love toward the Venerable Fr. Pio Bruno Lanteri, a love manifested in prayer and imitation of his heroic virtues. The sick are especially urged to seek his intercession. Miracles that have sometimes been ascribed to Brother Gino, he in turn, would rather ascribe to the intercession of the Venerable Lanteri and to God's Mother.

Fr. Lanteri's Oblates of the Virgin Mary describe themselves in the following manner:

"The first aim of the Congregation is the salvation and sanctification of its members by the close imitation of Jesus Christ and by the modelling of their actions on the example of 'their dear Mother Mary Most Holy'.

"The Congregation establishes religious houses where the Oblates can withdraw, like hermits, to apply themselves to prayer and study in order to go out and preach the Good News of salvation more effectively to the world. The Oblates wish to possess as one their principal characteristics, a reciprocal love and union. This they propose to guard well.

"It is the new commandment that the Lord has given. 'Love one another even as I have loved you... By this will all men know that you are My disciples, if you have love for one another" (John 13:34-5). The Rule of the Oblates can be reduced to the two major principles of charity and obedience."

The second aim of the Congregation is the salvation and sanctification of others. The Oblates are a missionary Congregation and have established themselves in seven countries of the world; besides several establishments in Italy, the Congregation has houses in France, Austria, Argentina, Uruguay, Brazil and the United States. In recent years the Oblates have been receiving vocations also from Canada, East Ceylon, Ireland and Nigeria.

In their training, the Oblates look to St. Thomas Aquinas as their teacher. Their guidelines on moral and pastoral theology present St. Alphonsus Ligouri in prominence. According to their Rule, the Oblates of the Virgin Mary propose to fight today's current errors, especially those among innovators of dogma and morals. They have frequent recourse to the Blessed Virgin Mary, "who has overcome all the world's heresies" in order to achieve this goal. They also profess "a sincere, complete and inviolable obedience to the authority of the Holy See and a complete observance of its teachings."

The Oblates have taken St. Peter as their patron. On his feast days they renew their profession of faith, emphasizing the article: "I swear a real obedience to the Roman Pontiff." It is also in the adoration of the Eucharistic Lord that Oblates find a major source of their spiritual strength and apostolic zeal. Postulants to the Oblates are infused with an evangelical spirit and are formed in a spirit of piety based on a solid devotion to the Cross of Jesus and the Rosary of His Blessed Mother.

According to the teaching and example of Fr. Lanteri, the Oblates of the Virgin Mary:

- are particularly docile and obedient to all the Pope's, Bishops' and Catholic Hierarchy's directives;
- they profess a particular devotion to the Blessed Virgin Mary, Mother of God;
- they are sensible to the new opening in theological, moral, liturgical and pastoral fields which are accepted and approved by the Pope and the Catholic Hierarchy.

They are a Congregation of priests and lay-brothers who devote themselves to the service of Christ under the guidance and care of the Blessed Virgin. Their apostolic work includes:

- Fraternal assistance to the clergy: spiritual direction, confessions, confraternities, preaching of the Spiritual Exer-

cises;
- Spiritual aid to the laity: parishes, missions, lay organizations, residences for students;
- Spreading the Word of God in mission territories;
- Service of the truth: corrections of current errors; distribution of sound Catholic literature, publications.

Father Lanteri, called also by Pope John XXIII, "precursor of Catholic action" is credited as an innovator and initiator of the most modern methods for the defense of the cause of God and the salvation of souls.

Despite all this, the Oblates were thought to be dying just ten years ago. But in recent years, they have manifested new life, and even doubled their numbers with an influx of new vocations. There can be little doubt that this is due in part to the prayers, sufferings and example of the Stigmatist Brother Gino, who would, of course, ascribe everything to the intercession of Venerable Lanteri and the Mother of God.

Be that as it may, it is into this religious Congregation that God and His Mother have drawn a modern Stigmatist, placing him in a house at San Vittorino near Rome. That house is near the Sanctuary of Our Lady of Fatima, "celebrated for its many miraculous cures and conversions", and for the presence there of Fratel Gino. It is there that he answers the call of heaven.

"For you alone are my hope, Lord, Yahweh, I have trusted you since my youth, I have relied on you since I was born, you have been my portion from my mother's womb, and the constant theme of my praise." (Psalms 71:5-8)

II. The Boyhood of Gino Burresi

Blandina Artemisi Burresi, mother of Brother Gino, stood to the side of the pilgrims at San Vittorino as each one was anxious to approach the Brother, now ordained a deacon, kiss his hand with the wound near the wrist, and perhaps have a word with him. Doubtlessly, few if any of the pilgrims knew that the lady standing so humbly to the side, saying nothing, but beaming a wide smile, was the mother of the Stigmatist they were so anxious to encounter.

Her husband, Angelo, had made himself even less conspicuous during that week which he and his wife were able to spend near their son at the Seminary and Sanctuary of Our Lady of Fatima at San Vittorino. Angelo is quiet and slight of build, not short, but hardly the type of man one would expect to be the father of the princely Brother Gino who is six feet in height, walks erect and has penetrating eyes. His mother too was humble, gentle, smiling a friendly welcome, possessing compassionate eyes, but noble in bearing. The morning after I first interviewed this lovely lady I decided to participate in another holy Sacrifice of the Mass in the lower crypt church of the Sanctuary. Some minutes before the holy Mass began, I happened to turn toward the entrance to be greeted by a most friendly smile of Blandina, arriving for the holy Sacrifice alone. She took her place and knelt in prayer before our Eucharistic Lord. She participated in the divine Liturgy in unaffected manner. Her son was not present. There were no efforts on her part or that of Angelo to relate to the pilgrims that they were the parents of the famed Stigmatist whose prayers, sacrifices, interventions had been instrumental in the Shrine dedicated to Our lady of Fatima and where conversions and miraculous cures were no longer a rarity. The devotion with which Blandina received the Lord Jesus in Holy Communion revealed, without ostentation, a deep faith and reverence for the Real Presence of the Body, Blood, Soul and Divinity of Jesus Christ, the Bread of Angels, which one receives in this august Sacrament of the altar.

The Mass completed, Blandina's extended thanksgiving included an approach to the front of the chapel to light votive candles. Blandina dropped her coins to pay for a candle. Again the coins dropped and more candles were lighted. It was as if she wished to leave her love burning strongly and brightly behind her as she must leave behind in the tabernacle the Presence of the God of Love Incarnate.

"How sad, how beautiful," I thought, "the parents of Brother Gino come to spend a week at San Vittorino and hardly seem to see their son. His time is taken up with the pilgrims, the mail, with prayer, with the likes of me asking endless questions for a book he would rather not see published."

The day Brother Gino, Fr. Joseph Breault and myself with another priest of the Mammertine of Rome went to visit the temporary Novitiate, high on the mountain, we first offered Holy Mass early in the small sisters' chapel, where Brother Gino served as deacon. His parents were not present at that Mass. We returned late in the evening that July summer day, when the lights of Rome were seen in the distance, lighting up the sky, and only after dark did Brother Gino's parents have the opportunity to sit with their son, outside under the stars and with others gathered around as well.

When the pilgrims had departed, I approached this lovely lady, recorder in hand. That I was writing a book on her son's life seemed not to impress her, but her respect and graciousness accompanying the privilege of talking with priests was evident.

"Mrs. Burresi, did you sense anything supernatural in the young Gino?"

"Yes, he saw the Madonna when he was five or six years old. He came home from the chapel, called and said, 'Mother, at the chapel I found a Lady who had a Child at her neck and she was weeping. I said to him, since I was busy, 'You should have asked her what she wanted.' He replied that she only said this while she wept: 'Only you will save me.' "

"And before this? What was he like even earlier in life?"

"He was always good, religious. He would take my Rosary and wanted me to teach him the Rosary because he was small and did not know it. He was always good."

I further asked Mrs. Burresi a pointed question as to whether she noticed anything unnatural, or supernatural, at the birth of Gino. This was her answer:

"As I think it over now, at an older age, I think that there was something mysterious about this because he was born without pain. While I was laughing he was born. He also was smiling. All the others were born in pain."

"Mrs. Burresi, were you aware at the time that he was born that there would be something special about this child?"

"At the moment he was born. After two months he got sick and the doctors were telling me that 90% of the babies who had this disease would die. Then I said to the Madonna, 'This is my first son. You could save him for yourself, but please save him.'"

"Were you afraid, Mrs. Burresi?" I asked.

"Yes, because he was so sick. I was holding him in my arms. I prayed and prayed, knowing out of one hundred, ninety would die. 'Madonna, save him, save him for yourself,' thinking that she would save him for me, too."

Then Brother Gino's mother made her point: "But She took him all for herself."

Gino Burresi was born of Angelo Burresi and Blandina Artemisi in Gambassi, in the province of Florence, on July 7th, 1932. The humble parents were workers of rented land. Gino was to be the first of five children: Gino, Sergio, Maria Luisa, Renzo and Maria Teresa. By eight or nine months old his mother decided to take him to Holy Mass for the first time. In his late forties, he still recalled the event.

"I remember. Along the way I saw a white flower and asked my mother what it was, since I did not know the word for it. When I got to the Mass I was not too quiet."

Mrs. Burresi said: "When I brought him to the altar of Our Lady, he began to look at the statue of Our Lady with the Child Jesus and became quiet, such that I was able to follow the Mass."

Brother Gino, recalling the same first Mass, says: "I remember too that there was a little nun there with a little basket of roses. I asked my mother, 'What is she doing with them?' Mother told me, 'They are roses of St. Rita. The nun had them blessed by the priest.'"

Mama Blandina was surprised that her tiny son could remember the details of these things of his first Mass. In later years she asked Gino how he could remember these things. Gino replied by surprising his mother yet more. He described how he was dressed.

"I had on white clothes, white socks, black shoes with a buckle."

Looking back during middle age, remembering such events in detail, Brother Gino had to admit, "To this extent there was something special." It became obvious to me why Brother Gino, who is so observant of people and things, has been gifted with the talent of being an artist. Brother Gino seemed most anxious, however, to convey the idea that he had been a normal child.

The earliest recollection Brother Gino has of his childhood concerns that first Mass and the Madonna of his home parish Church. "I always looked at the Madonna with the Child in her arms. I also liked the angels. These baroque churches have angels."

Mrs. Burresi recalls also the unusual acceptance for suffering her son had at the age of ten. "One day Gino hurt his arm. He had a fracture and the arm was never put back into its normal position. He was taken to the hospital. There he asked for a spiritual book to read. 'Mama! Ask the Sisters if they will give me a book of religion to read.'" When Mrs. Burresi came to the hospital to visit her son, the Sisters took her aside and said to her: "This boy Gino has something different about him. We do not understand it. It amazes us. However great the pain of his arm, he will never complain." The teachers at school noticed something different about Gino as well. They told his parents: "Whatever that child wants to do when he grows up, let him do it."

Looking back on his own childhood, Brother Gino prefers to think of himself as a normal child. "My mother taught me from childhood, in a very special way, the devotion to Our Blessed Mother. She taught me to have great trust in Her. The first prayers I learned were to Her. This was always the greatest devotion. Our Lady certainly helped me to have faith, even if I was a child.

"For example, to do an act of charity was a joy. When a poor person passed by I would go to my mother and ask for a piece of bread. Then I would go to give it to the beggar. My mother told me that Our Lady and also St. Francis would multiply the bread for us. So when a friar or beggar passed by, I tried to give a large amount of bread, thinking that Our Lady and St. Francis would multiply it for us. Thus I would go to look where we kept the wheat since I had given it to passing priests or to beggars. When the month of June came and the new sheaves of wheat formed, I would go to my mother and say, 'Mother, it is true. Our Lady and

St. Francis have multiplied the wheat because now there is new wheat and there is still the old wheat too.'''

Looking back at his family life, the training and the atmosphere of religion in the home, Brother Gino recalls, "Everything was done in this climate of faith. And when we helped a poor family, my mother said that I should not talk about it but do it quickly. Therefore, I would ask my mother for bread to give to a poor family which we often helped." The boy Gino prepared the bread in paper, which his mother gave him for the poor. Going to the poor family's door, rather than knock, he would leave the bread at the door and run off, making sure that the poor family did not see him. The boy thought, "If they see me, they will thank me. Then I will get no reward from Our Lady since I will already have been thanked."

It was these simple things, this practical charity for a supernatural motive, "the things which I learned from my mother," said Brother Gino, which developed "the devotion toward the Blessed mother which led to the consecration."

In these words, spoken by Brother Gino in his late forties, as he reminisced, one discovers the deep and lasting roots which grow in the home through the medium of the parents, the first teachers of the child, where education and formation are most effectively given and received. The consecration to God through the Immaculate Heart of Mary which typifies his entire life, started, he claims, in the home, especially through the practical guidance of his mother. Little did Blandina Burresi realize, in the performance of her daily duty as wife and mother, that her own love for the Madonna would educate and form a son in personal consecration to God's Mother which would touch souls throughout the world. Brother Gino gives credit, too, to the school and the dedicated nuns who taught him.

Along the way to the parish church there were two small chapels. The boy Gino would gather flowers along the way, before he got to the chapels. Arriving at the metal grate entrance to the chapels, he would place his collected flowers at the door. He would take off his hat and say this prayer: "I greet you, Mary, and I ask of you to pray to Jesus for me." His mother had taught him this prayer. Then Gino would put his hat on again, and off he would go. He had another prayer when he passed by in the evening. This time it was: "Jesus, Mary and Joseph, protect me along the way." Then he would sing a song to Our Lady and run on.

There was much poverty among the people. Many women

had to go into the woods to gather wood as a material from which to make charcoal. The road was long, about two kilometers, and it was very steep.

The young Gino, seeing the ladies collecting wood, would feel sorry for the poor women who had to carry such a weight on that steep road. The boy would go to the road and wait for the ladies to pass by. Then he would say, "May I carry that sack for you?"

Many of these women Gino helped are still living as this book is written. They remember the charity of young Gino well. They recall that when they got near the village, they would thank the boy and say to him: "You must go home now. You have done enough already. It is getting late. Hurry home or you will be afraid." Gino would answer: "I am not afraid because I shall pray, sing and run."

While the strong and growing devotion to the Mother of God in the heart of the young Gino is attributed for the most part to his mother, yet his father, Angelo, agreed with this spirituality, and it was obvious to the boy that the spirituality of his mother was very much a part of his father's heart, even if expressed less frequently or vocally.

Blandina Burresi did not hesitate to reprove her son Gino when necessary. There was a mutual agreement about discipline between Blandina and Angelo Burresi. If the father scolded Gino, never would the mother come to the child's defense. If it appeared that the boy had not really done wrong, yet, in respect for the authority of her husband, Blandina said nothing. On occasion, Blandina would know for certain that it was some other child who had done the wrong, not Gino. Hearing her husband reprove Gino, she nonetheless kept her silence. Only later when she was alone with Angelo would she in private discuss the matter with him. Angelo Burresi followed the same procedure with his wife. Should she seem to be mistaken, never would he take sides with the children in opposition to the mother. Respect for both parents must be safeguarded at all costs.

The temperament of Angelo in relationship to his children tended a little toward severity. One might not guess this, seeing the quiet, humble Angelo Burresi today, yet such is the loving recollection of Brother Gino.

Angelo Burresi did not want his children hanging about along the way, a pest to others, and made sure they were constructively occupied. There was school in the morning, and Gino did not return home for lunch. He went to the Sisters of the Child Mary at noon for lunch. Then the children were free to play. At four o'clock the Sisters would call the children in and help them with the work assigned by their teachers. At times the Sisters of Mary taught them in advance. The next day when the regular teacher met with the children, the teacher would be surprised as the children already knew what was being taught.

A ritual frequently heard in the Burresi household was the words spoken by Angelo to his children on Saturday evening. "Tomorrow I shall be going to holy Mass. I shall talk to the pastor to discover first of all how you have behaved in church. I shall want to know if you talked or argued, and whether you have been to catechism. Then I shall go into town to get what we need at the stores. I shall ask the shopkeepers if my children have bothered people." Gino and his brothers and sisters listened well to their father, and they were afraid that some Sunday their father Angelo would come home with a bad report. But always the good Padre could report to Angelo Burresi, "Your children have behaved. All is as it should be."

Come Sunday evening Angelo would say to his children, "Now you must go to church for vespers." If there was any solemn function taking place at the parish it was the same, his family must be present. He would say to his children, "Do you see the sun? You are to be home before it sets." Gino watched the sun closely. When he saw that it was going down, off he would take, running for home lest he be disobedient and arrive after sunset.

Angelo was no one to spoil his children or waste money for them on needless things. "I will not buy you many toys. I will buy you clothes, but not toys. When children have everything, they grow up to be content with nothing. Nothing will satisfy them as adults. When instead some things are wanting, children feel the matter of life much more. This way you will learn to save some money instead of wasting it. If you have all, nothing will ever satisfy you."

It was not that Angelo was stingy with his children. He loved them too deeply for that. It was that he wished to teach his children not to be materialistic but to place their highest values on things of the spirit. While his instructions may not have been as direct in mentioning the spirit as the words of Blandina, yet his motive was the same and they complemented each other. The lessons of Angelo Burresi had the desired effect on his son Gino. His attachments were indeed chiefly not materialistic but spiritual.

One of Gino's teachers, 83 years old at the time of the writing of this book, recalls incidents in the life of her former student. It was the teacher's custom to have every student write a composition on some subject each day. The teacher was surprised that every day Gino would write on the Blessed Mother. "Today I went to find flowers for the Madonna…Today I went to find flowers for the Madonna…" Every day Gino wrote on this same subject. There was already this great attachment to the Blessed Mother. "The others go off to play, but he always goes to collect flowers for the Madonna," Gino's teacher would say. After gathering his flowers for the Madonna, Gino would go to play, too.

One day Gino went to collect flowers, and he found the flower of St. Mark. Flowers of St. Mark are green on the outside and appear beautiful, but nature has provided them with a protection. They give off a bad odor. Gino nonetheless took the flowers of St. Mark to school. There he gave them to the sister for the Madonna.

Sister said, "You bring these for the Madonna? Why, they have a terrible odor. I must throw these out." The boy protested, "Sister, these too are created by Jesus and therefore too are beautiful. I could not find roses or other beautiful flowers, so I brought these which I could find." The sister studied the boy and thought seriously. "All right, we shall keep them. They do give forth a bad perfume. Nonetheless, let us place them before Our Lady all the same."

Thinking on this later in life, Brother Gino said, "So there was something which made me a bit different from the other children." Indeed, he was the first among the children playing to say, "Now we must pray." But the other children did not want to take off too much time for prayer, and so he would settle for ten Hail Marys.

Sometimes Gino would motivate his playmates to do acts of penance. Off they would go to the woods to gather flowers for the Madonna. "I am going to take my shoes off so that I can find the thorns and suffer for the Madonna." But the other children did not want to take off their shoes, so Gino would say to them, "I am going to take them off and say a Hail Mary, and you will see that Our Lady will not let me step on any of them. You who don't want to take off your shoes and who will not say the Hail Mary, you will see that you will find the thorns.

And sometimes it happened just so. Gino with the bare feet would not be touched by the thorns and the others would get cut by them on their legs. Then Gino would remind them, "You see,

I who did not have any shoes didn't get touched by the thorns, and you who didn't want to offer this little penance for the Madonna got cut by them.'' When Brother Gino related this, he solemnly added, "Our Lord was even then already beginning to draw me to himself.''

The Burresi children, three brothers and two sisters, with Gino being the oldest, were very united in their religion and among themselves. It was a very beautiful family relationship. They would play together, but it was the eldest of the Burresis who would organize the games, not only with his brothers and sisters, but among the neighboring children. At times there would be ten or more to play in the fields or to gather flowers for the Madonna and to play.

The boy Gino was by no means all sanctity, nor did he have a false sanctity, with a long face and folded hands. In fact, "mischievous" would hardly be a strong enough word to describe some of the games of which Gino Burresi was the leader. His young mind was capable of devising games that were far from right in every respect.

Once, for example, Gino killed a snake. He said to his brothers and other companions, "Let's wrap it up in a package and leave it along the side of the road to see who comes to pick it up." In those days, meat was scarce and people walking along the roadside could easily think that someone had lost a choice package of meat from their groceries.

Gino managed to find some paper that butchers use. He made a neat package with it, leaving little traces of blood which came from the head of the snake. Then he wrote "meat" on it and the price that would have been normal for such a size package of meat. Gino and his companions laid the package to the side of the road and then hid in a ditch, looking up every so often to see if anyone were coming or had taken it. Soon an old lady passed by, carrying a load of firewood. She saw the package and looked every direction to see if anyone were watching. Gino, his brothers, and other playmates had to place their hands over their mouths to keep from laughing.

The lady picked up the package, put it in her apron, and went on. The boys in the ditch watched her closely. After walking for some time, the lady put her wood down. Then she took the package to see how much meat and what kind she had found. When she opened the package, the serpent fell out. The lady shrieked with fear, picked up her wood and ran off, much to the amusement and laughter of Gino and his playmates.

We learn of another game from the Sisters of the Child Mary, who still point out for visitors "The Window of Brother Gino." Gino used to gather his brothers, sisters, friends, and any other children, and they would go to that window, which was along the only road to town. The sisters being away, Gino would say to the other children, "Wait to see who will come by. You make an ugly face. You make ugly eyes...," and so on.

Thus prepared with their assortment of faces, the children would await a passerby, hoping the sisters would not return. The children would tap on the window, and the passersby would see a collection of ugly faces. Then the children would await with delight the next person to pass by, so as to put on their show again.

Eventually, the sisters discovered the sideshow their students had been putting on under the skilled direction of Gino Burresi. Henceforth the children were no longer permitted to go to the place, but the sisters affectionately gave the window a name.

Gino, having finished the fifth grade of elementary school, prepared to go into the first year of middle school. At this time there was a lady who taught several children at her house. She had an extremely stingy mother, so stingy that the woman even made her daughter suffer from hunger.

This was in the post-war times, and there was rationing of everything, even bread. The teacher's mother had a great amount of land, yet Gino's teacher used to ask the children for bread. The children were surprised and wondered why, since her mother had so much land and grew so much wheat.

Discovering that the teacher's mother was very stingy, Gino said to his companion, "You know what we will do? When at Christmas the tenants of the land that her mother owns bring her the hens, we will kill them all."

Christmas time came, which Gino anticipated for a purpose not entirely spiritual. The mother received her hens and put up a high fence around a terrace which she had, so that the hens would not fly out and escape. In the terrace was a cistern which contained water to clean the hen yard and from which water could be drawn for the chickens to drink.

Gino carefully made his plans to teach the stingy woman a lesson. He said to his companion, "You know what we will do? When our teacher goes out and the old lady is out, too, we will go with a broom, and the hens will have no place to escape except through the open door of the cistern. Then they will all go into the water and die."

But there was the problem of the little girls who studied with Gino and his companion. They were told, "You all keep quiet, because if you speak up after we do this, we will let you have it."

One morning the teacher announced that she would go out to get the mail. The children were left alone. Before leaving she gave the children a logical analysis to work at. The old lady was out as well. The long-planned venture could now be realized.

Up to the terrace went Gino and his companion. They opened the door to the cistern and went after the hens with a broom. The first hen went down into the water. Splash! The others followed the first hen. The children could hear them as they hit the water. Splash! Splash! Splash!...

Every hen having made its attempted escape, Gino and his companion closed the cistern, put everything back as normal, and went back to do their classwork, working out the logical analysis. When the teacher returned, her students had finished their work. She let them go home as a reward.

When the teacher's mother returned home, she noticed that her hens were missing. She began to ask the neighbors if they had seen hens flying around in the nearby fields. She thought she had made the fence high enough so they could not fly over, yet they were gone. They must have escaped. But no neighbor had seen any hens flying around. The mother said, "I'll bet those students of yours are responsible."

Returning to school the next day, the children were quizzed about the hens which had disappeared. "Gino!...What do you know about those hens? Where have they gone?" He knew nothing. "Girls! You were here with the boys. What do you know about those hens? They knew nothing. The mysterious disappearance of the hens was given up for a lost cause. It appeared that no one would ever know what had happened to them.

Then a man came to the well to draw water for his horse. He dropped a bucket and drew it up. He found a hen in the bucket with the water. He dropped the bucket again and got another hen. Upon investigating the cistern it was discovered that every hen had drowned and could be seen floating in the water. But all the children who knew kept their silence. The girls, whether in loyalty or fear, kept their silence over the years along with Gino and his companion.

Brother Gino's companion and accomplice in crime grew up to marry the niece of the teacher. Twenty years later, the first time the same teacher came to visit Brother Gino at San Vittorino, she said to him, "Do you know, Andrew told me that it was you with a broom who put all the hens in the well?"

It has never been revealed whether the boy Gino ever made his confession, under the Seal which forbids any priest to ever relate the slightest sin of any individual, or whether he rationalized in his young mind that he was God's instrument of justice for a stingy woman, but Brother Gino did reply to his teacher of 20 previous years, "Yes, it was I. I did it because your mother was too stingy, and I, even as a child, had understood that she didn't give you enough to eat. So to defend you, we put all the hens into the well."

When Brother Gino recounted this to me, he commented, "It was not just."

The boyhood of Gino Burresi was much like that of any other rural lad of his time. He had to work on the farm, and often he was chosen to take care of the younger. He would play with them while their mothers were busy working. Their fathers were at war.

World War II was a time of great crisis and tragedy mixed with much sorrow for Italy, as for the rest of the world. Among other war experiences that touched very close to Gino about the age of nine was an event he was never to forget and of which he, when he will speak of it, prefaces the account by saying, "I saw the heart of a man."

It happened in his home village. The Americans were taking over. They were flying over low, signaling to the German soldiers that they had to give up their arms and that they were prisoners. One German soldier got excited and nervous with fear. He jumped into a plane to get off the ground and into the air, hoping to escape. As soon as the German soldier got off, the American fighters began to pursue him. Seeing that he was going to be hit, the German soldier jumped from his plane with his parachute.

As the German soldier was descending with his parachute, another fighter plane came along and shot the soldier. The boy Gino watched this sad tragedy from under a tree. The German soldier fell to the ground very close to Gino. The boy crawled on the ground, lying low, going close to the man to help him, to discover that the man was seriously mangled. The soldier's parachute then settled upon the soldier and Gino and covered them both so completely that it was difficult to see or to breathe.

The plane of the German soldier crashed to the ground about

one thousand feet from Gino and the soldier. There was a terrible explosion, as there was ammunition aboard, and the gas of the plane burst into flame.

Gino felt he must get clear of the parachute and enable himself to breathe and do whatever he could for the soldier. His tender heart had been formed by his mother from pre-school days to care for those in need. The whole experience was terrifying for the young boy, learning first hand the horrors of war. Getting the parachute pushed back, hearing the terrible explosion of the plane nearby, and feeling the heat from the wild flames, Gino was finally able to behold the soldier he had come to assist. The soldier was dead. His side was all open, and the heart of this man was lying on the ground beside the body. The nine-year-old Gino, realizing the soldier was dead, carefully placed the man's heart back into his body.

About twenty years later, the mother of that German soldier who for long years had retained the love of her son in her heart, was determined to come to Italy to find the grave of her son and discover any information she could about him. The soldier had been buried in the cemetery of Gino's village.

Arriving in Italy, the woman learned of the village cemetery where her son had been buried. Attempting to get any information she could, she was told that there was a young man from the village who had joined the Oblates of the Virgin Mary who might know something. The German mother went to the Burresi household. She was desperately in need of any information she might discover about her son killed in the War. Gino was at home on vacation, visiting his parents.

The mother had to learn every detail as described above. Finally, she asked Gino, "When you saw him dead there, was all the body in one piece?" Sensitive to this mother who for many years had borne the wounds of the Second World War in her heart, not wanting to hurt the poor mother any more as she had already suffered enough, in his charity, thinking he had already given her sufficient information, he answered, "Yes, he was all in one piece. He died because, when he jumped from the plane, the parachute did not open. He just hit the ground like that, and that's the way he died."

Another incident illustrates Gino's trust in God. Previous to the take-over by the American soldiers, the Germans had taken some American soldiers prisoner and were intending to take them to Germany and eventually kill them. Gino said to his father, "Those Germans intend to kill the Americans. It is not right to kill those many young men. You must free them."

Angelo Burresi replied to his boy, "It is too dangerous. The fence which surrounds the prison camp is electrified."

Gino said, "Father, do not worry. I will pray to the Blessed Mother. You go ahead and free those soldiers. Nothing will happen to you."

The boy kept insisting until Angelo Burresi, together with his cousin, went to see what they could do. They cut the wire so that the young prisoners were able to escape.

Next Angelo called several Italian families together and came to an understanding with them that the American soldiers would be kept hidden from the Germans. These families would see that sufficient food was given to the Americans. Gino was assigned to represent the Burresis by taking food to the American young men. It was necessary to pass the Germans to reach them, and at times he had much difficulty, as he had to make several river crossings.

Then the boy remembered what his mother had taught him. "When you are afraid, you should say, 'Jesus, Mary, Joseph, accompany me along the way." Blandina Burresi had also given her son a Rosary and taught him to say it. With the Rosary and the frequent recitation of "Jesus, Mary, Joseph, accompany me along the way," the boy safely passed through the Germans every time without fear and brought food to the Americans in their place of hiding.

At school, Gino organized his companions, even the youngest, to keep quiet about the soldiers. Understanding the principle of mental reservation, he said, "You must not tell the Germans anything you know. Do not tell them the truth about where the Americans are hiding or that the Italian families take food to them. The Germans have given orders to the police to search for the Americans. If they ever find the families which are helping the American soldiers, our entire families will be killed by the Germans."

This, of course, worried the children, but the situation was not an imaginary one. One cannot help but look ahead of our story of this true situation in Italy during World War II, and, remembering the charity extended by the boy Gino to young American men, note how as an adult religious Brother Gino continues to welcome many other American young men who come to Italy to begin their studies for the holy priesthood at San Vittorino. Is God years later rewarding the generosity of Gino who helped American boys in great need?

In fact, the police did pass by, and they asked the children questions like this: "Have you seen the prisoners that escaped, the Americans? They are very bad men. They eat children. Tell us, have you seen them?"

All the children, even the youngest, replied to the Germans according to Gino's instructions: "No. We have not seen anything."

"Come now," the Germans insisted. "Tell us. Have you seen anyone?"

The more the Germans insisted, the more the children replied, "No. We have seen no one."

Finally, the Germans turned and left. The backs of the Germans turned toward the children, the children all made a gesture indicating, "You all are pretty foolish."

The American front grew closer and closer. Gradually, these American soldiers, a few at a time, escaped through the woods and rejoined the other Americans. When the Germans left the zone in which the Burresi family lived, it then came under American occupation, and an American camp was set up on the Burresi property. Gino, remembering that his mother had taught him always to be charitable, began to bring buckets of water to the soldiers so that they could wash and have clean water to drink. "What a great little Italian boy. Here, have some pieces of candy. And here's some chocolate." The soldiers enjoyed offering various other gifts, as well. Sometimes the American soldiers offered cigarettes, and one time they got a laugh out of having Gino smoke one as well. It was the last time Gino ever tried to smoke.

Some of the soldiers had fun joking with the boy Gino and even took advantage of his lack of knowledge of the English language and the apparent good will and innocence of the lad. They taught him a bad word, and he had no idea what it meant. The word was "goddamn." Gino, admiring his newly-learned English word, in his charity passed among the soldiers with his bucket of water which he graciously offered them. Along he skipped, feeling sorry for the soldiers, and so bringing joy to their hearts when he used his few known English words taught him by mischievous American soldier boys. With his innocence and Italian accent, not knowing he was speaking of "cursed by God," he walked among them singing, "Goddamn sonofabitch."

One day Gino was carrying out his mission of mercy mingled with the song which delighted the soldiers, when one soldier, rather serious-looking, called out to the young Italian lad, "Hey, little boy, come here." He spoke Italian so Gino understood. "Come here. Don't say those words. They are bad words."

Gino replied, "But the others tell me they are *good* words."

"No," said the serious soldier. "They are *bad* words."

The boy was surprised that this one soldier would take exception to that which brought laughter and seeming joy to the soldiers from America, who were so far from home and had been risking their lives.

"Who are you?" Gino asked that different type of soldier.

"Come in here." Then the soldier opened his tent and Gino, curious to see what was inside, saw a large crucifix and a book and realized that this very special soldier was a priest, the Catholic chaplain.

The priest-soldier said, "Here is a holy card for you. It is of Jesus crucified. Now don't say those bad words anymore or sing them either." Gino, with profound respect for the priesthood, obeyed and never said them again.

Many years later, when the American students began to come to San Vittorino, Brother Gino remembered his experience as a boy with other American young men. Now he was becoming well acquainted with American seminarians who were becoming fluent in Italian. Brother Gino even demonstrated how he would skip along, singing the words. "What do they mean?" The young seminarians told Brother Gino what the words meant. Embarrassed now at the discovery, Brother Gino could also see the humor.

As a boy, Brother Gino used to set up on the family's property different little grottoes and shrines. Each shrine, dedicated to a different saint, was assigned a special section of their farm land. On one ocassion, a terrible storm was coming, of which his mother to the present day says that she has never seen the equal. They knew the storm would do much damage. All the people in the village were very much afraid.

Brother Gino was still a very young boy. Hearing of the great fear of his parents, he said, "I have all these saints. They are going to take care of us and our property. Do not worry." His mother, hearing her son's expression of faith and confidence, herself being a strong woman of faith, still placed little stock in what the boy Gino was saying. The storm proved to be a very severe hailstorm, destroying all the crops in the area. Yet all the property where the boy had set up his tiny shrines was untouched. His mother then recalled the assurance her small son had given her. Gino's little statues and holy cards on trees had pleased Heaven.

His mother tells still another story about the ants during the war. Sugar was severely rationed. The Italians considered sugar important, considering the shortage of food. They were living in a pit in the ground because of the bombings. A town next to them had been completely destroyed; not a building remained. Storing the sugar in their underground shelter, the Burresis had suffered such an infestation of ants that there were almost more insects than sugar. When Blandina picked up the sack of sugar and saw the ants, she dropped the package in surprise. She became greatly depressed, as there was no way to separate the ants from the sugar. The boy Gino had a little religious object, and he composed a little religious, child-like poem which he recited a second time, making an M and a Cross in the sugar. All the ants left, leaving a pile of pure, white sugar.

There is yet more to relate of the boyhood of Gino Burresi and his innovative mind in inspiring other children and playing religious games. Upon discovering his types of games, with their religious overtones, one cannot help but remember what the survivor of the Fatima apparitions, Sister Lucia of the Immaculate Heart, writes of her girlhood. She tells of the religious processions and unusual music the children of the village of Aljustrel produced in imitation of what they experienced at their parish church. It was Lucia who led and directed the children in this. Lucia, being an extrovert, would have her band of children process down the village street.

Gino Burresi's favored game was called "Family." He preferred to play it with his brothers and sisters. He would say to the other children, "You build your home here. You build a home there. Over here we shall build a church." Gino was careful to see that a little statue of the Madonna was placed in the toy church.

Gino, already inclined toward celibacy, would always take the safest position. He would say to the other children, "You form the families. You, you be the husband...Here, you can be the wife..." Meanwhile, Gino would attempt to dress as a priest. Off he would go to find the needed materials to give the necessary effect. Some black material from some old lady's dress would suit the purpose. "Here, this man's white shirt will look like a surplice." Then he would remember that Father Pagani wore a biretta when he came out to offer the Sacrifice of the Mass. "Yes, I can use this shoe box to make a biretta for my head, like the one Father Pagani wears.''

"Husbands'' and "wives'' selected by Gino for his game of "family,'' which involved their own make-believe village of homes and a parish church, solved the problem of meals created by his early respect for celibacy. He would say to the other children, "For me, I cannot get married. Therefore, I must come to your houses to eat.''

Then young Gino would get some ink, and, so that the children's imaginations did not have to work too hard, he would make some pictures of the church with the ink. "Here is a little stick. We'll put a fig at the end and then three or four feathers, and look, we've got a sprinkler for the asperges. Get some water...Here, see, it sprinkles very well.''

Thus prepared, Gino would officiate at a pretend wedding and bless the couple with the aspersion. Then the children would have a procession with make-believe concoctions imitating the feast of Corpus Christi. Gino would say to the children on the occasion of such major feasts, "Tomorrow morning we must all go to Mass. In the afternoon we cannot go to the parish procession because we shall have our own procession in our own little church.'' So the children all had to gather flowers to decorate along the road where their children's procession with the Madonna would come. All this was done in the woods, decorating a path where they would carry the Madonna.

Gino would also supervise the making of a bell. The children were instructed to go look for American shells from the War which were then hung on trees. Hitting the improvised "bell'' made a loud noise. When the bells rang in the parish church, the children would run to ring their bell. It had the effect of scaring the birds away, it rang so loudly. Then all would say the Rosary in front of the little statue, and Gino would line the children up for a procession. A man who lives in Gino's home village still tells of the processions he used to witness. "In front of the procession there would be a little boy carrying some flowers.''

Similarly, on the way to school and returning home, Gino used to walk with a companion. Whenever possible, however, he was pleased if his companions would leave him so that he could walk that kilometer and a half alone. Walking along the road, with his school bag on his back, Gino would open his arms wide and start to sing the Pater Noster (Our Father). People would be working in the fields and would hear a boyish voice singing the Latin Pater Noster, such as the priest sang at holy Mass. The people would call to one another, "Don't you hear that little boy who is always singing the Pater Noster?'' Older farmers living in the area still recall the little boy Gino whom they frequently heard singing the Lord's Prayer.

This singing of the Lord's Prayer stemmed from the time that a young priest, Father Ilario Bruni, a native of Gino's home town, was ordained. He returned to his village to celebrate his first holy Mass. Gino was sick and could not go to the first Mass. When Sunday came, Gino went to holy Mass with his mother. Father Bruni was the celebrant. When Father sang the Pater Noster, Gino listened well and was deeply impressed. It was to have a deep effect on Gino's life.

Gino was still very young, not having made his first Holy Communion, as at that time children could not receive Holy Communion in Gino's village until they were eight or even ten years old. About this time, Blandina Burresi sent him to the store with a bag and an empty bottle with instructions to have the bottle filled with a liquid, a bleach which, when mixed with water, served to clean bathtubs.

Along the way to the store, Gino began collecting flowers for the little chapel, the "Chapel of the Madonna" which was along the roadside. As he was placing his flowers in the chapel, Father Ilario, the young priest who had impressed Gino by singing the Pater Noster so beautifully, was also walking along praying the Divine Office. The priest was very impressed to see this young lad place some flowers near the statue of the Blessed Mother Mary.

Just then, Gino, sensing someone was near, turned around to see the priest of the Pater Noster.

"What is your name?" the priest asked.

"Burresi," replied the boy.

"We are relatives," said the young priest. "I know the Burresis. And you, you love the Blessed Mother? In that case, you must always say your prayers every morning and at night, too. Have you made your first Holy Communion?"

"No," said the boy.

"Here, I want to give you something. Here is a little holy card, a souvenir of my first holy Mass."

The boy Gino put the holy card into his pocket, happy at the encounter, and off he ran for home to share the good news with his mother.

Bursting into the house, Gino called to his mother, "Look, look! Here is what the priest gave me. It was the priest who last Sunday sang the Pater Noster."

Gino did not see Father Ilario Bruni again for many years until the priest returned to his parish in 1946. Nonetheless, the boy preserved the precious holy card to remember the priest of the Pater Noster. In later years as a deacon, Brother Gino considered the little incident with Father Ilario to be an important event in his young life.

Thus passed the boyhood years of Gino Burresi, attending primary school at Gambassi, which is in the province of Florence. The first year was with the Sisters of the Child Mary; then he briefly attended the State School, returning later to the Sisters. In June of 1945, Gino obtained the elementary license and diploma of admission to middle school. For a year, as indicated earlier in the chapter, he studied privately under the care of a tutor because there was no middle school in the town. But while his teachers had a deep effect on his education, the greatest education and formation of all came from his parents.

"...And this is what he said on coming into the world: You who wanted no sacrifice or oblation prepared a body for me. You took no pleasure in holocausts or sacrifices for sin; then I said, just as I was commanded in the scroll of the book, 'God, here I am! I am coming to obey your will.' " (Hebrews 10:5-7)

III. Seeking the Will of God

During adolescence things began to change somewhat for Gino Burresi. As a child his relationships with other children had been very easy. He was their leader in games and had much influence over them, even in a religious manner. But from the ages of thirteen to fourteen this became more difficult because his childhood companions went the ways of the world. With Gino it was different. His interests were becoming more strongly religious. Rather than try to mix with his former companions, who were now becoming more aware of what the world had to offer, Gino preferred to remain alone when necessary and go his own way. Not that Gino forgot his companions in their adolescent years, but when he came into contact with other teenagers who were inclined toward immorality, he would experience mental pain out of concern for their immortal souls. Indeed, God was forming the soul of the adolescent Gino more and more into the image of His Son. Always it was the Mother of Jesus who remained his chief spiritual teacher. With the passing of childhood and the approaching of manhood, Gino's love for the Madonna grew not less but greater.

The teen years are often called "the dangerous years," for adolescence is intended by God to be the bridge between childhood and adulthood. For the successful teenager, faith during this period, while strongly tested, does not lose its simplicity but becomes a far deeper spiritual experience.

Gino Burresi saw teenagers taste the pleasures of the world. He tried to bring them to pray to the Blessed Mother and to St. Joseph, but too often they would not listen. To them he found it necessary to say, "Goodbye," and he would find new friends.

Gino himself as a teenager experienced some temptations, but these were given to the Lord, and in beseeching the intercession of the Blessed Virgin Mary, he grew ever closer to Jesus Christ. Gino, like any noble teenager who gives his heart to Jesus Christ, was willing to be different at times and even to stand alone.

In the spring of 1946, the fathers from the Oblates of the Virgin Mary of the community of Pisa came to preach a Mission at Gambassi. At the end of the parish mission, a sermon on death was preached at the cemetery which the altar boy Gino was long to remember. Gino talked to one of the missionaries and decided he wanted to go with him. He was fourteen years old, an age when most teenagers are rather thinking of beginning to reach further out to experience the world.

The seeds planted by his parents were now beginning to take firm root. A vocation is like a small bud. The bud grows. If well nourished with good soil and watered sufficiently, it will eventually begin to blossom, slowly, gradually, imperceptibly— but eventually the blossom will come to full bloom and then to fruit.

A few years previous to this writing Brother Gino revealed a sign that affected his future. Such secrets seldom slip from Brother Gino's lips. The Brother had gone to Gambassi to visit his parents. A priest friend relates the following:

"While we were at Gambassi, Brother Gino wished to see a small chapel in the countryside. He stood silently for a long time before the little chapel. 'This is the little chapel that I passed on my way to school each morning. I used to leave flowers at the door, as it was usually locked. One day it was open. I entered and knelt before the altar. I was five years old. I began praying, but shortly after, I heard crying. I turned around, and there on the chair in the corner was a beautiful lady. She was crying and had a baby in her arms. The baby boy constantly looked at his mother and shared in her grief. ''Why are you crying? Has someone died?'' I asked. She answered: ''Because men blaspheme me.'' I asked, ''What must I do?'' She responded: ''Give me your heart, sacrifices and prayers.'' Our Lady instructed me in the message of Fatima from my earliest years.' "

What Brother Gino is sasying here is not that Our Lady revealed herself as Our Lady of Fatima when he was at the age of five, but that the same message of Fatima, from the same Mother, was made known to him at this very tender age. Our

Lady of Guadalupe, Our Lady of Lourdes, and Our Lady of Fatima are all one and the same Mother of God, and Our Heavenly Mother does not contradict herself but gradually unfolds an ever-deepening message, reaffirming the gospels.

Obviously, the supernatural experience at Gambassi had an effect on the five-year-old Gino that burned itself into his young spirit, never to be forgotton, much like the experiences Sister Lucia described years later when, under obedience to her Bishop, she revealed secrets which she had kept in her heart since the apparitions at Fatima, treasuring them, not wanting to display them before the world. Only when she understood clearly the will of Heaven that she must do so, as explicitly stated by her Bishop, the representative and spokesman for Jesus Christ, did she give up her secrets. One can understand, then, that Gino Burresi has secrets in his heart, from a very tender age, which he is reluctant to share with the world.

In this matter of private revelation, a word of caution is in order. Authentic revelations are nothing more than a reaffirmation of the Gospels and of the doctrines of our Divine and loving Lord's holy Church. They never reveal anything new, although sometimes what has always been the faith of the Church is made contemporary, expressed in a mode, so to speak, in which modern man can more easily grasp the message and realize the application of Gospel and doctrines in today's world. Likewise, no authentic angel from heaven and no authentic apparition of the Mother of God will ever teach contrary to the Scriptures or to God's holy Catholic and Apostolic Church. No angel of Heaven and no true voice of the Mother of God will ever ask or suggest to anyone to be disobedient to legitimate Church authority: "I implore you, brothers, be on your guard against anybody who encourages trouble or puts difficulties in the way of the doctrine you have been taught. Avoid them. People like that are not slaves of their own appetites, confusing the simple-minded with their pious and persuasive arguments." (Romans 16:17-19).

Finally, Mary is not simply a friend, as some would present her, or one to be simply admired. She is in fact our spiritual Mother. She is the perfect Model and Mother of the Church as Sacred Scripture and Vatican II present her, the perfect exemplar of everything the Church is and hopes to become. She is the Mediatrix of grace. In no way is Mary in competition with Jesus Christ, her Son. Mariology, understood correctly, leads to Jesus Christ, the one essential Mediator. In authenticated apparitions of the Mother of God, such as at Fatima, the reparation called for to be directed to the Immaculate Heart of Mary was never understood by the recipients, even by young children such as Jacinta, Francisco and Lucia, as an end in itself and in isolation from Jesus Christ, the Invisible Head of the Church, the Redeemer of Mankind. The ultimate end is always God, the Blessed Trinity. Authentic devotion to Mary is always Trinitarian. Mary is the daughter of God the Father, Mother of God the Son, and Spouse of the Holy Spirit. True devotion to Mary obtains from the Spirit the capacity to engender Christ in one's soul and in that of others. Can it be Satan himself, that other angel, fallen and essentially evil, that will place in the hearts of some the idea that devotion to Mary somehow distracts from the role of Jesus Christ? At the dawn of creation, at the fall of our first parents, Adam and Even listened when Yahweh (God) announced the punishments. He said to the serpent, "I will make you enemies of each other: you and the woman, your offspring and her offspring." Satan is indeed an enemy of the Woman Mary. He will present her even as an obstacle to Jesus Christ, the Son, the Seed of the Woman who crushes his evil head. The father of lies knows that true devotion to Mary leads to Jesus Christ and to loyal participation in the life of His Church, the Mystical Body of Christ of which the Woman of Sacred Scripture, now reigning as Queen and Mother in Heaven, is also the Mother of that part of the Communion of Saints still upon earth. Now a five-year-old Gino Burresi of Gambassi and a six-year-old Jacinta Marto of Fatima could not, at their tender ages, expound these truths in theological terms to please the best or worst of theologians, but the end result is the same: union with God in the indwelling of the Most Blessed Trinity in the soul in grace when reparation is properly made to the Sorrowful and Immaculate Heart of Mary, which is inseparable from the Sacred Heart of her Divine Son. Five-year-old Gino saw a beautiful Lady in tears, with the Baby in her arms. The union of Jesus and Mary is depicted simply in this Baby Boy constantly looking at His Mother and sharing in her grief. The Mother is sorrowing over the fall of many who reject the saving graces of her Son.

The sorrowing Mother asks the five-year-old for total consecration to Her Immaculate Heart in the words a pre-schooler can understand. *"Give me your heart."* The Mother leads her children, all of them, as this child of five, to the Son of Her Womb, the Fruit of the overshadowing of the Holy

Spirit sent by God the Father at the word of Mary and the Angel.

"The Holy Spirit will come upon you," the Angel said, "and the power of the Most High will cover you with its shadow. And so the Child will be holy and will be called the Son of God..." "'I am the handmaid of the Lord,' said Mary, 'Let what you have said be done to me.' And the angel left her" (Lk. 1:35-38).

However, even a soul that receives extraordinary graces of mystical experiences must still live by faith and is capable of rejecting all. Lucia reports that in 1915, the year before the Angel of Peace appeared to Jacinta, Franciso and Lucia, she was with other companions who experienced some sort of angelic apparition. The other girls related the event hastily and were ridiculed. Whatever be Heaven's reason, it is known that subsequent mystical experiences of Lucia switch from her first companions to be shared with Jacinta and Francisco one year later. Thus, the experience of Gino at the age of five did not deprive him of normal boyhood experiences and mischievous deeds, as related in the former chapter. Yet his efforts to lead not simply himself but others to God through devotion to the Madonna was obvious in the child-like way he led his playmates.

As Gino passed into his teens, then, he was inclined to practice charity toward fellow teenagers and even help some with homework. To the present day, he has many friends from that time, for as a young boy Gino had learned to share with others. Bread had been scarce during the War, but the Burresi home always had plenty of bread. He found it very easy while going to school to give his bread to some companions who lacked, or even to the teacher, and to give bread to the soldiers he met.

When soldiers were passing by in groups, Gino would run down the road, open his school bag and give them some bread, usually. He would give it willingly because, even if he would have to suffer a little bit of hunger, he wanted to offer this to please the Madonna, who had asked him at the age of five for sacrifices.

Remembering his close relationship with Mary, Brother Gino says: "The Madonna has been for me some kind of a Guardian. Even my mother remembers how much I used to observe others, even when I was very small. After she took me to another house, for example, I would tell her all of what I had seen. I had even noticed the wrong things or the ugly things. Therefore, I should thank God that I never became occupied with something wrong because the Madonna protected me."

A further example of Brother Gino's keen sense of observation is found in something that took place very early in his life. One day a lady came to the Burresi home to re-do the mattresses because the wool inside of them had become very lumpy and very uncomfortable for the family. The wool had to be taken out and refreshed and made as new. The boy Gino watched the lady closely. With her hands she would stretch the wool. Having taken it out of the cover she would beat it with a stick to remove the dust from the wool. The reworked wool would be replaced into the cover, making the mattresses like new.

One day Gino saw the Sisters of his village who were attempting this kind of work. He could see that their manner of approach left much to be desired. The boy approached the Sisters and said to them, "Let me do it because it has to be done this way." He proceeded to show them exactly the different methods which must be employed. After many years one of these Sisters came to the Burresi household to visit with Blandina. She said in the course of conversation, "Your son Gino taught me how to fix mattresses." Mrs. Burresi replied, "How could he do that? I never knew that he knew how."

The good example of the Sisters, after that of his parents, served the oldest child of the Burresi family well, and we shall see that a certain priest and lay apostle played an inspirational role in his direction toward the Oblates of the Virgin Mary.

The Sisters prepared Gino in such a way that he was motivated toward Catholic Action, desirous of serving the Church for the honor and glory of God and the salvation of souls. The first step in this direction was to join the Association of St. Aloysius, who is the patron of Catholic youth. This association was for younger children.

After passing successfully through the Association of St. Aloysius, young people could join the next group which was aspiring to work in Catholic Action. At the time that Gino was about twelve years old, he met a young man who was leader of the group and who had been a prisoner in Russia during World War II. This young former soldier had succeeded in escaping the Russians and the Germans and had had a very good formation for his leadership role in Catholic Action. He was gifted with the knowledge of uniting boys for the cause of Jesus Christ and His Church.

One day this youth leader in the territory of the Parish of Gambassi met an Oblate of the Virgin Mary, Father Ilario Bruni. "I tell you, Father," he said, "there is a young man here in my

Action group you must speak to. His name is Gino Burresi. There is something special about him. The finger of God must be placed upon him in a special way." Father Bruni was the same priest of the Pater Noster who, years before, had met Gino at the wayside shrine of the Madonna. He was now to be the priest chosen by the lay leader to direct the young Gino. The year was 1946. Father Ilario had returned to the parish of Gambassi for a parish mission, but he did not recognize Gino Burresi as the same little boy he had met while saying the Hours of the Divine Office.

Gino Burresi had been contemplating a religious vocation, and it was at the end of the mission, after the memorable sermon on death held at the cemetery, that the altar boy Gino met with Father Ilario and decided that he must go with the Oblates of the Virgin Mary. It was the spring of his fourteenth year, and Gino was determined that he must follow this calling as soon as possible.

But the summer of 1946 was one of struggle for Gino. God was calling him. Our Lady was beckoning him. The words of Jesus had become ever stronger, "Come follow me." Yet there was parental opposition. Not that his parents were not good parents or that they were opposed to a religious vocation from among their very own. Blandina, his mother, had prayed and hoped, from the time she herself was but a girl growing up, that if marriage were her vocation and God should give her a family, at least one of her sons should be called to the Holy Priesthood. But Gino, the oldest of the Burresi household, was still so young. He had hardly entered his adolescent years. There was plenty of time. He must be more certain and not leave home to attempt the religious life on the spur of the moment.

What must have been the thoughts of Blandina at the strong insistence of her son, insisting he must leave now to join the Oblates of the Virgin Mary. There was that time when he was only five and she had been so busy and he had come home saying that the Lady at the chapel was crying and had talked to him. And there was the time he ran home from the same chapel holding his precious treasure of a holy card memento of Father Ilario's ordination, and his singing the Pater Noster as he walked through the woods, along the paths, to the amusement and amazement of the farmers in the fields. They had heard his piping voice, as Blandina had more than once, singing, *"Pater noster, qui est in caelis: Sanctificetur nomen tuum: Adveniat regnum tuum: Fiat voluntas tua, sicut in caelo, et in terra..."*

But Gino was young. There had hardly been time to see this her firstborn even begin to approach manhood. It was Gino's father who put his foot down by saying his son could not go. Gino was crushed at the decision, and, while obedient, he was determined to find a way. The call of Heaven in Gino's heart had become so strong he could delay no longer giving his heart completely to the Madonna in prayer and sacrifice so she could present it to the Lord as together they approached the Divine Majesty. With a Mother so tender, so mild, so pleading, why delay? The Sisters of the Child Mary agreed. "The love of Christ overwhelms us..." (2Cor. 6:14).

Gino Burresi determined to leave home to join the family of the Oblates of the Virgin Mary. It was not that he loved his parents and his brothers and sisters less—he loved God more. The greater family of God was calling him. The Mother of the total Christian family was now beginning to take him all to herself.

Separation from loved ones is always painful. There seems to be something of death in every change of status in life. The son who leaves home for employment, the daughter who marries: "Unless a wheat grain falls on the ground and dies, it remains only a single grain; but if it dies, it yields a rich harvest" (John 12:24).

It is doubtful that Blandina and Angelo Burresi had much selfishness mixed with their refusal to give consent to the young Gino, hardly more than fourteen years of age. Blandina remembered that she gave this son to the Madonna when still in her arms; she likewise recalled his preoccupation with God's Mother from the tenderest age. In fact, the first reaction of Blandina was to be pleased with the request of her son. The mind of the father, Angelo, was another matter. As if the refusal of his father were not enough opposition, the news of the intention of fourteen-year-old Gino to leave home and join the Oblates, who had just preached a parish mission, spread to the relatives of the Angelo Burresi household. "Angelo is right. His son is too young. How can one decide at the age of fourteen what he wants and what he will do for a lifetime. Let the boy grow up, see more of the world, and when he is older he will be in a better position to know his own mind. He's hardly past thirteen." Neither father nor relatives were pleased about Gino's decision.

But how could Angelo Burresi and relatives who resisted the decisions of the handsome young Gino know what God had in mind for this son and cousin? Perhaps mother Blandina detected a special plan, a special call of Heaven for her son, since it was she that was immediately pleased. Mary, too, had had to stand back as her Son gave Himself to public ministry all the way unto death on the Cross. Even when He was twelve years old, just entering into adolescence, She had suffered the pain of losing Him for three days only to hear Him reply to her joyful discovery in the temple, "Why were you looking for me? Did you not know that I must be busy with my Father's affairs?" (Luke 2:49).

Luke concludes: "But they did not understand what he meant" (Luke 2:50). There was much that Blandina did not understand, but she was willing to place her trust in the Madonna. That same Madonna had heard from the prophet Simeon the first time Jesus was presented in the temple: "You see this child: He is destined for the fall and for the rising of many in Israel, destined to be a sign that is rejected, and a sword will pierce your own soul, too, so that the thoughts of many may be laid bare" (Luke 2:34-35).

In any case, with the angels doubtlessly assisting, especially the guardian angel of the fourteen-year-old Gino, the summer and fall of 1946 presented ways for Gino to keep up his contacts with the Oblate Missionaries. Accomplices were found in the Sisters of the Child Mary, and communications by letter with the Oblates continued after the parish mission. The months before the departure of his son were short for Angelo Burresi but seemed long to a fourteen-year-old son who beseeched his Madonna for assistance. With God's Mother and mother Blandina to influence her husband in a gentle, supportive and respectful manner, Gino finally won the permission of both parents in the fall.

On December 10, 1946, the fourteen-year-old, eldest of Blandina Artemisi and Angelo Burresi, entered the Oblates of the Virgin Mary as an "aspirant" in the house of Pisa, where, with help of the Fathers, he completed his study in the first class of Inferior Middle School. On October 2, 1947, on the Feast of Guardian Angels, Gino entered the Apostolic School that the Oblate Fathers have at Chiavari in the Province of Genoa. There he continued and completed Middle School.

It came as a surprise to the Oblate superiors in the summer of 1950 when they learned for the first time that Gino Burresi did not aspire to be a priest. Having just passed his eighteenth birthday, the young man revealed to them his intention to interrupt his studies and become, instead, a lay brother in the same congregation. Father Moscarelli, Gino's Superior at the time, had a great spiritual love for this promising student. It was both a surprise and a shock to him to learn that the Burresi lad no longer aspired to the priesthood. Interiorly, Father Moscarelli suffered much at Gino's decision to discontinue his studies. Yet he did not want to stand in the way if God's call were other than his own desires. And so, after much insistence, the desire of the young man was granted. He remained some months longer at Chiavari in the college in order to gain practical experience for his new way of life.

On February 13, 1950, Gino entered the novitiate house which the Oblates have at Ivrea in Piemonte, near the Sanctuary of Our Lady of Monte Stella. On March 19, 1951, the Feast of St. Joseph, he made his first investiture and began the first year of the novitiate. On March 22, 1952, he was transferred to Pisa for the second year of novitiate. There he was given work in the service of the parish church of St. Michael, cleaning areas and rooms of the university students, preparing children of the parish community for their first Holy Communion and preparing the altar boys to serve the Holy Sacrifice of the Mass.

As Gino advanced in his years of postulancy and novitiate, he was always asking the Lord to make him understand what He wanted of him. As a result, the desire to become a lay brother had become so strong that consultation with Father Moscarelli had resulted in his decision to pursue the brotherhood. As a brother, Gino felt, he could more easily perform some activities with people than as a priest.

The period of novitiate was a happy one, yet not lacking in temptations. If the good angels assist one in discovering and following a vocation from God, the devil is also active and cunning. Of course, for one accustomed to prayer and penance from pre-school days, the devil must be more subtle in his attacks and temptations. With Gino the temptations took the form of "divide and conquer."

The young Gino experienced attractions toward more than one religious congregation. Gino had already changed from the initial studies which would have led to the Holy Priesthood, and now the knowledge that the young man was considering another religious congregation, then another, and still another, would give fuel to the doubts experienced among those at Gambassi who had objected when he decided to enter the Oblates at the early age of fourteen. Thus, the devil in his cunning now attracted Gino toward several orders—the Capuchins, the Fathers of the Consolation, the Franciscans, even the missionary orders. Gino was in danger of falling into that impractical idealism which never matures, permitting himself to be pulled in many directions, never settling on any one.

Still, Gino was on the right track. As St. Paul said, "For whereas I was free as to all, I made myself the servant of all, that I might gain the more. So though I am not a slave of any man, I have made myself the slave of everyone so as to win as many as I could...For the weak I made myself weak. I made myself all things to all men in order to save some at any cost, and I still do this, for the sake of the Gospel, to have a share in its blessings" (1 Cor. 9:19-23). Gino simply had to *decide*, to commit himself to the hard, lifelong, quiet work of a particular way of life— and to stick to it.

The struggle that went on inside him was pitiful. Unfortunately, some Franciscan confessors, seeing how confused the young man was, attempted to pull him their way. Rather than advise Gino to "do what you are doing" and that "God first called you in this direction and there is no clear indication that you should switch congregations," they attempted to have the water flow their way. A contemporary way of saying, "Do what you are doing," has it, "Bloom where you are planted."

Gino was at Ivrea when the struggle became especially intense. Father Pagani, who was the Secretary General of the Oblates of the Virgin Mary, had come to Ivrea, and, when midnight came, since Gino was unable to sleep and could bear the inner struggle no longer, he went to Father Pagani's door and knocked until he gained attention. The door opened. "Would you hear my confession, Father?" "Why at this particular hour? Well, come in." The young man made his confession, sharing the inner turmoil of his soul. Father Pagani listened and advised well. Finally, the young man knelt to receive sacramental absolution. "I absolve you from your sins in the Name of the Father and of the Son and of the Holy Spirit." The young man rose from his knees, the temptation and confusion vanished forever.

When I interviewed Brother Gino before beginning this volume, he said, "If I had followed the temptation, I believe yet today that I would have acted against the will of God. It is evident that the devil was trying to deceive me. I understand now that God permitted that I should go through such a strong temptation. It was good for me to have gone through this trial because I would otherwise never have understood that all this difficulty was just to confuse me and prevent me from doing the will of God. It is even possible that if I had listened to the temptation and followed it, I would have found myself back in the world."

The opportunities to give in to the temptations of the world had not been totally lacking in Gino Burresi's life. From a time even before going to the Oblate novitiate there had been a girl at the neighbor's house who had always hoped for marriage. She even wrote to Gino after he left home. One day the novice master read one of the letters from the girl. Concerned and surprised that Gino Burresi would receive such a letter, he called the young novice to his office: "What is this letter from this girl all about, Gino?" Somewhat embarrassed by the whole event, Gino, who had been pained by the attentions of the girl, answered, "Oh! That letter is from a poor retarded girl. I really don't know how she found out where I am."

Again, when Gino was about twenty-one, he had to return home to his village for a medical examination. In some strange way, the same girl discovered that he was back home. He had gone to his uncle's house where he took off his habit and put on a civilian suit in order to go for the medical examination. As Gino came out of the clinic, there stood the girl on the sidewalk waiting for him. Looking at Gino, she immediately proposed that he should marry her.

Gino answered, "At 1:00 p.m. I must return here to get the results of the doctor's examination. If I return in my civilian clothes, your request will be proper. But if I return in my religious habit, you'd better not show up, because then I'll throw you over the bridge." With that Gino never saw her again, and she stopped causing trouble.

On March 22, 1953, in the parish church of Gambassi, which has as its patroness Our Lady under the title of Our Lady of the Assumption, Gino Burresi pronounced his first religious vows, that is, his first temporary profession. He thus ended his novitiate and began the life of a religious in the Congregation of the Oblates of the Virgin Mary as a lay brother.

The Superior General of the Oblates had desired that the young man make his temporary religious profession for three years at the end of the novitiate in his own parish church of the Assumption, where he had been baptized and had made his first Holy Communion. Parents, brothers and sisters, relatives and friends, gathered at the Piere di Gambassi, Our Lady of the Assumption Parish, as Gino Burresi came home with the

Superior General for his temporary vows. It was a solemn occasion, and the young man pronounced his vows with the greatest seriousness. The Divine Liturgy accompanying the occasion was a moment of joy and edification for all present, including relatives who, more than seven years before, together with Angelo Burresi, had entertained grave misgivings about Gino's entering the Oblates so young. Twenty-six years later, Brother Gino was to look back on that March day of 1953 and remember the opposition he had received when first desirous of entering the Order. He laughed and said, "On that day everything was pacified."

Twenty-six years later, Blandina, his mother, was also able to look back as I questioned her about that day. She remembered still her son Gino at the age of two months when she prayed to the Madonna, "This is my first son. You could save him for yourself, but please save him." How those thoughts must have been on Blandina's mind the day of her son's profession—they have remained throughout the years as she beholds how the Blessed Virgin Mary has taken him ever more to herself.

Blandina looked back at her other children also and said, "On the religious point of view, they were good children, but they cannot compare with Gino. The others got married and are solid Christians, but he has been different." Blandina added: "From the time I was a little one I have practiced my faith. I have always desired to have a priest from my children. Even as a little girl I was saying that if I got married, I would be happy to have a priest." Part of being a good practicing Catholic is accepting the will of God. Having discovered the will of God for her son, who at this point seemed destined always to be a lay brother, Blandina Artemisi Burresi rejoiced, as she rejoiced, too, that her other children, Sergio, Maria Luisa, Renzo, and Maria Teresa, remained true to the faith she and Angelo had worked to see formed in them.

When asked, "Why do you think your son did not become a priest?" Blandina only replied, "That answer I don't know." But God knows: "...For My thoughts are not your thoughts, My ways not your ways; it is Yahweh who speaks. Yes, the heavens are as high above the earth as My ways are above your ways, My thoughts above your thoughts" (Is. 55:8-9).

Some who do not interpret vocations as a call from God may look upon the religious brotherhood as a waste. "Why, when a young man has determined to give up his life in celibacy to the service of Jesus Christ, would he not enter more fully into the

mission of the Church and be ordained a priest of Jesus Christ?"
Some might even think that a brother is one who was not
intelligent enough for the long studies in preparation for the
Holy Priesthood, but Brother Gino's experience, like that of
other brothers, including teaching brothers, testifies that the
vocation God gives us is not determined solely by intelligence.
From childhood Gino Burresi was gifted with many talents and
could well have mastered studies leading to ordination. He
explained his own thoughts on the subject of being a lay brother
rather than a priest in the following words: "I believed I could
then approach the people with a lot more simplicity and esteem
and could be closer to the people, either while working in the
sacristy or doing some works of charity as my family had taught
me in the past."

At the time Gino aspired to the brotherhood, they were not
using the word "lay" brother, but rather "adjutor" brother,
which was probably to distinguish between religious priests and
those who were not. "Adjutor" would signify that the brother
could "help" in the work of the Church and obviously be of great
assistance in bringing people closer to Jesus and to His
priesthood. In this fashion, Brother Gino did humble work, such
as in Chiavari, where he went to visit the sick in the hospitals
and visited the poor of the city. He would be seen carrying the
poor some wood. Looking back at this, he told me with a smile,
"If the priest had been seen carrying wood under his mantle, he
would have been excommunicated, but for a brother nobody
would make any remark."

Some have said that Brother Gino had wished to become a lay
brother like St. Francis of Assisi, who died October 4, 1226,
having received the Stigmata about a year before, and who
deemed himself unworthy to become a priest. This, however, is
not the reason why Brother Gino discontinued the studies which
would have led him to the priesthood. For who is worthy of even
receiving the Sacrament of the Holy Eucharist, the Body, Blood,
Soul and Divinity of Jesus Christ in Holy Communion? Who, in
fact, is worthy of Baptism and Confirmation? No man merits any
of these gifts, not even salvation. What Brother Gino sought was
simply God's will. That same will, moreover, was to lead him
after years of brotherly service to resume his studies for the
priesthood, as we shall see.

His new life as a lay brother began at Pisa in the parish where
he continued performing such tasks as keeping the church clean
and teaching catechism to the acolytes. Here Brother Gino

remained for three years, winning the deep love and affection of the youth and adults whom he inspired to live the Christ-life and have a deep devotion to the Mother of God. After these years, he made his final profession, happy at his choice, perfectly content that in the humble life of a lay brother he had discovered the will of God—loving the Madonna, adoring her Son, and serving the people of God in whatever humble assignments were given him.

Perpetual procession on April 17, 1956, was a glorious day for Gino Burresi. He had long before given his heart to the Heart of God and to the Immaculate Heart of God's Mother. Now that gift was consecrated in solemn vows before the representatives of Holy Mother Church, in a perpetual gift he intended never to relinquish. Having once given God the gift, he would never take it back.

"And Mary said:
'My soul proclaims the greatness of the Lord
and my spirit exults in God my savior;
because he has looked upon his lowly handmaid.
Yes, from this day forward all generations will
call me blessed, for the Almighty has done great
things for me.
Holy is his name,
and his mercy reaches from age to age for those
who fear him.
He has shown the power of his arm,
he has routed the proud of heart.
He has pulled down princes from their thrones
and exalted the lowly.
The hungry he has filled with good things,
the rich sent empty away.
He has come to the help of Israel his servant,
mindful of his mercy—according to the promise
he made to our ancestors—
of his mercy to Abraham and to his descendants
forever.' " (Luke 1:46-55)

IV. Brother Gino and Our Lady of Fatima

The remarkable story of Brother Gino's association with Our Lady of Fatima is the story of his early manhood. It begins with his assignment as a catechist at St. Michael's Parish in Pisa. His students were learning that they were children of God and spiritual children of Mary. There was no abstraction in Brother Gino's approach: simple, humble, direct, in the language children understand. The love for Jesus and His Mother was both deep and personal in the humble, quiet lay brother, and the simplicity of faith and deep love for God and His Mother became personal for the children as well.

There are all kinds of modern audio-visual aids for the teaching of children and youth, but there has been found no substitute for the living voice coming from a teacher whose soul is penetrated with faith and love and reflects the Lord Jesus:

"The word that is the faith we proclaim is very near to you; it is on your lips and in your heart. If your lips confess that Jesus is Lord and if you believe in your heart that God raised Him from the dead, then you will be saved. By believing from the heart you are made righteous; by confessing with your lips you are saved. When scripture says, 'Those who believe in Him will have no cause for shame,' it makes no distinction between Jew and Greek: all belong to the same Lord, who is rich enough, however many ask his help, for everyone who calls on the name of the Lord will be saved.

"But they will not ask His help unless they believe in him, and they will not believe in Him unless they have heard of Him, and they will not hear of Him unless they get a preacher, and they will never have a preacher unless one is sent, but as scripture says, 'The footsteps of those who bring good news is a welcome sound.' Not everyone, of course, listens to the Good News. So faith comes from what is preached, and what is preached comes from the word of Christ" (Romans 10:8-17).

For the few years of his first teaching assignment, Brother Gino enjoyed the children of his catechism classes and the boys he trained and guided in the serving of the Sacrifice of the Mass. "The footsteps of those who bring good news is a welcome sound," says God's word, and the footsteps of their beloved teacher, in his early twenties, tall and handsome, brought, in turn, a gentle, soft-spoken joy to the young people of Pisa. Indeed, what a joy it was to prepare the children of the Parish of St. Michael to receive their first Holy Communion and make their first Confession. Brother Gino could assure these little ones that the priest represented Jesus Christ and had the indelible mark of Jesus the High Priest on his soul. From that indelible mark or character of Holy Orders, stamped upon the soul of the priest, came the power for the very Person of Jesus Christ to act to forgive sins and to change bread and wine into the living substance of the Body, Blood, Soul and Divinity of Jesus Christ.

Brother Gino found simple and direct ways to teach children profound truths of faith. It was Jesus Christ, their loving Lord and Savior, that they would receive in Holy Communion. Jesus is God and Jesus is Man. Jesus is so kind, loving and humble that He comes to us in the form of a little round wafer. But when at Holy Mass the priest, who is another Christ, says those sacred words of Consecration—"This is My Body...This is My Blood..."—there is no longer bread and wine. Brother Gino taught these truths by example. Kneeling in prayer before the

Real Presence of Jesus in the Most Blessed Sacrament, genuflecting with love and a spirit of adoration, and witnessed by the children and youth of the parish, he communicated as much as, or more than, is written in the pages of a book about the Holy Eucharist. Whether he was preparing the students for Penance or simply teaching the Sign of the Cross, Brother Gino taught from his heart with the childlike faith that was his own.

Three years is a long time in the life of a university student. To Brother Gino, spending the first years after his first profession with these children, it seemed as though it would last forever. He was their special teacher whom they loved and understood and who loved and understood them. But it was not only the small children that occupied his time at Pisa. There, besides looking after the church, he dedicated himself to helping the poor. He also had the responsibility of cleaning the rooms of students who were in residence at the university—students who were easily attracted to the ways of the world and who often put God out of their minds. Brother Gino used the opportunities he had while cleaning student rooms to meet these young men and to guide them. His kindness and concern for their souls was the occasion of many conversions among the university students.

Then one day the sad news came that Brother Gino was being transferred to the college of Chiavari, where he had done his first studies. The altar boys and the children of the catechism class were greatly saddened and decided that they must not let Brother Gino go without some small remembrance of them. They must buy him a gift. And so these poor children gathered their precious coins together and looked hard for just the right gift that would please the religious lay brother who had taught them to love God and His Blessed Mother. Finally, they came to a store that had second-hand objects. Their eyes became enchanted by a little golden statue of the Madonna, forty centimeters high. The little statue with the folded hands, the Madonna in prayer, the white mantle of Our Lady with its gold border, held the children in rapture. Did not Brother Gino have a great love for the Madonna? Had he not often spoken of her to the children? How he loved her. Surely he would be pleased with this gift. And, best of all, they could afford this used statue.

The children presented their gift to Brother Gino, knowing nothing more of what the statue represented than that it was the Blessed Virgin Mary. When Brother Gino saw their gift, he was pleased with the generosity and thoughtfulness of the children. However, with the Madonnina itself he was not pleased. It was not his favorite, Our Lady of Lourdes. But it was a gift, so he examined it more closely. On the pedestal of the little statue, he found the words "Our Lady of Fatima." He had not heard of her "Why that title?" he asked. "What does it mean?"

Brother Gino had never heard before of Our Lady of Fatima. It was many years since Our Lady had appeared in central Portugal with a message for the entire world. Brother Gino had been well instructed by his mother, Blandina, to know and love the Mother of Jesus. The Oblates of the Virgin Mary are especially devoted to Mary, but never could he recall hearing one word about Our Lady of Fatima.

Brother Gino had followed the advice of his mother well. When he left home she had said to him, "Gino, always turn to the Madonna of Lourdes, and you will see that she will always help you." Many years before, she had inscribed Gino under the special patronage of Our Lady of Lourdes. Later, Blandina described to me the gradual shift in Gino's interest to Fatima: "The little statue of Our Lady which is at the Mammertine now was given to him by the children, and he did not want it. He said to me, 'If only they had given me that of Our Lady of Lourdes—because when I left home you commended me to her.' Gradually, however, he came to love Our Lady of Fatima, and he has continued the apostolate under the name of Our Lady of Fatima. While I told him, 'Always turn to the Madonna of Lourdes,' it is the Madonna of Fatima who has helped him more." But his love for Fatima was to grow slowly, a new blossom in his garland of devotion to the Mother of God.

At this time, he was well acquainted with, and influenced primarily by, the Lourdes events and the message God gave the world in France in 1858, just four years after Pope Pius IX had infallibly defined the dogma of the Immaculate Conception. It will be remembered that on March 25, 1858, Bernadette, a young girl from the mountain village of Lourdes who had seen the beautiful Lady from heaven before, was on this occasion to follow the instruction of her parish priest and ask the Lady her name. Having received Our Lady's answer, Bernadette took off like a flash, running toward the parish rectory. Along the way she repeated the words over and over again so she would not forget them. She must tell them exactly to the pastor as the Lady had spoken them, although Bernadette had no idea what the words meant. At last she arrived at the priest's house. Bursting in upon him, she shouted, "*I am the Immaculate Conception.* The Lady, she told me. She gave me her name like you asked. She said, 'I am the Immaculate Conception.' " The pastor was dumbfounded. Here was a poor, simple girl, pious, but not gifted intellectually, blurting out that glorious title, giving that name to her Lady in the grotto, when she did not even know what she was saying. The pastor was somewhat of a scholar himself, and he immediately recognized the profound implications of the title. It had truly to be the Mother of God. St. Bernadette was canonized by Pope Pius XI on December 8, 1933, the Feast of the Immaculate Conception. Gino Burresi was not quite one and a half years old at the time of the canonization, but the seventy-five years since the miraculous events at the Rock of Massabielle, and the subsequent canonization and devotion to God's Mother and her Immaculate Conception which spread, were sufficient for Blandina Burresi to instill into her young son Gino a great devotion to Our Lady of Lourdes. Devotion to Our Lady under that title was devotion to the Immaculate Conception.

Nonetheless, Brother Gino, who brought only a few personal things with him to Chiavari, did bring the little statue of the Madonna which the children of Pisa had given him. His newly assigned tasks included the duty of working in the small chapels of the Sacred Heart of Jesus, doing janitorial work in the college and cleaning the areas near the church and the janitor's room.

Quietly going about his duties, Brother Gino came into contact with people in the area. Eventually, many people began to note the devoted attitude of the brother, and his humble manner which led them to open their souls to him. They began to ask his counsel and prayers for their spiritual and temporal needs. For everyone who came to him, he found words of comfort and he invited them to turn with faith to Our Lady. Meanwhile, he himself was seeking to unravel the mystery of his little statue by reading whatever books or articles he could find on the subject of Fatima.

What was to follow was the beginning of astonishing events in the life of Brother Gino. All that he knew about Our Lady of Lourdes was to remain very much a part of his spiritual life. But now his love and reverence for the Immaculate Conception was to expand to include the Immaculate Heart of the Virgin Mother Mary.

The lay brother was to learn that for six continuous months, May through October of 1917, the Mother of God had appeared to three shepherd children in central Portugal in the parish of Fatima. The events took place atop a mountain of the Serra de

Aire. Two of the children were brother and sister, Francisco and Jacinta, ages nine and seven at the time. The third was their cousin Lucia, age ten. It was in the Hollow of Irene (Cova da Iria) where God's Mother appeared as a woman of light.

Two of the children lived only a short time after the apparitions, fulfilling the prediction of Our Lady that she would soon take them to heaven. Lucia would have to remain upon this earth for many years in order to spread devotion in the world to the Immaculate Heart of Mary. The Lady from heaven said that on October 13, 1917, at noon, she would perform a miracle so that all could believe. This she did—the miracle of the sun, witnessed by people from up to thirty-five miles away and seen by approximately 100,000 people in some estimates. None place the number below 70,000.

The children were far from Russia and had no knowledge of the events taking place there, and yet the Lady mentioned Russia, and the children related what she said. During the same months as Our Lady's appearances, the Russian Revolution was taking shape—the beginning of Communism's atheistic, totalitarian attempt at world domination. It was in the third apparition on July 13, 1917, that Our Lady mentioned Russia both as a scourge of God to punish the sins of the world, and as the object of Divine Mercy, by the promise of its conversion through the intermediary of the Immaculate Heart of Mary.

The events went like this. Our Lady appeared over the little holm-oak tree, after the flash of light, as she was to do each of the six months. "What do you want of me?" Lucia asked. She continued: "I want you to tell us who you are, and to perform a miracle so that everyone will believe that you have appeared to us."

The Lady replied, "Continue to come here every month. In October I will tell you who I am and what I want, and I will perform a miracle so that all may believe." She also said that certain persons must say the Rosary in order to obtain the graces of their requests during the year. "Sacrifice yourselves for sinners, and say often, especially when you make sacrifices, 'Oh, Jesus, this is for love of You, for the conversion of sinners, and in reparation for the sins committed against the Immaculate Heart of Mary.' "

Saying these last words, Our Lady opened her hands, as she had done during the two previous months. The light from them seemed to penetrate the earth, and the children saw a great sea of fire. Lucia describes the vision of hell as follows:

"Plunged into this fire were demons and souls that looked like transparent embers, some black or bronze, in human form, driven about by the flames that issued from within themselves together with clouds of smoke. They were falling on all sides, just as sparks cascade from great firs, without weight or equilibrium, amid cries of pain and despair which horrified us so that we trembled with fear. (It must have been this sight which caused me to cry out, as the people say they heard me exclaim aloud.) The demons could be distinguished by their likeness to terrible, loathsome and unknown animals, transparent as live coals. Terrified and as if to plead for succour, we raised our eyes to Our Lady, who said to us kindly but sadly:

"You have seen hell, where the souls of poor sinners go. In order to save them, God wishes to establish in the world devotion to my Immaculate Heart. If you do what I tell you, many souls will be saved, there will be peace. The war will end, but if men do not cease offending God, another and more terrible war will break out during the pontificate of Pius XI. When you see a night lit up by an unknown light, know that it is the sign God gives you that He is about to punish the world for its crimes by means of war, hunger, and persecution of the Church and the Holy Father. In order to prevent this, I shall come to ask for the consecration of Russia to my Immaculate Heart and for the Communion of reparation on the first Saturdays. If my wishes are fulfilled, Russia will be converted and there will be peace. If not, Russia will spread her errors throughout the world, promoting wars and persecution of the Church. The good will be martyred, the Holy Father will have much to suffer, and various nations will be annihilated. But in the end, my Immaculate Heart will triumph. The Holy Father will consecrate Russia to me and it will be converted, and a time of peace will be conceded to the world. In Portugal the Dogma of Faith will always be preserved...Do not tell this to anybody. You may tell it to Francisco.

"When you recite the Rosary, after each mystery say: "Oh, my Jesus, forgive us; save us from the fire of hell; lead all souls to heaven, especially those who are most in need."

A short silence followed and Lucia asked, "Is there anything more that you want of me?"

"No, I do not want anything more of you today." As in the previous and following apparitions, the Lady began to ascend toward the east, until she finally disappeared in the infinity of space.

As Brother Gino studied the accounts of Fatima, he

meditated on the events and began to see beyond the story. Many have read the story of Fatima, even have seen the movie of Fatima over and over, and still miss the rich doctrinal content of Fatima and its message for the world and for each one of us. Pius XII has called it a "reaffirmation of the Gospels." The lay brother, now at Chiavari, was to penetrate the story that merely entertains or edifies some and find motivation for himself and for others for an authentic spiritual program of life in harmony with the Gospels.

In Fatima Brother Gino discovered the Mystery of the Most Blessed Trinity and the profound sense of annihilation experienced by the children as they adored the all-holy God. He saw the Providence of God as He directs and governs the world and presides over human history, knowing future events and able to intervene with extraordinary signs. Brother Gino also saw that God is the Rewarder Who also punishes, but One Who is infinitely merciful toward repentant sinners and most anxious for that repentance. He also noted that Fatima confirms the reality of heaven, hell and purgatory.

At a time when the world was growing cold to the love of God and faith in the Real Presence of Jesus in the Most Blessed Sacrament was growing weak, Fatima reminded Brother Gino of the Real Presence of Jesus Christ in the Most Blessed Sacrament of the Altar and the necessity and meritorious value of Holy Communion and adoration of our Eucharistic Lord.

Fatima further reveals that sanctity is a necessary condition for true happiness, even on this earth, and that sin brings misery already in this world. Brother Gino was to meditate on all these events so that frequently he would advise souls, as he advised the author of this book, "Be holy."

Our Lady's protrayal of the reality of sin as an offense against God and the Immaculate Heart of Mary, and of its tragic consequences for sinners, led Gino to come gradually to a deeper understanding of devotion to the Immaculate Heart of Mary as the great revelation of Fatima. Fatima further revealed to Brother Gino that flight from sin and amendment of life are indispensable conditions for the state of grace. As he dug more and more into whatever he could find on Fatima, he began to realize that the Mother of God was the Mediatrix and Dispensatrix of all graces from Jesus the Source. The expiatory value of penance and prayer became ever more clear, and the prime importance of Eucharistic Reparation became ever more appreciated.

The lay brother was to grow continuously in his love for the Rosary and in his ability to meditate on the mysteries ever more profoundly. Our Lady had insisted each time she appeared on the praying of the daily Rosary. She had taught that the proper praying of the Rosary required meditation on the mysteries. Brother Gino grew in spirituality until one, two, or three Rosaries a day would not be enough. Like Francisco, he must say as many Rosaries as possible each day.

The action of grace transforming the Fatima children had led them to great union with God. After the terrible vision of hell, the spiritual transformation of the children greatly intensified, thus contradicting modern theories which would have us hide from children the reality of hell and the terrible consequences of sin. Sister Lucia herself noted years later that whereas some think we ought not teach these truths to children, yet Heaven did not hesitate to reveal the reality of hell to three little children, one only seven years of age. Brother Gino, as he grew in spirituality, was to have direct and visible confrontations with the devil.

The necessity for the sanctification of the family is seen at Fatima in imitation of the vivid scene of the last apparition. Loyalty and devotion to the Pope is very much a part of the Fatima message, as it is of the spirituality of the Oblates of the Virgin Mary. For Brother Gino, the importance of the papacy and undivided loyalty to the Pope was reaffirmed in the Fatima message as already taught by the doctrines of the Church and emphasized so vividly by the Oblates' founder, Father Pio Bruno Lanteri.

The necessity of purity and modesty as reaffirmed at Fatima and as taught by the Gospels and the Church, were virtues the lay brother was to emphasize, at times most frankly, to certain pilgrims who would come to him in the years ahead, some of whom would be reluctant to change their style of life, so identified with the world.

Brother Gino saw in the Fatima message what many have missed. The simplification of the message as merely a directive to say the Rosary each day is far from the position which sees Our Lady of Fatima as a catechist presenting the truths of our Holy Catholic Faith, one by one, in such clarity that children can understand and in such profundity that theologians would have to meditate on the Fatima message for decades to even begin to plumb its depths.

Brother Gino would see Communism gain a foothold in his

own beloved Italy and remember that Our Lady of Fatima had said that if her message were not heeded, "Russia will spread her errors throughout the world, promoting wars and persecution of the Church."

Consecration to the Immaculate Heart of Mary, especially as lived by Jacinta, the youngest of the Fatima children, was a part of the Fatima message which became ever more dear to the heart of Brother Gino as he contemplated the sweetness of his Mother's Heart and all that she had said. Understanding now the meaning of the Madonnina, the little statue of Our Lady of Fatima given to him by the children, Brother Gino developed a loving devotion to her and began to share it with others.

At Lourdes, Our Lady had held the Rosary over her elbow and smiled constantly. Bernadette said that it seemed that all Our Lady did was smile. At Fatima, Our Lady holds the Rosary in the palms of her hands. The world situation is more desperate now. The urgency for prayer and sacrifice is even more needed. Our Lady of Fatima smiled but once and that is when she said to the children, "God is pleased with your sacrifices." If Our Lady was the Joyful Mother at Lourdes, when the same Blessed Mother came to Fatima in the following and present century, she who is the Glorious Mother of heaven came as the Sorrowful Mother.

Meanwhile, more and more of the faithful came to Brother Gino with their problems, large and small. For everyone he continued to find words of comfort, and he now invited them to turn with faith and love to Our Lady of Fatima. Every evening in the recollection of his small room, before the small statue of the Madonna of Fatima, he repeated the requests of the faithful presented to him that day.

With the permission of his Superior, he went periodically to visit the sick in the nearby Civil Hospital, bringing to them his words of comfort. Always Brother Gino would invite these people to prayer and faith in the maternal intercession of Mary. To everyone he gave small objects of devotion, such as medals, little rosaries and holy cards. Not only the sick but also the doctors and infirmarians enjoyed, desired and awaited his visits. Some of these would later come to visit the lay brother secretly at the college of Chiavari.

Very soon many souls began to tell how they had obtained unusual graces which they believed to be the result of the efficacious prayers of Brother Gino. There were cures and important conversions that took place that seemed to have no explanation other than the miraculous. And so the humble lay brother of Chiavari could no longer remain hidden. The knowledge of this quiet lay brother and the seeming power of his prayers spread through all the towns and villages of the Gulf of Tigullio. Still, Brother Gino continued his humble tasks. Twice a week he went to visit the sick in the hospitals. He would also visit the poor of the city and would even carry them some wood under his mantle.

The people knew that he was helping the poor, and so they would call out to him on his way to the market place, "Fratel Gino. Come over here. Here, I have something for you to give to your poor people." The charity of Brother Gino was contagious. Humbly accepting these gifts for the poor, he would in turn leave the donors with some good spiritual thoughts, food for the soul. Always important in his advice was that they must pray to and trust in Our Lady of Fatima.

The people continued to appreciate Gino's exceptional goodness. More and more people came to him to solve their problems of conscience and to confide to him their sorrows, their worries and their doubts. Brother Gino would take these people before the statue of the Madonna of Fatima and say: "Let us pray together. Our Lady will help us."

Thus it was that at Chiavari, helped in a special way by Our Lady of Fatima, Gino began his special apostolate: conversion of sinners through counseling, direction of good souls, and care of the sick. All this he did with such discretion and humility that even his superiors did not at first realize the magnitude of his charitable works and the great effect he was having on so many souls, near and far.

It became more and more obvious why God had called Gino, at least for a time, to the vocation of the brotherhood. He was able to touch many as a humble lay brother who might have shied away from ordained priests. Brother Gino served as a beautiful bridge to and representative of Christ, in touching many souls and moving their hearts to repentance. Thus, through his influence, souls were motivated and opened to approach the priests of the Church for the Sacraments of Reconciliation and Communion with our Eucharistic Lord.

Brother Gino was moving more and more in his Marian spirituality from a focus on the grand and unique privilege of the Immaculate Conception, Mary conceived without sin, to contemplation of her Immaculate Heart. He was moving more and more from Lourdes to Fatima without being unmindful of the former. Mary, after all, was conceived of her parents, Anna and

Joachim, in an immaculate state, free of any stain of sin, and this was beyond the will of parents or child. She is indeed the Immaculate Conception. Yet, her Immaculate Heart requires an ongoing response. As she lived upon earth, of her own free will she believed, and she loved and became Model of Martyrs in a life of reparation. God made the first act of will. He would create this Creature immaculate. Mary willed to continue living that life of being completely free of all stain of sin. The former is her Immaculate Conception. The latter is her Immaculate Heart. That the Immaculate Heart of Mary is inseparable from the Sacred Heart of Jesus, and that there is superabounding love in these two Hearts—such is the great revelation of Fatima.

In the third apparition, on July 13, 1917, Our Lady mentioned her Immaculate Heart at least four times. "Sacrifice yourselves for sinners and say often, especially when you make some sacrifice: 'Oh Jesus, this is for love of You, for the conversion of sinners, and in reparation for the sins committed against the Immaculate Heart of Mary.'

"...God wishes to establish in the world devotion to my Immaculate Heart...I shall come to ask for the consecration of Russia to my Immaculate Heart, and the Communion of reparation on the first Saturdays...In the end, my Immaculate Heart will triumph..."

Jacinta developed to a profound degree devotion to the Immaculate Heart of Mary, while Francisco was consumed with the desire to console his God. During the second apparition of Our Lady at Fatima, Jacinta and Francisco were seen in the light which rose towards heaven, revealing that they would soon be taken to heaven. Lucia was in that light which poured out over the earth, revealing that she must remain many years yet on earth to be an instrument of God in spreading devotion to the Immaculate Heart of Mary.

On October 13, 1942, Pope Pius XII, observing the twenty-fifth anniversary of the apparitions of Our Lady of Fatima, broadcast a message to the Portuguese nation, and while praying for peace, for the Church and for the entire world, used the opportunity to consecrate the Church and the World to the Immaculate Heart of Mary. His address ended with these words: "Even as the Church and the whole human race were consecrated to the Heart of Jesus, that they might place in Him all their hopes and that this Heart might be for them a token and assurance of salvation, so may they also forever be consecrated to you, to your Immaculate Heart, O Mary, our Mother and

Queen of the World, that your love and your protection may hasten the triumpth of the Kingdom of God on earth, and that all nations, reconciled to each other and to God, may proclaim you blessed and, from one end of the earth to the other, may sing together with you the eternal Magnificat of glory, of love and of gratitude towards the Heart of Jesus, in Whom alone they can find Truth, Life and Peace'' (*Acta Apost. Sedis,* Nov. 23, 1942, p. 346).

As Brother Gino so well understands and teaches, devotion to the Immaculate Heart of Mary does not mean simply honoring her *physical* heart. While certainly we do *honor* the physical heart of Mary, as we do her entire holy body, and as we *adore* the entire Body of Jesus as hypostatically united to His Divinity, yet, devotion to Mary's Heart means much more. Her physical heart is the symbol of her love for God and for men, of whom she is the Mother. Thus, on May 4, 1944, the Sacred Congregation of Rites issued a decree extending the Feast of the Immaculate Heart of Mary to the universal Church. It stated: ''By this cult, the Church renders to the Immaculate Heart of the Blessed Virgin Mary the honor which is due to her, since, under the symbol of this Heart, she pays homage to her eminent holiness and particularly to her ardent love for God and her Son Jesus, and to her maternal love for men, redeemed by the Blood of God'' (*Acta Apost. Sedis,* Vol. XXXVII, p. 50).

Already in 1857, three years after the definition of the dogma of the Immaculate Conception, and the year before the apparitions to Bernadette, the Consultors for the Sacred Congregation of Rites had approved of devotion to the Immaculate Heart. In the liturgical prayers for the Sacrifice of the Mass and the Divine Office approved on that occasion, the focus was almost totally on Mary's love for God. The Mass and the Liturgy of the Hours approved for our present times, however, emphasize the love of her Heart for men and encourage our trust in Mary's intercessory power.

The formal and essential object of devotion to the Immaculate Heart of Mary then is the love of God's Mother for her Divine Son, Jesus Christ, and for all mankind. This devotion includes, too, the total Person of Mary, her entire inner life, her virtues, her love of purtiy, her humility, all her affections, and, as Brother Gino learned from his study of Fatima, all her sorrows.

The connection between the Sorrows of the Blessed Virgin Mary and devotion to her Immaculate Heart was prophesied already by the prophet Simeon. ''You see this child: He is destined for the fall and for the rising of many in Israel, destined to be a sign that is rejected, and a sword will pierce your own soul, too, so that the secret thoughts of many may be laid bare'' (Luke 2:34-35). And how many thoughts are laid bare as they react to devotion to the Mother of Jesus, the Son of God made Man!

What is important is that we realize that devotion to the Immaculate Heart involves the total Person of God's Mother—all that she is and has in the fullness of grace, as she is Mediatrix of Grace, something recognized by Vatican Council II. While the essential object, if we must make distinctions as theologians are wont to do, consists in the love of the Virgin Mother of God for her Divine Son and men, the secondary object of the devotion involves her whole inner life, for, as the Angel Gabriel said, she is "full of grace."

Brother Gino's detailed study of Our Lady of Fatima brought him face to face with all these truths, and so to a greater devotion to the Immaculate Heart of Mary and a deeper understanding of the living of one's consecration to God's Mother. As he grew spiritually, the people of Chiavari continued to come to this man who spent himself assisting the poor, the sick, and the troubled. He directed them all to the Madonna of Fatima.

But he was not to remain at Chiavari forever. On Easter Monday, 1955, by order of his superiors, he was transferred to the community of the Oblates of the Virgin Mary which is attached to the parish church of St. Helena. Again Brother Gino packed his few personal belongings, including the little statue of Our Lady of Fatima, and left for a new, more prominent assignment, for St. Helena's was a church of Rome.

> "How rich are the depths of God—how deep his wisdom and knowledge—and how impossible to penetrate his motives or understand his methods! Who could ever know the mind of the Lord? Who could ever be his counsellor? Who could ever give him anything or lend him anything? All that exists comes from him; all is by him and for him. To him be glory forever! Amen." (Romans 11:33-36)

V. The Finger of God

At present, many seminarians live at St. Helena's in Rome during their years of theology, prior to ordination. When Brother Gino arrived in 1955 he was given care of the church and the job of cleaning the house. He was also of some assistance to the children of the parish oratory. But his reputation followed him to Rome. Friends and the devout of Liguria continued to turn to him through letters, through relatives they had in Rome, or through those near the parish. Some of the people of Chiavari called their friends in Rome to tell them how the lay Brother Gino had a special concern for the poor. "Help that brother in his apostolate. He does much good for souls. He needs your help in order to help the poor."

And they did. Good people in Rome began bringing things to the lay brother. Never one to make issue of his charity, he worked quietly at his special apostolate, and he found that he needed some place to hide the things people were giving him for the poor. Now, the old pulpit with the steps leading up to it, raised over the people, was no longer used. Who would look there?

Placing the things received from the people in bags, Brother Gino hid them on the pulpit steps. It was his charge to keep the church clean, and it was unlikely that anyone else would discover his supply center for the poor since no one ever used that pulpit for preaching. But one day Padre Luigi Torezani decided the old pulpit should be used again. He went to the pulpit to preach and found the bags which contained food, shoes, and clothes. It was only with difficulty that he could mount the preacher's platform.

Gino had been discovered.

The lay brother's stay at St. Helena's in Rome was to last approximately two and one-half years. On November 4, 1957, the Rector Major called Gino to be near him in the house of the General Curia that is next to the Mammertine Prison in the heart of Rome. The Oblates still have charge of the Mammertine Prison where, almost two thousand years ago, St. Peter and St. Paul were held. There at the Mammertine, across from the Forum, Brother Gino continued his efforts. There the friends and devout of Liguria met him, along with new friends he had made at St. Helena's.

Daily, those who came to see the brother grew more numerous. His reputation for holiness had spread, and more and more people came to ask graces through the intercession of the "Madonnina." Many returned to give thanks for favors received. Almost everyone who came wanted to see the little statue of Our Lady of Fatima. All wanted to touch it and to pray before it. The superiors at the Mammertine allowed the little statue to be exposed over a side altar in the church dedicated to St. Joseph.

Brother Gino did not forget his poor in the heart of Rome. There, too, he gathered things, keeping them in his room, which had a window on the facade of the building. Emphasizing secrecy, he would say to the poor, "You come after 10 p.m. If you come at night, I will lower down in a basket through the window what you need." Thus, Brother Gino was able to supply poor people with cheese, various foodstuffs, or the little bit of money he had.

One day, unknown to Brother Gino, now in perpetual profession, Father Ilario Bruni, who had had a great effect on him at the age of six and again at the age of twelve, returned from the Argentine mission. Father Bruni is the priest Brother Gino considers that God used to direct his vocation as an Oblate, because he had been thinking of joining some religious like the Salesians or the Franciscans, but none of them came along. The first Oblate he met to discuss such a vocation with was Father Ilario.

Father Ilario had been in Argentina for 15 years when he returned to Rome and walked into the Mammertine, where the Rector Major of the Oblates lives and directs the Oblates of the Virgin Mary, now existing in seven nations. Brother Gino had been working about the premises. He was just coming out of the kitchen when he heard a striking voice coming from the sacristy of the chapel which adjoins the living quarters. Brother Gino stopped in his tracks, thinking: "I know that voice." Then Father Ilario appeared and, seeing Brother Gino, asked the Superior, "Who is this priest?"

The Superior answered, "This is Brother Gino."

Brother Gino looked joyfully at the priest who had so inspired and guided him in the brief meetings of his younger days. He spoke to Father Ilario: "You are the one who brought me to Chiavari. You are the one who introduced me to the Oblates." Brother Gino then reviewed for Father Ilario the events of his first Mass—how he had come to Gino's parish church when Gino was only six years old, and how they had met later when Father Ilario came for a parish mission.

Yes, Gino still preserved that first Mass card. "Here, Father Ilario. Here, look, it is your ordination and first Mass holy card I've kept all these years. Do you remember the little boy who was putting flowers at the shrine of the Blessed Mother on the road? You asked me if I were saying my morning and night prayers, and I said, 'Yes, I say them well,' and now I am myself an Oblate."

What little things God uses to draw men to himself. The Lord doubtlessly had looked into the soul of the young Gino from the earliest years and said, "Come follow me." As the Lord used His Mother to give Gino the call, so the Virgin Mother Mary is today an instrument to call many young men and women to her Son. And the Lord uses often the simplest means, as he used Father Ilario with his singing of the Pater Noster and the first Mass card for Gino Burresi. God is using Gino Burresi today, as shall be evident in the pages ahead, to help the scales fall from the ears of many a young man and woman so that they might hear the call of Heaven.

The faithful who came to Mammertine kept increasing, as they wanted to recite the Rosary before Brother Gino's little statue. Many went there every day and thus became friends and thought to unite themselves in an organization to work more efficaciously with Brother Gino so as to make known the devotion of the Madonna of Fatima and her message. Seeing the importance that the movement was taking on, and fearing that the ecclesiastical authority (Vicariate) might show some concern, Brother Gino decided that perhaps permission could be obtained to found canonically the "Pious Congregaton of Our Lady of Fatima" for the conversion of sinners.

With the aid of Monsignor Crovella, a member of the

Brother Gino at the age of fifteen—taken just as he entered the Oblates as a student.

Brother Gino at prayer, age 33, in the first chapel at San Vittorino.

Brother Gino with a dove which befriended him.

Brother Gino with Mother Teresa of Calcutta, Fr. Joseph Breault, and seminarians of San Vittorino.

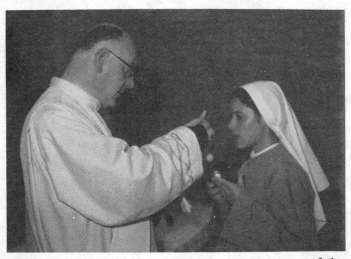

Brother Gino, a deacon, gives Holy Communion to one of the sisters of the Order he founded.

Brother Gino assists Fr. Fox (author) at Mass at San Vittorino.

Brother Gino with young men on Fr. Fox's pilgrimage to Fatima.

Two of Brother Gino's paintings, originally done in color. On the left is the "Mother of Sweetness" which he gave to Fr. Fox.

San Vittorino

Carissimi Giovani

Per mezzo del Padre Fox sono venuto a conoscenza del vostro gruppo animato da buona volontà di volere onorare il Cuore Immacolato di Maria. Ebbene, cari giovani fatevi coraggio in quest'ora così difficile in cui tutto il mondo viene tormentato dal materialismo. Cerchiamo di essere dei veri devoti della Madonna, e noi per primi cerchiamo di vivere con autenticità il suo grande messaggio di salvezza e di pace. Cerchiamo di essere i primi a tenere in mano la dolce catena del Rosario da Lei tanto raccomandata, e l'assidua frequenza ai santi Sacramenti; offerti per la salvezza nostra e degli altri. Un vero devoto della Madonna, non può trascurare l'Eucaristia, ma ogni giorno si unisce con Gesù Cristo per mezzo di questo grande Sacramento di amore. La Madonna vi guidi sempre, affinché possiate essere la vera luce che illumina ogni momento questa povera terra così avvolta nelle tenebre. Preghiamo e offriamo le nostre sante Comunioni, i nostri Rosari e tutti i nostri sacrifici, affinché il Cuore Immacolato della Madonna salvi tanti nostri fratelli che sono nella morte orrenda del peccato, e ottenga finalmente a tutto il mondo la tanto desiderata Pace, pace nel cuore di ogni uomo e pace in ogni angolo della terra. Vorrei che il vostro gruppo diventi sempre più numeroso, e porti sempre tanto bene in particolare a tanti altri giovani che vivono nella schiavitù del peccato – e non pensano che solo il peccato e la causa di tanti mali, fisici e morali – egli porta sempre all'odio e alla separazione, e così la pace è sempre più lontana.
Vi auguro che possiate fare sempre tanto bene
e Vi assicuro il ricordo della mia preghiera
Fratel Gino O.M.V.

Brother Gino's letter to American youth (see page 124) in the original handwriting.

Secretariat of the Vatican State, a rule governing the association was proposed. There was a careful examination of the actions of the faithful in the new devotion. The Statute was officially approved by the Vicariate of the Holy Father, Cardina Micara, on February 28, 1958. Thus, through the initial instrumentality of the sacramental of the little Madonna statue, the movement grew and won official Church approval. In fact, Pope Pius XII, himself greatly devoted to Our Lady of Fatima, met in audience with Brother Gino and personally blessed the little statue and his work in the Fatima apostolate.

Meanwhile, the number of devotees in the Pious Congregation of Our Lady of Fatima continued to grow, not only in Italy, but also in France, Belgium, Germany and other European countries. Likewise, the Pious Congregation of Our Lady of Fatima grew at the Mammertine, beginning with only a few persons but growing very large. There are now members in all parts of Italy, and they are called Prayer Groups of Our Lady of Fatima.

In the beginning, in addition to praying and spreading devotion to Our Lady of Fatima, there was an additional aim: to provide for the material development of the work, which eventually grew into the apostolate headquartered at the Sanctuary of San Vittorino, the subject of another chapter. At present, only the spiritual aspect of the association remains. They are purely prayer groups which bring groups of pilgrims to the Sanctuary of San Vittorino. The use that Heaven made of the tiny statue of Our Lady of Fatima is indeed a lesson in the valid use of sacramentals, which are holy things or actions of which the Church makes use to obtain spiritual and temporal favors from God. Unlike sacraments, the power of sacramentals does not come from the objects themselves, but from the intercessory prayers of the Church.

The Fatima prayer groups arising from the little statue, in collaboration with the Oblate Fathers of the Virgin Mary, have gone on to organize Marian missions in many parishes in Rome, Lazio, Tuscany, Liguria and Abruzzo. From these beginnings grew the desire to raise a sanctuary to Our Lady of Fatima in Italy. Here is where Brother Gino's junk collecting proved useful. He and his fellow Fatima group members cooperated in collecting funds, organizing pilgrimages and cultural and artistic showings, and giving their own professional work to obtain the necessary approvals and realize their plans for a special shrine of Our Lady of Fatima, a sanctuary to this great message and devotion in Italy.

And yet, all this activity was very hard on Brother Gino. One of the summary accounts of his assignments tells us that he was transferred from St. Helena's to the Mammertine because "his precarious health," in fact, did not permit him to do all the work he was asked to do at St. Helena's. Paradoxically, however, it is this report, amid Brother Gino's exertions for the poor and for Mary, that gives us our first glimpse of the extraordinary blessing of God which was to unite Brother Gino even more intimately in Christ's suffering for the salvation of souls. For it was while at St. Helena's, twelve years before the wounds of Christ became visible on his body in 1956, that Brother Gino began to experience the pain of the stigmata.

The stigmata are the reproduction in a person of the wounds of Christ, corresponding to the wounds of His hands, feet, side and head, or some of these, which may be gradually added until all the wounds of Christ appear. The wounds appear spontaneously. In certain persons they have been known to disappear and then reappear on other occasions. They are accompanied by bleeding, at least at times, and also by pain. The invisible stigmata causes considerable pain in the wound area, but no wound is seen. There have been approximately 325 recorded cases of stigmatists, the best known being St. Francis of Assisi. St. Catherine of Siena is reported to have suffered the pain of the invisible stigmata.

To the present day Brother Gino, like his brother Oblates, is most reserved in speaking of the stigmata. In interviewing Brother Gino, however, I learned that the report of Brother Gino's "precarious health" refers to the pain he experienced in the invisible stigmata, which made his physical work difficult at St. Helena's. Brother Gino reported, for example, that his only carving at that time was a wooden *bambino*, because of the difficulty of working with his hands.

In this context, Brother Gino's holiness and attractiveness for others interested in Marian devotion is not at all surprising. The crowds who gathered around him at St. Helena's and the Mammertine soon became too large to be accommodated in the existing shrine. Hence the goal of establishing a major shrine was conceived. It was to be at San Vittorino, outside Rome.

The dates given in different accounts written in Italy as to when Brother Gino first went to San Vittorino vary from 1957 to 1960. However, Brother Gino stated in an interview that he came in 1959 for brief visits, but was not a resident until 1964: "I lived for two years in the back of the crypt, lower church. Because of the first pilgrims who were coming, I did not want to leave the church by itself because there was this movement and the people started to come here to pray. The seminary was built two years later." Brother Gino, however, would not answer *directly* inquiries as to the origin of his deep devotion to Our Lady of Fatima, as associated with the particular area of the San Vittorino shrine: "I will say this," he said. "The devotion had spread so much at the Mammertine and St. Helena's that it was no longer possible to receive all those who wanted to pray to the Blessed Mother. The idea came to have a greater sanctuary to accommodate all those people."

I then said to Brother Gino, "Why did you come out here? Why this God-forsaken, isolated spot?"

The answer came with laughter. "In fact we have started everything. To start everything we have to start where there is nothing."

An official brochure put out by the Sanctuary at San Vittorino shortly before the writing of this book explains it all this way: "At San Vittorino, near Rome, one of the efforts to further the spreading of the Fatima tidings is growing largely on account of Brother Gino Burresi of the Oblates of the Virgin Mary...At Pisa in 1953, some of the catechism students of Brother Gino gave him a small statue of Our Lady of Fatima as a parting gift. He kept the statue with him wherever he went until it was eventually put to stay on a side altar of the Church of St. Joseph of the Carpenters near the Roman Forum. As time passed, more and more of the faithful began to gather there regularly with Brother Gino to pray the Rosary and offer their requests to the Blessed Mother. Eventually, as the number of devotees grew, it became clear that the small church was neither sufficient for their needs, nor was the locale well suited for quiet prayer and meditation. From this came the idea to search for an area where a true sanctuary devoted to Our Lady of Fatima could be built.

"It was on account of an injured man in San Vittorino that Brother Gino came to know this small, isolated village at the eastern edge of greater Rome. Signore Angelo Colista, bedridden since he had been crippled by a serious fall, asked Brother Gino to come and visit him. It was December 8, 1960, the Feast of the Immaculate Conception, when Brother Gino, after spending some time with the sick man, went with some children of the town to recite the Rosary in a nearby meadow. It was at this time that he came to understand that the Blessed Mother wished the sanctuary to be built there, from where she would grant many spiritual favors and make her message of Fatima better known.

"So it was that in January of 1961 Brother Gino brought a statue of Our Lady of Fatima to the parish church in San Vittorino and immediately the people of the town begn to share his enthusiasm for the new sanctuary. In the field that had been chosen for the new church a little shrine was built and a small statue of Our Lady of Fatima was raised on May 13, 1961. In the meantime a study was undertaken for the construction of a small chapel (the present "crypt chapel") as the first serious work toward the building of the sanctuary. Inaugurated in May, 1964, it quickly became the focal point of the growing spiritual life of San Vittorino.

"In 1965 the design for the main work above ground was begun, but it was not until December 2, 1969, that the authorities approved the plan. On the seventeenth of September, 1970, ground was broken for the construction of the new sanctuary. Originally, it had been hoped to build the new church above the crypt chapel which had been put up in a huge pit cut out of the earth. Studies revealed, however, that the ground lacked sufficient support, and so the work was undertaken about one hundred yards above and to the east of the crypt.

"In 1974 the walls were finished and the first Mass was celebrated in the new church by the Bishop of Tivoli, Monsignor Guglielmo Giaquinta, on the night of October 12. In the following years the interior work was continued with the placing of the marble floor, the erection of the main altar and tabernacle, and, above all, the solemn crowning of the statue of Our Lady of Fatima on December 8, 1977. Finally, on May 13, 1979, the anniversary of the first apparition at Fatima, the church was consecrated. However, there are many parts of the sanctuary that will be developing as the years go by and the various apostolic works that are planned take shape. The Oblates hope in the future to be able to add a house for the sick who visit, a center for retreats and special conferences, and whatever else may become a means of deepening the spiritual life and strength of the pilgrims who come to the sanctuary.

"There are many activities at the sanctuary which keep Brother Gino and the Oblate priests devoted full time to their work. Every day several busloads of pilgrims from all over Europe arrive to visit the new church and to talk and pray with Brother Gino. Once a month there is the penitential pilgrimage

when thousands converge on San Vittorino to pray together and
process through the nearby village. Each month there are also
special days set aside for the sick and elderly who come to the
sanctuary seeking the help of the Mother of God and a word of
encouragement from their brothers in Christ.

"Near the sanctuary in an olive grove is the seminary of the
Oblate of the Virgin Mary...Young men from literally all parts of
the world have been coming here to prepare for a life of complete
commitment to Christ and His Church in this religious family.
The majority of the seminarians have come from the United
States seeking a form of consecrated life devoted to the Mother
of Jesus and firmly convinced of the need to renew the Gospel's
call to salvation as the Church wishes to be done in the world of
today."

In the case of Our Lady of Lourdes and Our Lady of Fatima,
when God's Mother wanted a chapel built at Massabielle and
again at the Cova da Iria, the Church authorities were
understandably hesitant to act at once until there was sufficient
evidence of the authenticity of the heavenly request. By the same
token, in the case of the Sanctuary or Church of Our Lady of
Fatima at San Vittorino, it is *not* in the mind of the Oblates of the
Virgin Mary or of the Bishop of Tivoli, in whose diocese the
Sanctuary exists, to convince the faithful that there was a direct
call from Heaven that such a shrine exist in this area. Officially,
they make *no* such claims or judgments. It is rather viewed as the
overflow to many pilgrims of the great love and devotion of
Brother Gino for God's Holy Mother, his devotion to Our Lady of
Fatima, to the Immaculate Heart of Mary, and the desire that
people come to the Sacraments of the Holy Eucharist and
Reconciliation and thereby discover God's love and mercy, and
that sinners be converted. At the same time the brother inspires
many young men to make a total commitment to Jesus Christ in
their call of Heaven to the Holy Priesthood. More recently,
young ladies are also being inspired by Brother Gino to join the
Oblate Sisters of the Virgin Mary of Fatima, as they, too,
experience the call. It must always be remembered that private
revelations are but a reaffirmation of the Gospels and of the
constant teachings of the Church. They are never the source of
our faith. They only reaffirm what is our faith. Still, Guadalupe,
Lourdes and Fatima give that special touch of human testimony
that God is still with us, that Mary is our Mother, too. When
studied from prudent sources and reliable reporting written in
harmony with the faith of the Church, their messages warm the

heart, indeed, can inflame the spirit. Moreover, the very strong faith of one person may be so firm that it serves as an inspiration to others. It can help those whose act of faith is weak. One person may hear God speak within him so strongly that he will in turn speak to others in prophecy. The Holy Spirit surely uses certain men to attract unbelievers to the Church, even through special miraculous gifts. God uses men to lead others to repentance and to greater love for God and fellow man, and to concern about the salvation of all. With all of these things in mind, readers are asked to interpret the accounts below in proper perspective.

Signore Angelo Colista tells the story as follows as he sits in a wheelchair, his legs completely lifeless: "It was I myself who asked him to come here to San Vittorino. I was dying at the Fratebenfratelli Hospital in Rome. The doctors realized there was nothing that could be done to save my life and therefore told my relatives to take me home. I was taken back to San Vittorino. My case moved the town with pity. I had small children, and my death would have left my family in great difficulties.

"Somebody told one of my relatives: 'Why don't you call Brother Gino? He is a religious brother. He lives in Rome and helps poor people. They say he is working miracles.'

"My parents ran to the parish priest. They begged him to go to Brother Gino. The day after, Brother Gino came to see me. As soon as I saw him I said, 'I don't ask to be cured. I am ready to remain an invalid forever, to suffer, but I wish to see my children grow and be able to be their advisor.'

"We prayed together. Brother Gino told me before he left, 'Be confident. Your wishes will be fulfilled.' "

Signore Angelo Colista adds, "I am not completely cured. But I am still alive, just as I asked. Brother Gino and I became friends. He came to see me often. His work left such a peace in my soul.

On one Sunday afternoon, after speaking to me, he went for a walk with my son and the other lads. When they reached the town where there is a chapel dedicated to St. Rock, Brother Gino said, 'Let us pray the Rosary.'

"They began to pray. All of a sudden an extraordinary thing happened; he had begun to speak alone and got transfigured.

"In fact, Brother Gino had seen the Madonna, who had requested that a church be built on that spot. The Blessed Virgin had told him: 'Many people will come here to be converted. You will have to undergo many sufferings, but I shall always be at your side. I will show you every time the solution of the difficulties you will meet.' And so Brother Gino moved from Rome to San Vittorino, where now the sanctuary demanded by Our Lady is being built."

Inquiries of the author revealed that Our Lady had appeared as Our Lady of Fatima. Another account from a priest acquainted with San Vittorino corroborates the above information: "San Vittorino is a small and very old hamlet of the commune of Rome, twenty-seven kilometers from the center, away from every transit road, therefore unknown to all. In the summer of 1960, a sick man of San Vittorino who had heard about Brother Gino while he was in the Hospital, asked the pastor to call him to come visit him. Brother Gino came on a Sunday afternoon and returned the following Sunday. It was a splendid day. After the visit to the sick man, he gathered the boys of the town and took them to a field near the town, where they often went to play and from which one sees the panorama of the whole Roman plain. He recited with them the Rosary. During the recitation he stopped: the idea was born to construct there a sanctuary of Our Lady of Fatima.

"Some time later, Brother Gino returned to San Vittorino, called by another sick person—Signora Maria Casina, owner of the field where Brother Gino had prayed with the boys and had thought to construct the sanctuary. The field was donated to Brother Gino. Another four pieces of property were acquired for a little money. The basis was ready to realize the dream of Brother Gino and of the friends of the Pious Congregation.

"On May 13, 1961, a small building was begun, and in it was placed the small statue of the Madonna of Fatima, at its feet a stone from the Cova da Iria.

"May 17, 1964. The crypt church was opened. (Construction had begun on February 18, 1962.) On this occasion a large statue was brought from Rome in procession destined for the new devotion in the crypt. The same day Brother Gino was transferred to San Vittorino to be custodian of the new construction and to meet and guide the pilgrims.

"May 12, 1965. During the night, Brother Gino, with about ten friends, began the tradition of the monthly procession of penance, on foot, reciting the Rosary, while walking the four kilometers of road from the crossroad of Capanella of Tivoli to San Vittorino

"September 17, 1970. They began work to construct the new sanctuary.

"May 12, 1975. The structure in fortified cement was

finished and ready to take in the many pilgrims that participate in the monthly procession of penance and other solemn celebrations.

"During 1977—the floor, doors, and altar were set.

"December 8, 1977. Another statue was solemnly carried from Fatima, destined for veneration in the new sanctuary.

"Every day many pilgrims come to the sanctuary, singly or in organized groups. They come to pray to Our Lady of Fatima and to have a talk with Brother Gino, telling him their problems, spiritual and corporal, to ask counsel and prayers, to request the intercession of him who is dearer and closer to God and to Mary His Mother."

Apparently, there was more to the growth of the sanctuary than meets the eye, as revealed by the following story about the college seminary which had been built at San Vittorino in the '60's but was empty by the beginning of the next decade.

In the summer of 1971 some young foreigners were on a trip through Europe. They were pilgrims visiting all the sanctuaries of the Madonna that they could. They were seeking the grace and spiritual light to see their vocation and discover what the call of Heaven was for each one of them. The young foreigners traveled in an old "600" Fiat. Their car broke down in Rome. The mechanic to whom they went to have the car fixed discovered why they were traveling.

"Why don't you go out to San Vittorino? There you will discover a new Sanctuary of Our Lady of Fatima under construction. There is an unusual holy brother there who people say has the bleeding wound-marks of Jesus Christ. Talk to him. You maybe can seek there the light which you have not yet found."

And go they did. They were met by Brother Gino, who showed them with sadness the large new house of the seminary college. It was empty. He said: "Let us pray that the Madonna will fill it again."

By October the young travelers and pilgrims with the "600" Fiat were taken into the empty house which was rebaptized, "Seminary of Our Lady of Fatima." There were eight students and all were foreigners who spoke the English language. The oldest was Basil Mendes, who was born in Colombo (Sri Lanka) on February 13, 1925, and who is now a priest in the Congregation.

The following year another 52 students arrived. Again all were foreigners coming mostly from the United States, but also from Canada, Ireland and England. In 1973 the new arrivals totalled fourteen; again all came from countries outside Italy. In 1974 there were Italian students among the 26 arrivals. In 1976 there were eight Italians among another 26 postulants. In 1977 there arrived forty-eight, thirty-one of which were from the United States, thirteen from Italy, and four from other nations.

Not all of the initial influx of foreign students remained. At first, there were difficulties with the foreign-speaking students adapting to the new environment and language, and the college seminary was not immediately prepared for the large enrollments or equipped to deal with a foreign mentality. During this period, there can be no doubt that the prayers of Brother Gino to Our Lady of Fatima were many, and in due time the problems were remedied; the students adjusted to the challenges and the Italian authorities learned to work well with the young Americans and the young men coming from other lands. By 1978 the first American and Canadian men were ordained. Since then ordinations for the Congregation take place each spring.

Father Joseph G. Breault, O.V.M., who came to the Oblates in Rome and at San Vittorino at the time young American men were coming to study for the Holy priesthood, was one solution to their problems. The difficulties of relating to one another in the early '70's, and the adjustment to linguistic and cultural changes required an older priest well acquainted with the American culture. Father Breault was experienced in various pastoral ministries for many years. Although originally a French Canadian, he had become an American citizen and had worked in the United States, including work with the Fatima apostolate. His brother had been quite active with the Fatima Pilgrim Virgin statue, which Father Breault sometimes accompanied. Although Father Breault was not finally professed in perpetual vows with the Oblates of the Virgin Mary until December 8, 1979, his many years as a priest equipped him for conferences, confessions, spiritual direction and retreats, especially as it pertained to the English-speaking seminarians. The Superior General of the Oblates considered Father Breault an answer to prayer.

In September of 1972 Father Breault had gone to see Brother Gino with the desire to ask him a few questions. When he entered the office of Brother Gino, the perfume from the wounds was so strong that Father Breault feared he would become sick. He tried very hard to control himself, and it became obvious to Father Breault that something important was going to happen between himself and Brother Gino. The request of Brother Gino that Father Breault work with the seminarians seemed to be the answer to the unusual experience he had at that first meeting. It gave him greater confidence that he was the man whom God would use satisfactorily for the position. Father Breault, like many others, even across the ocean, has experienced the perfume of Brother Gino at a distance. It has always made him feel as if Brother Gino must be thinking of him.

Of course, the Bishop of Tivoli keeps a prudent supervision on the whole work at San Vittorino and the private life of Brother Gino and approves of the apostolate at San Vittorino for the education of young men for the Holy Priesthood, of the Oblate Sisters, and of the pilgrims that come to honor the Mother of God and to participate in Eucharistic devotions and the Sacraments. The Bishop's interest is no doubt quickened by the fact that Brother Gino's visitors increasingly include churchmen of the highest rank and dignity, even Cardinals. Many seek his private counsel but must be sent elsewhere for absolution. It is apparently for this reason that in January, 1981, Brother Gino resumed studies which should lead to his priesthood by May, 1982. According to Brother Gino's superior, Father Piazzi, Brother Gino ''is not under obedience in this matter as he was for the diaconate. He felt that to be ordained was God's will for him. Priests and bishops, even Cardinals, have pleaded with him that he be ordained a priest.'' Indeed, when I asked Brother Gino himself why he was studying dogmatic theology under Father Grassi of Gregorian University, he stated simply: ''God may have more work for me yet.''

Meanwhile the pilgrims coming to San Vittorino from around the world continue to increase as the Sanctuary gradually becomes better known. The processions used to be held there on the evening of the twelfth of each month. At the time of preparing this book, the schedule had been changed to the first Sunday of each month at 3:00 p.m. during the winter months and 6:00 p.m. on Sundays during the summer. The processional ceremonies continue from about 6:00 to 8:30 p.m.

On the afternoon of the thirteenth of the month, however, there is still held at the Sanctuary the ceremony for the blessing of the sick. At that time Brother Gino blesses the sick with the Most Blessed Sacrament. Wheel chairs and casts have been left behind at San Vittorino by the deformed and the crippled who on occasion have been instantly healed. In one case on record, a lady who had been confined to a wheel chair for many years was instantly healed. After the sudden healing, the lady rose from the wheel chair and pushed Brother Gino, who then sat in the same chair.

This is but the beginning of the gradual development of the Sanctuary at San Vittorino, and it may be hoped that the story will not end for many decades to come. Let us conclude, for now, in Brother Gino's own words, from one of the interviews:

"Brother, surely all these pilgrims flocking here and coming to you must test your patience greatly. Why do you think they come to you?"

Brother Gino: "Certainly also to exercise a great patience. This is certain. (Laughter.) And also I think they come to receive a helping hand, a certain help so as to go toward God and rediscover certain values which materialism had made them lose."

"But why do they come to *you* rather than to someone else?"

Brother Gino: "I think that when God calls men to his service, He gives a certain task to each, and those who come to me were not destined for Father Murio, Father Bruno, or Father James (three names used to mean anyone else in general) but they were destined to me, and so, if I should return to childhood again, I would have to repeat the same path so as to meet these souls which have need of me."

"Brother Gino, what do you think? What do you make of all of the conversions and healings which reportedly are taking place here at San Vittorino?"

Brother Gino: "I think that the Finger of God is here and that there is the real presence of Our Lady."

"Do not be afraid of those who kill the body but cannot kill the soul; fear him rather who can kill both body and soul in hell. Can you not buy two sparrows for a penny? And yet not one falls to the ground without your Father knowing. Why, every hair on your head has been counted. So there is no need to be afraid; you are worth more than hundreds of sparrows. (Matthew 10:26-31)

VI. Enthusiasm for Souls

The supernatural occurrences leading to San Vittorino's choice as the site for the Sanctuary of Our Lady of Fatima have already been considered. But if something is truly supernatural, a result of grace, there is still the principle that "grace builds on nature," and Brother Gino had much convincing to do, combined with necessary prayers and sacrifices, before he would achieve his goal.

After many years of the apostolate of the prayer groups inspired by Brother Gino's devotion to Our Lady of Fatima, and having carried to different families the little statue of Our Lady of Fatima which he had received from the children, he felt that these people were ready to support him in establishing a Sanctuary of Our Lady of Fatima at San Vittorino. After the initial efforts to raise some money for the purpose, he still needed permission from his superiors. The first session of the General Council which discussed Brother Gino's proposal for a sanctuary brought unfavorable results. The General Council of the Oblates objected to such an apostolate under the guidance and direction of a lay brother. It was said that the man was not competent to take such a responsibility. The Council likewise expressed serious doubts about the success of the entire venture.

After considerable discussion by the members of the General Council, the Superior General, who had been listening intently so as to discern their opinions, finally chose a moment to inform his council of his own view: "I know that in Canada there has been a lay brother, Brother Andre, who started a work near

Montreal, on a mountain, Mount Royal. After he had developed this chapel, this shrine, the Oratory of St. Joseph, there were thousands and thousands of pilgrims who flocked to his sanctuary to pray. There have been so many conversions there that the whole world has looked at the apostolate of that little brother (the Miracle Worker of Montreal). If God wanted this little brother to accomplish an apostolate of conversions and prayer in Canada, couldn't it be possible that among us a brother would have a similar mission to accomplish an apostolate that might also bring many, many souls back to the Church and develop the devotion to the Blessed Mother?"These words of the Superior General had reference to the Shrine of St. Joseph, sometimes called the Oratory of St. Joseph, on the mountain near Montreal in Canada, where devotion to the virginal foster-father of Jesus of a humble and insignificant lay brother has resulted in St. Joseph's oratory, which is now the second largest church in all Christendom, exceeded in size only by St. Peter's Basilica in Rome.

Significantly, in the September, 1917, apparition at Fatima, Our Lady had announced to the children: "Continue to say the Rosary in order to obtain the end of the war. In October, Our Lord will come, and also Our Lady of Sorrows and Our Lady of Carmel. *Saint Joseph will appear with the Child Jesus to bless the world.*" Sister Lucia describes it as follows: "When Our Lady disappeared in the immense distance of the firmament, beside the sun we saw Saint Joseph with the Child Jesus, and Our Lady robed in white with a blue mantle. *Saint Joseph and the Child Jesus seemed to bless the world, for they made the Sign of the Cross with their hands.* A little later this vision vanished, and I saw Our Lord and Our Lady, who appeared to me to be Our Lady of Sorrows. *Our Lord seemd to bless the world in the same manner as Saint Joseph.* This apparition disappeared, and I saw Our Lady again, this time resembling Our Lady of Mount Carmel."

Hearing of the work of Brother Andre, the General Council decided to abandon all objections. They concluded: "If you desire, let him start his work."

Brother Gino then went to San Vittorino where he lived in a little room almost entirely devoid of furniture. His shack-like room was entirely outside the village in an area of the country where there was nothing but olive trees. For a couple of years Brother Gino lived under these severe conditions, and finally permission was granted to build the lower crypt church. The lower crypt was envisioned as a temporary chapel until there were sufficient funds for a larger structure.

As a humble lay brother in Canada was instrumental in the building of a sanctuary to St. Joseph, so, too, a humble lay brother in Italy has been instrumental in the building of a sanctuary to Our Lady in Italy—both related to the Fatima message.

There at San Vittorino, at the Sanctuary of Our Lady of Fatima, outside the village, in what once were fields, olive trees, and barren land, rises ever more extensively Gino's Sanctuary, manifesting what the enthusiasm, dedication and consecration to the Immaculate Heart of Mary of one humble lay brother can accomplish for the world. There, not only pilgrims from throughout the world now come, but young men study for the Holy Priesthood and young ladies, for the religious sisterhood. And these go forth, not only to Italy, but to other lands, to the missions to spread the Word of God, the Gospel, and the devotion to Our Lady of Fatima for the conversion of poor sinners. Indeed, this lay brother, now ordained deacon of the Church, is always especially effective when he meets a young man he thinks is directed to the Holy Priesthood. He will say, "What are you waiting for? Why are you not preparing in the seminary for the priesthood?" Many a young man who has had such thoughts in secret has been awe-struck to hear the Brother of San Vittorino enunciate his hopes, the private prayer which he feared to express publicly.

Plans are also in the offing as the Sanctuary expands to build a special building on the Sanctuary grounds at San Vittorino as a retreat house with about fifty rooms where priests or religious can come for a complete retreat or at least a day of recollection. As soon as such a building becomes available, Brother Gino will preach the retreats.

As a lay brother, Gino was already recognized for his gift of speaking to move people, but after his ordination to the diaconate, which brings the first stage of sacramental Holy Orders and a commission to preach, both Brother Gino himself and his audiences noticed the added power, the unction that now accompanied his sermons. One priest, hearing confessions as Brother Gino preached, told me that he could detect great emotion in the congregation—weeping, crying. When there was a lull in the confessional line, the priest was able to stop and listen to the preaching of Deacon Gino, and he said, "I could then tell why the people were being so deeply moved."

Brother Gino has from time to time met with youth groups. One day in particular, Brother Gino went to a retreat house with the Abbot of Subiaco, who is a bishop, and who had sent a fair number of his own Catholic Action youth, both boys and girls. There, youth from various parishes joined together in retreat, about eighty in all. Brother Gino was invited to address them:

"It is really easy to be a good Catholic. It is much harder to be a sinner. If you measure what it is to be good against those who are sinning and what they have to suffer as a consequence, you will find it much easier to be good. The sinner has to suffer sorrow and anxiety, into which his sins cast him. If sinners would weigh the happines of being good against the misery of being sinful, they would not desire to endure that but rather to be good young people. There is so much peace and joy in being good. I cannot understand why some accept the bad life and reject the good life which brings happiness."

As Brother Gino preached to the group of young men and women, suddenly one young man about twenty years of age was so touched with a spirit of repentance and conversion that he rose up and grabbed Brother Gino by the shoulder. He then put his head on the brother's shoulder in front of all the youth and began to sob loudly. All the others were deeply touched with emotion, having heard the brother themselves, and now witnessing this sudden conversion and repentance.

The young man said: "Brother Gino, I have never realized before, until just now, how miserable I have been and how I want to end this life of sin."

Brother Gino and the youth then walked around the yard. The brother explained to the lad what he could now do to compensate for his life of sin. "That is all past. Don't worry. Now that you are sorry, God will forgive you." The youth was directed to confession. "Let us live now in the present and for the future," was the advice of the Brother of San Vittorino.

One girl who observed the sudden conversion was so deeply touched that she too started crying for joy. In fact, all were thus affected with joy. It reminds one of Jesus' words in the Gospel: " 'Rejoice with me...I have found my sheep that was lost.' In the same way, I tell you, there will be more rejoicing in heaven over one repentant sinner than over ninety-nine virtuous men who have no need of repentance" (Luke 15:7).

Returning home in the car, Brother Gino said, "Bishop, don't you think it was worth the trouble to stop for a short while, even if there was only one young man who was helped?"

The same thing happens, of course, right on the grounds of the Sanctuary of Our Lady of Fatima at San Vittorino. At times entire groups are infected with enthusiasm to change their lives. Sometimes, when a youth seeking Brother Gino is refused in his desire to kiss the Stigmata, Brother Gino will say: "First, go to confession. You are not in a position to talk now." Then the brother will say to a priest nearby, "There is a young man here who wants to talk to you."

Why this effect that Brother Gino has on most people who come to see him with an open heart? Obviously, it is because this Stigmatist has so forgotten himself that he strives to be attuned to the will of God and because, with his openness to the Holy Spirit, he is an instrument in God's heart not only for his own sanctity but for that of others. When a man lives in the holiness of God, how deeply, how intimately can he influence other souls to come to Christ, that is, to Holiness Itself!

Brother Gino, in his concern for souls, is no respecter of age, but it is obvious that he is most happy, most himself, and most relaxed with youth. A young man now studying for the Holy Priesthood once read an account of Brother Gino that I had written. The lad then revealed to me how he had gone to see Brother Gino and had attempted to kiss the brother's hand. But the stigmatist pulled the hand back, saying, "No." Sensitive of heart, the lad went to confession, then to religious services— Benediction of the Most Blessed Sacrament. The brother and the young man knelt in positions in church where they could see each other. The brother looked at the youth and smiled. When they met again shortly afterwards, there was complete freedom to kiss the hand, from which a rich perfume exuded. The Brother asked, "Will you be a priest?" The youth answered, "If it be God's will." As the months passed the young man went to daily Mass and Holy Communion, frequented the Holy Sacrament of the Confessional, and made repeated all-night vigils before Our Eucharistic Lord in the Most Blessed Sacrament. This mode of life represented a more intensive spirituality, as the youth had already practiced his faith regularly before the encounter with the Stigmatist of San Vittorino.

At this writing, the same young man continues his studies. One day he shared with me his soul regarding the refusal of Brother Gino to let him kiss his hand before confession. Admittedly, my imagination had run wild, although I could not ask the youth what it was he had needed to confess. It was far, far less than I had imagined, but it was not what should have been in the soul of a young man destined for the Holy Priesthood of Jesus Christ—nor, for that matter, in the soul of anyone seeking perfection and close union with God. There are many other incidences of people, obviously in very serious sins of impurity of the worse kind, who have approached the brother and who have been directed to confess their mortal sins so as to be washed in the Precious Blood of Jesus Christ.

That is what happens in confession when one properly disposed with sorrow for sin and with a firm intention of amending one's ways is willing to do penance for one's sins after a thorough examination of conscience and a willingness to confess. The young man above was surprised when the brother refused to permit him to kiss his hand. He then realized that he had not sufficiently examined his conscience and had looked too lightly on the sins of the world. Isaiah the Prophet had already looked forward to the power of Jesus Who lives and acts in His Church today to forgive sins and to give grace when he wrote: " 'Come now, let us talk this over,' says Yahweh. 'Though your sins are like scarlet, they shall be as white as snow; though they are as red as crimson, they shall be like wool' "(Isaiah 1:18).

In the history of the Church there have been holy souls who could detect when certain persons were in mortal sin. They experienced a terrible odor when one in mortal sin came into their presence. It is not the purpose of this book to describe how Brother Gino sometimes discovers the secrets of souls so as to help them. The most pertinent information I received from Brother Gino himself was that he discovers things by "a little telephone call" to heaven. But souls should never be afraid to approach one who may have *authentic* charismatic gifts. If the individual is acting truly of God, as a representative of Jesus Christ, then he will act in a Christ-like manner for the glory of God and the good of souls. That Brother Gino is influencing many souls can only come from his love, his openness to the Holy Spirit, and to the Immaculate Heart of Mary, who herself is described as the Spouse of the Holy Spirit. Enthusiasm? Yes. But remember the word *enthusiasm* comes from the Greek word *en-theos*, meaning "God within."

Some years ago, a very active Mormon by the name of Mr. Luciano Passaro went to see Brother Gino. His wife first had contact with the Stigmatist and for some time attempted to get Luciano, who had left the Catholic Church, to go out and see Brother Gino. Finally, to please his wife, he did go out to San Vittorino. At that time, Brother was receiving visitors in the little wooden building called "the barracks."

Generally, when Brother Gino talks to people, it is only for a few minutes, because of the great number of people coming. However, the first time Luciano Passaro went to see the brother he was kept for forty-five minutes. Luciano recollects that on that occasion he smelled very strongly the perfume of roses. Brother started telling the Mormon things about the man's own life. Luciano says that he turned pale. Finally, Luciano said to Brother: "How do you know these things? These are things that not even my wife knows!" He then returned home, shaken. Along the way home he continued to smell the roses. At intervals, at home, he continued to smell roses, the same perfume that came from the wounds of Brother Gino.

That was the beginning of his conversion back to the Catholic Church. He returned to San Vittorino several times to see Gino. He has since grown very close to the Stigmátist and has become a very good Catholic, after leaving the Mormon Church, and he spends a great deal of time at San Vittorino, helping the American students learn Italian.

This brings up a further point about Brother Gino. When the American young men first came to San Vittorino with the intention of studying for the Holy Priesthood, the change of country and culture was very much of a challenge, and most of them had very little opportunity to communicate with their own superiors, the priests, since none of the students yet spoke Italian and none of the superiors spoke English. That is where Brother Gino made a tremendous effort for the students from America and other lands.

Brother Gino became like a father to the students, and his love for them became a great support. Because he could not speak their language, he would communicate in other ways, playing little jokes with them, and spending time with them after meals. A newly ordained priest, Father Timothy Gallagher, one of the early arrivals at San Vittorino, recalls: "To find someone like that when you are away from everything you are familiar with was a real support to all of us."

For some students who come only out of curiousity, no real relationship with Brother Gino develops. Other students who come in sincerity but discover they have no vocation have no need for guilt; they simply find they have no vocation and leave. A very good relationship still develops between Brother Gino and some who leave. Indeed, Brother Gino has an uncanny ability to weld bonds, as seen each year as more young men come from outside of Italy, especially from America. They settle first at San Vittorino, then in St. Helena's in Rom for theological studies, and finally reach ordination to the Holy Priesthood and receive assignments in the vineyard of the Lord.

This enthusiasm which Brother Gino has for souls reaches not only committed seminarians, but even atheistic communists as well. Once a Communist leader from Naples, a fanatic for the Communist cause and very anti-Catholic, converted all of his family to Communism. His entire family stopped going to church. One day the Communist leader had an automobile accident and was very badly injured, especially in his leg, which was broken in three different places.

At the hospital, the doctors decided to amputate the leg. The Communist leader refused to permit this saying, "I want to save my leg." The doctors responded: "We might try to save it in this way. We would have to put a metal bar throughout the entire leg. It will remain still. You would never be able to bend your leg."

The Communist replied, "I prefer that rather than losing my leg." A few months after the operation, however, the leg was not healing too well and the man suffered very much. His friends came to see him and said, "The hospital has not succeeded too well. Why don't you go to San Vittorino and ask the Blessed Mother to cure you?" The Communist replied: "Me? A Communist? I don't believe. There is no use going there."

The others kept insisting. "It does not cost anything to go there. You can ask. You don't know what could happen." Finally, they convinced him at least to go out to San Vittorino. The Communist arrived at San Vittorino in his wheelchair with his leg out straight, due to the bar. When he came to the door of the crypt church, he did not want to go further. "I won't go there. I don't want to pray." But the others insisted. Finally, he permitted himself to be pushed into the church. They pushed his wheelchair all the way to the front. They whispered to the Communist, "See the statue of Our Lady above the altar? Ask her to cure you." The Communist then sat there in his wheelchair with the injured leg which refused to heal. He did not ask to be cured, but he prayed in this manner, "Blessed Mother, give me faith." Immediately, the man felt a change in himself. He got up. He knelt down as if he had two natural legs.

While this was happening, Brother Gino was kneeling to the side of the altar in the sanctuary. The brother observed the man getting up and kneeling down, knowing that he had the iron bar in his leg. The man remained there for some time praying to the

Blessed Mother. Then he got up and walked by himself to the confessional, bending his leg back and forth in the process of walking. There in the confessional the now-converted Communist knelt again and made his confession.

After his confession, the man returned to the center and knelt in front of the altar where Our Eucharistic Lord was present in the tabernacle, with the statue of Our Lady of Fatima above. The man looked at Brother Gino. Brother Gino, knowing what was going on in the man's mind, made a little sign. "Come here. Remain beside me for the Mass." The man walked to the prie-dieu beside Brother Gino and attended Holy Mass there. During the readings of the Mass, the converted Communist kept moving his leg up and down with the idea: "If I stop moving it, maybe it will get stiff again or straighten out so I can't move it, so I'd better keep moving it." Brother Gino, knowing what the thoughts of the man were, could not help but smile. After Mass, everything remained normal. The former Communist continued to use both legs.

The man said to Brother Gino, "What am I going to do?" The Stigmatist replied, "Well, if you are able to act like this, it seems that you do not need that iron bar anymore. Go to see your doctor and do whatever he tells you." The converted Communist returned to Naples. When the doctor saw that the man could bend his knee and walk, he said, "You don't need the iron bar anymore. We have to take it out." The man was readmitted to the hospital. They removed the bar, which was about a half-inch thick. The man said to the doctor, "I want this bar so that I can give it to the Sanctuary of San Vittorino as an *ex-voto* of my cure." (*Ex-voto* means a reminder of the grace received there in the Sanctuary.) The doctor replied, "No. We cannot permit that bar to go. *Now the bar is as stiff as before*, and we need it for someone else."

Not only was the former Communist leader converted, but all of his family returned to the Church, together with some Communist friends. Since that time he has worked to convert other Communists.

There is little wonder that Gino's religious congregation, the Oblates, thought to be dying, has doubled its population in a decade. The Brother of San Vittorino takes seriously the words of Our Lady of Fatima who, after showing the terrible vision of hell said, "You have seen hell, where the souls of poor sinners go. In order to save them, God wishes to establish in the world devotion to my Immaculate Heart..." That is the reason Brother Gino sought to have built the Sanctuary of Our Lady of Fatima. "God wishes to establish in the world devotion to my Immaculate Heart." Thereby sinners will be converted, and this is why Brother Gino has a special love for seminarians; to help in this work, holy priests and religious will be needed in the years ahead—priests and sisters enthusiastic for souls.

"I want no more trouble from anybody after this; the marks on my body are those of Jesus. The grace of our Lord Jesus Christ be with your spirit, my brothers. Amen." (Galatians 6:14-18)

VII. The Marks of Jesus

There have been no attempts in this book to compare the life of Padre Pio of San Giovanni Rotondo in Italy with that of Brother Gino. Considered the only priest known in history to bear the Stigmata, Padre Pio was no stranger to Gino, who recalls that he once saw Padre Pio staring at him from the head of a stairway, even though he knew the priest to be elsewhere in Italy (a possible bilocation). On one occasion, Padre Pio told Brother Gino, "Prepare yourself." Later, September 23, 1968, he died. A year later, in Holy Week of 1969, after having the invisible Stigmata for twelve years, Brother Gino received the wounds in a visible way.

A priest who has seen the wound marks at different times say that the first time he saw the Stigmata there was not much of a wound. Each was rather like a round red spot, a little pink on the outside, more red on the inside. Each wound was about the size of a quarter. Each had a red, bloody center. The same priest explained, "Each year the wounds increase with what was pink on the outside becoming red. The red spot in the center becomes much bigger. When I first saw the wounds, they were bleeding a little. On last Good Friday [1979], when I saw the wounds again, they were completely open. I saw the side, too, on Good Friday. I had the impression that the side wound was at least half an inch deep. The side wound was about one and a half inches long with redness around the wound, and the center was bloody. These wounds never become infected."

The wounds in the feet have been the last to become visible. In 1973 they were only little red dots. There were three or four red dots then. The skin on the feet was not broken. At present, the wounds on the feet resemble those on the wrist—round circles. The same priest who described the stigmata of the wrists above, speaks of those in the feet, today, as "open and bloody on both the top and bottom of the foot." As regards the placement of the wounds in the feet, the priest-confidant describes them as "Closer to the toes than to the heel."

When the wounds are unbandaged, the perfume of the Stigmata is "very, very strong. What is also remarkable during Holy Week was the brother's undershirt. We had to change it because he had been sweating so much. It was almost dripping it was so wet during the agony of Holy Week. But it did not have the odor of sweat at all. It was just perfume." A priest who experiences some difficulty smelling said, "The perfume at times is so strong it affects me greatly."

Beginning on the evening of Holy Thursday, Brother Gino goes into the intense sufferings of Holy Week. While the entire Holy Week is a time of special pain, the climax begins to arrive on Thursday evening. It was on the Thursday evening of that first Holy Week that Jesus instituted the Holy Eucharist as Sacrament and Sacrifice, whereby we may receive His Body, Blood, Soul and Divinity in Holy Communion and offer the two-fold consecration which perpetuates the Sacrifice of the Cross. Immediately after the Last Supper, "after psalms had been sung, they left for the Mount of Olives...Then Jesus came with them to a small estate called Gethsemane, and He said to His disciples, 'Stay here while I go over there to pray.' He took Peter and the two sons of Zebedee with him. And sadness came over Him, and great distress. Then he said to them, 'My soul is sorrowful to the point of death. Wait here and keep awake with Me.' And going on a little further He fell on His face and prayed. 'My Father,' he said, 'if it be possible, let this cup pass Me by. Nevertheless, let it be as You, not I, would have it.' He came back to the disciples and found them sleeping, and He said to Peter, 'So you had not the strength to keep awake with Me one hour? You should be awake and praying not to be put to the test. The spirit is willing, but the flesh is weak.' Again, a second time, he went away and prayed: 'My Father,' He said, 'if this cup cannot pass by without my drinking it, Your will be done!' And He came back again and found them sleeping, their eyes were so heavy. Leaving them there, he went away again and prayed for the third time, repeating the same words. Then He came back to the disciples and said to them, 'You can sleep on now and take your rest. Now the hour has come when the Son of Man is to be betrayed into the hands of sinners. Get up! Let us go! My betrayer is already at hand" (Matthew 26:30, 36-46).

In some way what Brother Gino goes through during Holy Week resembles the scriptural accounts of the first Holy Week. Luke 19:41-42 says: "As he drew near and came in sight of the city, he shed tears over it and said, 'If you in your turn had only understood on this day the message of peace! But, alas, it is hidden from your eyes.' " The Sacred Heart of Jesus, which came into being from the Heart of Mary, is greatly grieved as He beholds the city, materially so beautiful, yet spiritually so ugly. "Jerusalem, Jerusalem, you that kill the prophets and stone those who are sent to you! How often have I longed to gather your children, as a hen gathers her chicks under her wings, and you refused!"(Matthew 23:37). Jesus was dead on the Cross within the week. His Mother, with the youngest Apostle, stood by Him to the very end, agonizing beneath the Cross, suffering by compassion with Him in her Immaculate Heart.

What Jesus went through that first Holy Week, the Church in its Mystical Body goes through in history. Again and again Jesus in His Mystical Body, the Church, has been tormented, persecuted, rejected. At times it has seemed to die. In every century, in fact, there have been enemies of the Church who have risen to say the Church was dying and would not live to see another century, only to have history record that from out of the seeming ashes arose a stronger and more vibrant Church. Jesus rises again and again in the members of His Mystical Body.

But what pains and suffering and seeming death Christ's Body, the Church, must go through from time to time, especially in our own time! This is what we see expressed in the life of Brother Gino, especially during Holy Week.

While it has been noticed that at the beginning of Holy Week there is a definite change in Brother Gino, it is in the early evening hours of Holy Thursday that the intense sufferings begin. A witness has described it as "seeing a man die." From Holy Thursday evening until the climax during the three hours on Good Friday, there are periods of thirty or forty minutes of intensive suffering followed by relief. When the suffering is severe the Brother is, as it were, in another world. He trembles from the great suffering; he sweats. He prays most of the time: "Oh, Mother! Oh, Mother...!" During this agony he seems to be in some kind of conversation, but not with those around him. In this conversation he is heard to say, "I accept it...I want it..."

Gino goes through a heavy breathing process during the afternoon hours on Good Friday, as if he is suffocating. His chest goes up and down, and the breathing, the gasping for air, gets more rapid toward the end. His entire body is reacting as if every nerve were being affected.

There are always doctors present on Good Friday during the time of the extreme agony of the Stigmatist, especially when he approaches the final hours. From all biological points of view, Brother Gino dies and then gradually revives. After that he is very, very weak, extremely tired. He cannot walk alone but must be assisted in order to participate in the liturgical services late Good Friday afternoon. Medically, the doctors say he is dead. They have a needle ready, prepared to inject medication into the heart, such as is used with heart patients in extreme situations to stimulate the heart to beat, to keep one alive. If a patient's heart remains stopped for more than about four minutes there can be serious brain damage. Yet the doctors have *never* had to inject the medication into Brother Gino's heart. It has always revived. Slowly, without any aid from the doctors, his heart begins beating again after being completely stopped for some seconds.

Brother Gino has never been to Jerusalem, but he has described details of the city after the agony of Holy Thursday and Good Friday. He has described the streets in Jerusalem, the Way of the Cross. It is as though the walls of his room were no longer there and he were in Jerusalem. Likewise, from his sufferings on Holy Thursday he has described things about the Last Supper.

Some who have seen the opened side of Brother Gino during the agony of Good Friday have claimed they could see down to the heart. At other times the wound has been described as about one half inch deep. The appearance of the wound in the side is of the type that could well have been made by a sharp object, such as a soldier's spear.

St. Paul says of Jesus: "In your minds you must be the same as Christ Jesus: His state was divine, yet He did not cling to His equality with God but emptied Himself to assume the condition of a slave, and became as men are; and being as all men are, He was humbler yet, even to accepting death, death on a cross" (Philippians 2:5-8). In this way, Our Lord was obedient to the will of His Father. Likewise, the obedience of Brother Gino is noteworthy, suggesting that his apostolate is truly of God, for obedience is a necessary quality to religious authenticity. A test of an authentic stigmatist ought, then, to include the necessary quality of obedience.

In accepting obedience to his superiors, Brother Gino always answers "yes" twice: "Si. Si." He has a definite reason for this.

The first time is in obedience to the will of God. The second time is to express obedience with all his heart. That is, the first is in obedience because it was commanded by God as expressed by his superiors. The second is because his whole will is behind it. Through this obedience, Brother Gino is able to reflect Christ to others. This is seen nowhere more clearly than in the numerous miracles of faith. People who have come without faith, even hating the Church, have come away from San Vittorino seeking the truth, with their lives changed. The thing that inspires deeply those who know Brother Gino in the most profound way is that he gives Christ to the people he meets—not a superficial Christ, but the real Christ Who is Lord and Savior. This means, of course, a real acceptance of Jesus Christ as a personal Savior with a real transformation of life in Jesus.

And to those who already have Jesus Christ, the Stigmatist speaks of Jesus in such a way that they desire to do more. The example and the words of Brother Gino are eminently practical; the Jesus Christ he presents is not like the one sometimes encountered in the lives of some saints, which refer to "honey laid on their lips." Rather, the brother presents a practical example of a religious who seeks to live the life of Jesus Christ in everyday events. Thus, Brother Gino is seen by those around him as a holy man, one who does not desire to speak of the sensational, especially the unusual events connected with himself. He realizes he has been called into the particular work which he must do. Yet he remains very humble about the way God has used him. Once, when he was able to meet a nun, a founder of a religious order in Italy and known for her holiness, he was as anxious to kiss first the sister's hand as was the sister to kiss his own. Later he expressed similar thoughts with respect to the well-known Mother Teresa of Calcutta: "How fortunate I am that God should allow me to meet such holy people."

To observers, the words and manner of expression communicate that Brother Gino does not consider himself to be extraordinarily holy. He would never describe himself as a holy man. He merely considers himself as a man who has been given a work, a call by God which he is trying to fulfill. To do the will of God is the spirit that moves him, as with Jesus, who said, "My food is to do the will of the One Who sent Me, and to complete His work" (John 4:34).

Mother Teresa herself has admitted that there is a spiritual union between herself and Brother Gino and the Oblates in general. On one occasion when Mother Teresa came to visit the

Oblates she spoke as follows: "You have two ways of looking at everything, as problems or as gifts. I look at all my sufferings and problems as gifts of God's love. I believe our unity will come through the sharing of the Eucharist, the Bread of Life. Both our congregations belong to Our Lady...You are as one hand. We are as the other. Both belong to Mary. We are all alike because we are founded on the belief that we must give everything to Jesus, become totally His! Remember, you must have blind faith. Look at all that God has done for you...Remember, anything that disturbs you does not come from God. No matter how good or how holy something may seem, if your peace is disturbed, if you become anxious, this then does not come from Jesus. In the Gospel, when Jesus speaks of adultery, no religious thinks that this applies to him or her. But we who belong to Jesus commit adultery every time we place something between ourselves and Him—God. That is why we take very seriously our vow of poverty. We must be poor in order to live our other vows...We must give everything to Jesus. If you allow some attachment to come between yourself and God, then bit by bit you will drift away from Him."

When I inquired of Brother Gino about Mother Teresa, he admitted that he and she have a spiritual understanding, but he would add no more.

The Oblates to which Brother Gino belongs consider that God is using many instruments to draw them closer to the spirit of their founder, Father Bruno Lanteri, and to their own apostolate. Their spiritual union with Mother Teresa and her Missionaries of Charity does not turn upon their attention to an apostolate of primarily corporal works of mercy. Rather, as Mother Teresa gives bread to the starving body, so the Oblates must give Jesus directly to starving souls. This is what Brother Gino especially seeks to do in relationship with others. The Oblates are advised: "We, too, must give Jesus and only Jesus in spreading His Gospel and administering the Sacraments. We must adopt in our hearts the same intense charity for souls as the Missionaries of Charity and go forth to serve spiritually the 'poorest of the poor.' "

When Mother Teresa visited the Oblates she spoke of her dying lepers; she spoke of entire villages in India ready for conversion, but without priests. She said to the Oblates that they must remember not only to *speak* of evangelical poverty and chastity, but to "*live*" them first. People today want to *see* how we live the Gospel...We must be faithful in wearing the habit and in our prayer life." She also said that they must "thank God for the many good vocations He is sending" them. "We must continue to pray for each other. We both have the same Patroness in the Blessed Mother." Mother Teresa then said that she conceives of the union that God wishes to establish between their two congregations "to be a spiritual union, a union of prayer and sacrifice. We who have Jesus have everything, but we must make ourselves capable of *giving* Jesus, and *only* Jesus! Give only Jesus, not yourself, not what is human. Let it be Jesus Who gives Himself to others in you. Thus you will have nothing to worry about, for He will take care of everything, but we must be sure to give only Jesus!"

Here, then, is the secret of Brother Gino. He gives not himself. He seeks to give Jesus. When I asked Brother Gino for the secret to the success of Mother Teresa of Calcutta, he answered simply, "She forgets herself." And it is most certainly Mary, the Mother of God, who is the model of self-forgetfulness. She certainly believed it her role to give Jesus to us, to the world. That is why she is important in the economy of salvation. She teaches us how to give ourselves to Jesus so as to become one in Him and how we are then to give Jesus to others. That is what consecration to the Immaculate Heart of Mary is all about. And that is what Brother Gino strives to do in living his vocation, in living his call of Heaven.

The Word of God says that Jesus became obedient to His heavenly Father, "obedient unto death, even death on a cross." In an age when there has been so much scandal, even among some priests and religious who are not obedient, it appears that God has placed in our midst heroes like Mother Teresa of Calcutta, who would likewise avoid the public media if she could and Brother Gino, who in living his calling places great emphasis on obedience. "Si" once. "Si" twice. "Yes, I will do God's will as made known by my superiors. Yes, I will do it because I make it my will, too." Would God be calling Brother Gino to suffer with the very wound-marks of the crucified Body of His Son if he were not obedient? Would He be calling him to a seeming death every Good Friday, when he goes through the agony of a dying man, gasping for breath, and then has his heart stop and his body turn white like a corpse, if he were not willing to be obedient, even unto death?

What message is there in this for modern priests and religious, for those who aspire to the Holy Priesthood and the religious life? The lesson ought not to escape the laity either. The brother does not claim to be a saint, to be a holy man. He does not say, "Look at me, imitate me." He says, "Look at Mary. Look at Jesus. Be like them."

More than once officials of the Vatican have inquired about the reports of the Stigmatist and his apostolate at San Vittorino. Each time the results have been that the officials recommended no change. There was never found the need to suppress any of the activities. For example, some years ago when the Italian press carried articles on Brother Gino which were antagonistic not only to the work of San Vittorino but to the Catholic religion in general, the Vatican sent a clinical team to investigate Brother Gino but found all in order.

Brother Gino has been observed as having special difficulties on certain Fridays during the year, making it hard to meet with pilgrims. For this reason, his superiors decided that Friday should be the brother's free day. On Good Friday, however, his sufferings are worst of all. For the special Good Friday afternoon services in the Sanctuary, Brother Gino is carried on a chair. He is too weak to walk. His feet are excruciatingly painful and his body is extremely weak. He must be assisted in getting out of bed, in dressing, and in being placed on the chair to be carried to the Sanctuary for the special services. There have been as many as three doctors with the Stigmatist during this critical time of Good Friday. The doctors notice, minute by minute, the intensification of the sufferings. They observe the blood pressure getting very low, until his pulse disappears entirely for up to eleven seconds. They observe his pulse's gradual return. They have noted that, during the time his heartbeat is arrested, the brother's face becomes completely white and his head falls back on the pillow like that of a dead man. It is a matter of record that the aftereffects of these sufferings affect Gino for several days into Easter week.

Invariably in the case of reported stigmatists, the question will come up as to whether there could be a natural explanation, whether the stigmata are supernatural in origin or merely due to self-deception or mental suggestion. Despite the many clinical examinations of Brother Gino, no natural explanation has been forthcoming.

Indeed, there seems to be no self-deceiving thirst for glory here. Rather than enticing people to come to him, it is a great cross for Brother Gino constantly to have to meet the public, the pilgrims that come day after day all year long with their problems. Yes, he wants them to come to San Vittorino. He wants them to come in penance and reparation before the Eucharistic Lord and to find at the Sanctuary of Our Lady of Fatima compassion, mercy, love and forgiveness. But he does not want them to come for *his* sake. It would almost seem like a weakness that Brother Gino becomes so wearied at the people who occupy his time, each wanting to spend minutes in conversation. Hearing problems, constantly problems, would wear any man out. This was the thing that struck me strongly in the time I was able to spend with Brother Gino gathering material for this book: the weariness of it all, wishing he could escape from the constant pressing of the people upon him. "I am a man, not a machine," he would say.

Moreover, if Brother Gino's stigmata had arisen as the result of mental suggestion, one might well ask why he has the stigmata in the *wrist* and not in the palms like other stigmatists of the past have had. All traditional thinking would have them in the palms; there, then, is where Brother Gino would have induced them, not in the wrists, where he actually has the marks of the nails for the hands. Brother Gino had met Padre Pio. He is well aware of where the stigmata of the hands generally appear.

In November of 1979 a *Religious News Service* report was carried in papers across the United States which was entitled, "Shroud Raises Qestions About Those Saintly Wounds." The article was as follows:

"Scientific attempts to solve the mystery of the Holy Shroud of Turin have added a new mystery to be pondered—the mystery of those of saintly reputation who have what appear to be the wounds of Christ. Most recent studies of the Shroud, which is venerated as the burial cloth of Jesus, have drawn attention to the technical details of death by crucifixion. The Shroud, which depicts full length features of a man who has been crucified, indicates that nails had been driven through his wrists.

"And therein lies the problem. Throughout history, a small number of men and women of saintly reputation have carried what appear to be the wounds of Christ, but in their hands, not their wrists. The Shroud of Turin tells a different story. The marks are present, but are on the wrists. If the Shroud is proven to be authentic, a riddle remains about the stigmatists. Their wounds, although real enough, would be in the wrong place. Perhaps, as suggested by some medical authorities, the wounds are brought about by a state of spiritual ecstasy, akin to auto-suggestion...Medical experts, using freshly amputated arms, have scientifically proven that it is not possible for the hands to carry the weight of a human body when a nail is driven through the palms."

Obviously, those who prepared this release had not heard that Brother Gino in fact has the stigmata in the *wrists*. Although it is not our purpose here to examine the authenticity of the Holy Shroud of Turin, the report of one scientist, Thomas D'Muhala, published in January, 1980, by RNS, is worth noting: "A scientist who led the team which went to Italy last year to investigate the Shroud of Turin, the legendary burial cloth of Jesus, says that all the evidence amassed thus far indicates that the Shroud is authentic. And there is mounting circumstantial evidence, he said, that the image on the cloth is that of Christ and was 'projected' on the cloth, perhaps by a burst of radiation emanating from all parts of the body in one five-hundredth of a second.

" 'We all thought that we'd find it was a forgery and would be packing up our bags in a half hour,' Thomas D'Muhala told an audience at a breakfast meeting here of the Full Gospel Businessmen's Fellowship. 'Instead all of us who were there, at least all those I talked to, are convinced that the burden of proof has shifted. The burden is now on the skeptic.'

"... The scientists included representatives of the U.S. Army, Navy, and Air Force, the FBI, the Canadian government, the National Aeronautics and Space Administration, as well as the Los Alamos scientific lab and other private companies. The teams included 'born again' Christians, such as D'Muhala, as well as atheists, agnostics, Protestants, Catholics, and Jews...

"D'Muhala said the evidence seems to support Scripture in every detail, and that the radiation burst, if proven, could very well be connected to the Resurrection. 'Every one of the scientists I have talked to believes the cloth is authentic. Some say, maybe this is a love letter, a tool He left behind for the analytical mind.'

"As a result of the studies, he said, one Jewish participant on the team converted to Christianity."

That is what happens so often to those who come to the Sanctuary of Our Lady of Fatima at San Vittorino. There non-believers are often converted. There Christians who have been lukewarm, even living in sin and separated from grace, which is a sharing in the divine life of Jesus, repent and avail themselves of the confessional—the Sacrament of Reconciliation, and eat again of the Living Bread come down from heaven,

Jesus Christ. They leave with their souls radiant with the holiness of Jesus Christ.

It would seem that, now when people more generally think of the nails in the crucifixion of Jesus Christ as having gone through the wrists, that is where Brother Gino now has the wound marks. Whether that be Heaven's reason or not for having the stigmata of the hands in his wrists, in the case of Brother Gino, in fact, that *is* where they appeared in 1969, as he was kneeling in prayer in the sacristy. This was not a case of light piercing his body from a crucifix, as with St. Francis. No, he was simply at prayer, kneeling in the sacristy when he was overcome with pain. When he came to, he sank down in a chair, overwhelmed with what God had done. He had been chosen to share Our Lord's suffering; and now, the marks on his body were those of Jesus.

"The crowds got even bigger and he addressed them, 'This is a wicked generation; it is asking for a sign. The only sign it will be given is the sign of Jonah. For just as Jonah became a sign to the Ninevites, so will the Son of Man be to this generation. On Judgment Day the Queen of the South will rise up with the men of this generation and condemn them, because she came from the ends of the earth to hear the wisdom of Solomon; and there is something greater than Solomon here. On Judgment Day the men of Nineveh will stand up with this generation and condemn it, because when Jonah preached they repented; and there is something greater than Jonah here." (Luke 11:29-32)

VIII. The Sign of Jonah

What is the message that Heaven is sending us when it places in the hands, feet and side of a stigmatist the wounds of Christ? Why does the world have the tilma of a Juan Diego with the lustrous painting of Our Lady of Guadalupe which eminent painters and scientists tell us could never have been painted by human hands? Why does the world, moreover, have the Holy Shroud of Turin, with all the detailed descriptions of Sacred Scripture portraying the crucified Christ, and which scientists seem more and more to agree could not have been the work of human hands? And why, after hundreds of years, does the technology of modern science bring into the open only in modern times the deeper, hidden messages written in these cloths? And why, in our own times, do there seem to have been men and women who have become known the world over for being, as it were, living crucified victims bearing the bleeding wound marks of Jesus Christ in their bodies?

Do we need theses things? Are they essential to the faith? Do we not have all that is needed and essential in Sacred Scripture, in the dogmas, the doctrines, the traditions of Mother Church? Why these other things? A Guadalupe, a Lourdes, a Fatima, a Shroud of Turin, a Stigmatist of San Vittorino; are they really needed?

We must answer that they are not of the essence of the faith; they are by no means a part of Catholic dogma, not required as a divine act of faith on our part. Yet for human testimony, in that human faith we accord them, we must agree that obviously Heaven has decided that we do need these things to reaffirm what is of divine faith. What these things can do for us, and what Heaven obviously desires that they accomplish, is to reaffirm the Gospels, reaffirm the dogmas of our faith. They are then not the source but the reaffirmation of our faith. They are, as it were, letters from heaven, written or preserved for our own times.

How eloquently they speak and express themselves! For what can one say when one beholds a man with the wound marks written in his body and sees such wounds imprinted on a linen cloth thought to be two thousand years old, and then picks up the pages of Sacred Scripture and finds identically the same thing written about there? What most men say who have looked and seen and then read with open minds is: "I believe." And the "I believe" is often followed with "I love" as one looks to our Divine and Loving Savior, Jesus Christ.

In this connection, I have received written testimonies from throughout the United States and beyond of personal experiences in meeting the Stigmatist of San Vittorino. I select just one here to indicate the call of Heaven for us all. It comes from a permanent deacon in an eastern state, a police officer: "In May of this year [1979], two other police officers and myself made a pilgrimage to Europe. We visited Rome, San Vittorino, Ars, Assisi, Lourdes, FAtima...We had the great experience of meeting Brother Gino and spent more than an hour with him. I speak 'broken' Italian and conversed with Brother Gino for some time...We three police officers were aware of a beautiful fragrance that we could actually taste and feel...The amazing part of our trip was that this fragrance manifested itself off and on all the way to Fatima. This took place during Holy Mass or when we prayed before a statue of the Virgin...I have been aware of this fragrance even here in my home...It was Our Lady of Fatima that plunged me into the Catholic faith."

The mission that Brother Gino feels compelled to carry out appears closely related to the Virgin's Immaculate Heart as he attempts to imitate Jesus Christ, whose mission began in her under her Immaculate Heart. In this respect, note the words of the Holy Father, Pope John Paul II, spoken in front of our Lady of the Rosary Basilica in Pompeii, reminding those present that the

Annunciation was the beginning of Christ's mission: "The mission of this Son, the eternal Word, begins, then, when Mary of Nazareth, a 'virgin betrothed to a man whose name was Joseph, of the house of David' (Luke 1:37), on hearing these words of Gabriel, answers: 'Behold, I am the handmaid of the Lord; let it be done to me according to your word' (Luke 1:38). The Son's mission on earth begins at that moment. The Word of the same substance as the Father becomes flesh in the Virgin's womb...

"The mission of the Son in the Holy Spirit begins. *The mission of the Son and the mission of the Holy Spirit begins.* In this first stage the mission is directed to her alone: to the Virgin of Nazareth. The Holy Spirit descends first on her. In her human and virginal substance, she is overshadowed by the power of the Most High. Thanks to this power, and because of the Holy Spirit, she becomes the Mother of the Son of God, though remaining a Virgin. The Son's mission begins in her, under her heart. The mission of the Holy Spirit, who 'proceeds from the Father and from the Son,' arrives first, too, at her, at the soul that is His Bride, the most pure and the most sensitive...

"The Church is missionary entirely and everywhere because this mission of the Son and of the Holy Spirit, which had its historical beginning on earth precisely at Nazareth, in the Virgin's heart, remains continually in her."

This beloved Pope says further of Mary that the mission of the two Persons of the Most Blessed Trinity *"remains continually in her."* Mary is always at the very center of our prayer. She is the first among those who ask. She is *Omnipotentia supplex* [the omnipotence of intercession]."

These words remind me of the picture Brother Gino painted for me of the Madonna with the Rosary, which he named "Mother of Sweetness." He explained that he had painted the particular picture to inspire me to share the sweetness of Our Mother's Immaculate Heart with young people. "The sweetness of her face and the tenderness with which she holds the beads tells that Mary, Our Mother, will reveal the sweetness of her Immaculate Heart to those who meditate on the Mysteries of her Son in the Rosary." (See photo section for this painting.)

It is to the Rosary and the Holy Eucharist which Brother Gino directs youth—all people, for that matter—in the mission he considers Heaven has given him on earth. Emphasizing the Immaculate Heart of Mary, the spirituality of the Brother of San Vittorino, who also directs souls to unqualified loyalty to the

Pope, takes delight in the teachings of the Pope which see Mary praying with us and we praying with her in the Rosary. Brother Gino appears to understand the Marian needs of these times. We may take as an example the following letter, which he wrote on behalf of the Fatima Youth Apostolate and the Blue Army Cadets, which now exist in various countries, and for whom the stigmatist serves as a spiritual father in prayer and suffering (see photo section for original handwriting):

"Dear young people:

"Through Father Fox, I came to know about your group, so full of good will and wishing to honor the Immaculate Heart of Mary.

"Very good, dear young people, take courage in this hour which is particularly difficult for the whole world, tormented as it is by the spirit of materialism.

"Let us try to be really devoted to the Blessed Mother, being first in authentically living her great message of salvation and peace. Let us try also to be ahead of all others in taking up the sweet chain of the Rosary that Mary recommended so many times, along with the frequent reception of the Sacraments, both offered for our personal salvation and that of others.

"A true devoted son of the Blessed Mother cannot neglect the Holy Eucharist; on the contrary, he should, each day, unite himself with Jesus Christ in this great Sacrament of love.

"May the Blessed Mother be your guide forever, in order that you might be the true light able to illuminate constantly this poor earth, so enveloped in darkness.

"Let us pray and offer our Communions, our Rosaries, and all our sacrifices so that the Immaculate Heart of Mary may save many of our brothers, victims of the horrible plague of sin, and so that she may finally obtain for the whole world the peace we desire so much, peace in the heart of every man, and peace in each corner of the earth.

"I would be delighted to see your group increase in number and produce much good fruit, especially among the youngsters who are slaves of sin, forgetting that sin is really the cause of all evils, physical and moral, because sin always inclines toward hatred and separation, therefore ever pushing peace away.

"I wish you could always do much good, and I assure you of my prayers.

"Fratel Gino, O.M.V."

Mankind has lost its sense of mission. Becoming materialistic, victimized by what Our Lady of Fatima called the "errors of Russia"—the atheistic materialism which has spread throughout the world—many have neglected the grace of knowing God's will and realizing that every Christian is given a mission in this world. In the name of freedom, men look to the call of the world, not the call of Heaven. But being free does not mean one can go against the mission in life the Lord has given each one. We are not free when we act contrary to what is right. "The truth shall make you free"(John 8:32). If we attempt to live contrary to our mission, to God's will, to truth, then we are attempting to live a falsehood, and we become slaves of error, corruption and sin.

It need not amaze us, then, if there be a God in heaven, as indeed there is, and if He have a Mother, as indeed he has, that, in these times of atheism and a growing spirit of materialism, the worldly sign of the times, Heaven should send us other signs—letters, even a letter of God's crucified Son written in human flesh. And it should be no surprise that the man bearing the wound marks of the Crucified should point to the Immaculate Heart of that Mother who pondered the Word so perfectly that she conceived the Word of God in her Immaculate Heart before she did so in her spotless womb. As St. Bernard wrote long ago: "Through these sacred wounds we can see the secret of his heart, the great mystery of love, the 'sincerity of His mercy with which He visited us from on high.' Where have your love, your mercy, your compassion shone out more luminously than in your wounds, sweet, gentle Lord of Mercy?"

These things can help us in our mission, which is to witness Jesus Christ to the world as Lord, God and Savior. In different ways and through different vocations in life are we to accomplish this. In a man who bears the wound marks of Jesus Christ in his body, which open especially during Holy Week when he also undergoes all the throes of death, this witness to Jesus Christ is hard to miss, unless one be so callous, so cruel in rejecting Divine Love that one refuse to open one's eyes and see and to open one's ears and hear.

The crowds pressed upon Jesus. They almost crushed Him. Why? They wanted to listen to the Word of God. This is what happens yet today to those who witness Christ effectively. It happens to Mother Teresa of Calcutta. It happens to Pope John Paul II wherever he goes. Padre Pio could not understand why the crowds came to him. He would look out the window and ask, "Why do they come?" Brother Gino finds it difficult at times to understand why the crowds press upon him.

St. Paul the Apostle said, "I preach Christ and Him crucified." In 1 Corinthians 2:1-5 he says: "As for me, brothers, when I came to you, it was not with any show of oratory or philosophy, but simply to tell you what God had guaranteed. During my stay with you, the only knowledge I claimed to have was about Jesus, and only about Him as the crucified Christ. Far from relying on any power of my own, I came among you in great 'fear and trembling,' and in my speeches and the sermons that I gave, there were none of the arguments that belong to philosophers, only a demonstration of the power of the Spirit. And I did this so that your faith should not depend on human philosophy but on the power of God."

Here again I think we come to the reason why Heaven would place in our midst in these times a man with the crucified wound marks of Jesus Christ, Who is the Son of God and Our Savior. We live in a time lacking in faith, with the spirit of atheism engulfing the world as Our Lady of Fatima predicted it would if we did not heed her requests. Pope John Paul II, in October of 1979, came to America and spoke to the nations of the world, within the chambers of the United Nations, and said that atheism was "a sign of the times."

St. Paul discovered that human wisdom, human learning, demonstrating his own cleverness of philosophy in itself, did not win converts. But preaching Christ, and Him crucified, had merit. If atheism is a sign of the times, then God can send the sign of His crucified Son into the world so that men may see, not simply in the sign but in what is signified: God's power to save.

When Jesus worked miracles, when He gave signs, it was always to lead people to faith in the Father and in Himself as the one essential Mediator. He did not work signs to entertain. Those of good will, with open minds, disposed to believe, were given signs to change from sinfulness; those who were humble and willing to live free of intellectual pride were thus able to come to faith.

For our purposes here we especially focus on Pope John Paul's awareness of the *spirit of atheism*, a real drive in the world, a "mass phenomenon" unprecedented in the history of mankind. While Brother Gino would be the last to over-emphasize his importance, and while he himself would retreat, if he could, from the pressing of the crowds, he remains a sign of the existence of God as he, even silently, preaches Christ crucified. Word of him has spread to many nations, and peoples from throughout the world come to San Vittorino on pilgrimage; even seminarians from various nations have come there to study for the Holy Priesthood.

It was my privilege to once spend a week in Portugal with Brother Gino and 150 young men. Two of the young men came without faith in the Presence and Power of Jesus Christ in the Sacraments. One received the gift of the fullness of faith. The other returned home, still not believing and without receiving the sacraments, even though he experienced the perfume of Brother Gino's wounds. Looking at a man who bears the bleeding wound marks in his body, even in modern times when man has gone so far as to experiment with amputated arms to prove that nails placed through the palms could never support the weight of a full-grown man without ripping through, and seeing that this deacon has the wounds in his wrists, going in at an angle and reappearing in the palm on the inside of the hand, "as if a nail had been pushed in a slant through the hand and the wood to give it more strength against the pull of the body"—seeing these things one sees in this member of Christ's Mystical Body the crucified but risen Christ.

The marks of Brother Gino are signs, signs of Christ Crucified and Christ Risen. The risen Jesus still bore the glorified wounds as signs that He was the same Jesus they saw crucified, Who died and was buried. In heaven Jesus still bears the marks of the wounds in His hands, feet and side, glorified signs of our Redemption which angels and saints can behold for all eternity. If atheism is the sign of the times, as it is the heresy of these times, the stigmata are a reaffirmation of the gospels that God still gives men in a world approaching the twenty-first century, a sign of the crucified and risen Christ, "so that you may believe that Jesus is the Christ, the Son of God, and that believing this you may have life through His name" (John 20:31). Even given signs, however, it is still possible to reject true faith in Jesus Christ. Our Lady at Fatima promised a miracle in October so that all *might* believe. Jesus is recorded in the gospels as working many signs. Still, many did not believe. However, having been given signs, they had less excuse for their lack of faith, and their sin was greater. The Stigmatist of San Vittorino has, perhaps for these reasons, been associated with numerous miraculous signs.

Without probing the reports of bilocation which have reportedly occurred in the life of Brother Gino, for which perhaps the scientist might find a natural explanation, we report below a number of signs, in simple fashion, so that the reader may judge the purposes of God's work through Brother Gino.

A small child got seriously ill. The doctors said that a brain hemorrhage would bring his death. "If he does not die, the child will be paralyzed for life." The child's grandmother had heard of Brother Gino. She went to San Vittorino and begged Brother Gino to visit the dying child. The stigmatist, moved by the sorrow and the faith of that woman, went together with her to the hospital. He stood for some time by the bed praying for the recovery of the child, who was in a coma. Then he went back to San Vittorino. As soon as he left, the child completely recovered. It happened suddenly and unexplainably.

An American lady who came to Italy for a pilgrimage was suffering the loss of the use of a leg because of an auto accident. She could move about only with the help of crutches. She went to San Vittorino together with other piligrims. Having asked for a special blessing from Brother Gino, she stopped to pray. At a certain moment she realized that her leg was no longer without feeling. She threw away the crutches and began to walk. Later she was examined by the doctors, who found that her leg was perfectly normal. The cure could not be the result of self-suggestion, for the X-ray photo taken when she was injured showed that the tendons of the leg had been severed. After the cure they functioned regularly.

On a certain day a group of pilgrims came from Crotone, led by a doctor. Among them was a girl who was deaf. She was wearing an ear trumpet, by means of which she was able to hear only a few sounds. She received Brother Gino's blessing, prayed together with him and felt immediately better. As she was coming out of the chapel, she found she could hear well. She was thoroughly examined by the doctor and declared completely cured.

Some of the episodes in the life of the Stigmatist of San Vittorino have the simplicity and the charm of the "Little Flowers of St. Francis." I recount them as follows.

The Vinegar that Became Wine

One day when Brother Gino was going to Guidonia to visit a sick person, an old man stopped him and said, "Brother Gino, the wine of my cellar has become vinegar. You must help me because I am poor and cannot afford to buy any more wine. Brother Gino followed the old man into the cellar. He blessed the cask and said, "Your wine is good and will never become vinegar again."

After several months the old man went to San Vittorino in search of Brother Gino. A feast was being celebrated, and the bishop of the diocese was present. The old man entered the monastery dining room, threw himself on his knees before Brother Gino and said, "You are a great saint. My wine had become vinegar, but after your blessing it has become the best wine in Guidonia. Now you must do me another favor. You must make it last until the next vintage season."

Brother Gino, greatly embarrassed to have this happen before the bishop, was blushing. He said to the old man, "It is all right. Have faith. Our Lady will help you."

Summer and autumn sped by. One day in the month of November, the old man of Guidonia went back to San Vittorino. He found Brother Gino and said to him, "You are a great saint. As you promised me the cask never ran short of wine. When vintage came, I needed the cask for the new wine. Some of the old wine was left over. I poured it into another vessel and got it warmed up so that it might become vinegar. After a week I tasted it, but still it was good wine. Some friends told me to put bread into it. I did so, and the wine still tasted good. Then I mixed herbs with it; nothing happened. I had a big bottle of vinegar; I threw into the wine strong dregs that would turn even water into vinegar.

"Then I remembered that you told me, 'Your wine will never become vinegar again.' I have come back to ask pardon for the lack of faith, and I have brought you a bottle of the wine you blessed."

The Escaping Dove

In the monastery garden a man was feeding the doves which were enclosed in a big cage. One of the doves managed to escape. The man started to chase it, but he could not catch it. He was scolding and cursing the dove.

Brother Gino, who was walking in the garden, said, "Why don't you pray for Our Lady to help you?" "If I started to pray the dove would go still further," said the man. Brother Gino smiled. "This is the way," he said. The dove descended gently and rested on Brother Gino's arm. Brother Gino gave it to the man, who was looking on, stupefied. From that day on, the dove lived in freedom, and whenever Brother Gino walked in the flower garden, the dove followed him, flew about him, and often rested on his shoulder.

Petting the Fish

Brother Gino was once on a Marian Mission in Altopasso, in the province of Lucca. At the end of the mission there were a couple of days left over before they were expected anyplace else. Some friends asked Brother Gino if there were anything that he would like to see in the area before leaving. He said that he had always wanted to see the house of Carlo Collodi, who wrote Pinocchio. After seeing the house, they walked by a little lake, which was full of fish. Raising his hand, he made a sign of the cross and said, *"Venite creature di Dio."* ("Come, creatures of God.")

The fish came immediately to the bank in such clusters that some were actually lifted out of the water by those under them. Brother Gino bent over and petted them. Those present were astonished but managed to take a photo of this marvel. This photo is now preserved at the Sanctuary of Our Lady of Fatima.

After petting the fish, Brother Gino said to the men present, "Look, for these beings without intelligence two words are enough to make them come, while twenty-eight days of retreat are needed to carry a man back to God."

Then he gave some crumbs of bread to the fish. Each, after obtaining a crumb, left. Finally, all were gone except some fish who had remained all the while out in the deep. They then came in to receive the food that was being handed out. Brother Gino said to the fish, "To you, *nothing*, because you didn't come immediately when called to hear the word of God." To the men present he said, "It is this way in the Reign of Heaven. Those who do not come immediately will not be given the recompense of eternal life."

The Miracle of the Rosaries

Brother Gino had given a retreat in the Church of St. Augustine at San Gimignano for the people and the Augustinian Brothers. At the end, he desired to give the people rosaries. He had a little basket filled with about two hundred rosaries, some pink and some blue.

The brother said to the people, "Those who promise to be

faithful in the daily recitation of the Rosary may come forth and take one. The others need not come forth." The church was large and there were many people. The people had been moved to spiritual fervor, due to Brother's sermon. Thus, many more people than expected came forward.

Soon only a few rosaries were left, but still many were coming forth to receive them. Brother Gino then asked the Augustinians if they had any more to give the people. The answer came, "We have none."

At that point Brother Gino turned in prayer to Our Lady. A Hail Mary was said that God's Mother might provide. Immediately, the basket filled with white rosaries. The priests present were astonished. They continued handing the rosaries to the people. When the people had taken all that they wanted, there were only a few rosaries left in the basket. These were given to the priests who had witnessed the event. Some of those very priests had previously abandoned the recitation of the Rosary for some years.

The Gas of Grace

Brother Gino had been commissioned by Our Lady of Fatima to construct a sanctuary at San Vittorino. He spoke about it to his superiors. They told him that they had no funds. Brother Gino, together with some friends, began to go from house to house in the village, and even in Rome, to collect rags, old newspapers, and scrap iron. He resold these things and put the money aside for the buildings of the sanctuary church.

To go about making his collections of what others considered junk, the brother used an old, borrowed 600 Fiat car. The car often came to a dead stop. The driver, who was a friend of Brother Gino's, would get out, have a look at the petrol tank and say, "We are out of gas, dried up. There is not a drop left."

Brother Gino would answer, "And I have no money to buy gas. But drive on. I shall pray to the Madonna, and we are sure to get home safely." The driver would then start the engine and the car would move on and run for several miles. This wonder was repeated on more than one occasion.

Cures and Rescues

A Roman priest reported the following:

"I have known a gentleman who, until a year ago, did not believe in Brother Gino's power of intercession. His wife, on the contrary, made it a point to join the monthly nighttime processions organized at San Vittorino in honor of Our Lady of Fatima. She tried to convince her husband to join the processions.

" 'You should come,' she would tell him. 'Brother Gino and the Madonna perform miraculous cures. If you pray with faith, you may perhaps be cured of bronchitis.' 'If the doctors haven't been able to cure me after so many years, how can Brother Gino do it? Besides, I might catch cold and run the risk of losing my life.'

"His wife continued to insist, and the husband finally gave in. They came to San Vittorino and waited with the others for the procession to begin. It was cloudy and cold. At last the procession began to move. When the people had gone half way, it started to rain. Nobody carried umbrellas. The rain came down in torrents.

"The man got furious and cursed his wife. 'I shall catch pneumonia, and that will be the end of me,' he said. They came back home, soaked to the skin. They went to bed with the conviction that he had a high fever. The doctor was called. The doctor found his temperature normal. He said that there was nothing wrong with him. The next day, the man got up and felt quite well. Even the bronchitis which he had tried to cure for years had now disappeared."

Brother Gino had been called to Florence to take part in a feast in honor of Our Lady. Knowing his reputation for holiness, the organizers asked him to go about in a helicopter to bless the families, the houses and the countryside.

During the flight, the helicopter went out of control. The pilot radioed a messaged to the base. It was necessary to make a forced landing. "I do not think I can make it," said the pilot over the radio. On the ground, the fire brigade, the police and the first aid unit got ready for the worst. The aircraft began to descend, out of control.

"We are lost," said the pilot. "Do not worry. Our Lady will help us," answered Brother Gino. At that, the helicopter began to descend slowly, as if held from above. It gently alighted on the ground.

In the journals of Belgium there was widely reported the cure of a Belgian man who in 1975 visited the Sanctuary of Our Lady of Fatima at San Vittorino. His name is Francois.

In the first week of August, 1975, Francois, some members of his family, and a few friends set out on a pilgrimage to Rome from Antwerp in a green Volkswagen bus, bearing the words *"Legio Mariae"* boldly on its sides. Nineteen seventy-five was the Holy Year, and pilgrims came to the Eternal City by the millions. Thousands of these pilgrims also came to San Vittorino.

When Francois arrived in Rome and at San Vittorino, he was confined completely to a wheelchair. He was paralyzed from head to foot, being capable of only slight movement of his head. He had already spent fifteen years in a wheelchair and had been ravaged by a deteriorating nervous disease that was destroying his freedom of movement and impairing his eyesight, hearing and the normal functions of many of his internal organs. He was a physical catastrophe when he arrived at San Vittorino. His doctors did not see much of a lifespan remaining for him.

Arriving at San Vittorino with the others, Francois spent most of his time in intense prayer in the crypt chapel at the Sanctuary. More than once, those of his company declared that they would not leave until he had found a cure. Several days passed during which time those close to Francois noticed that he remained constantly in the highest spirits and seemed especially happy just being able to participate in the Sacrifice of the Mass from his wheelchair, say the Rosary as well as he could, and receive the blessing and encouragement of Brother Gino.

On the day before the Feast of the Assumption of the body of Mary into heaven, Francois travelled with his small group into Rome, so as to visit some of the holy places in the city, in particular, the Holy Stairs of Jerusalem—the stairs Our Lord is said to have ascended to be judged by Pilate.

During the visit, Francois experienced an intense desire to climb the Holy Stairs on his knees, as is the custom of pilgrims who come to this shrine. With great effort, he made his way to the top, but was so exhausted that he had to be returned to San Vittorino on a stretcher. All the same, this exertion of the wheelchair victim proved to be already a great sign of the man's indomitable faith and the beginning of a complete recovery.

The next day, after seeing Brother Gino again and receiving assurance from the stigmatist of many prayers, the party returned to Rome and visited the Church of the Seven Holy Founders of the Servite Order. As they were praying in the church, Francois, assisted by a friend, approached the main altar and knelt there before a portrait of the Blessed Virgin Mary. After a moment, he rose by his own power and went over to a statue of Our Lady to light some candles.

Later in the day, Francois returned to San Vittorino to thank Brother Gino and everyone there for their help and intercession. Above all he thanked the Blessed Virgin Mary. Francois then promised to devote his time and newly found strength to spreading the message of Fatima through his work in the Legion of Mary. He has also returned repeatedly to the Sanctuary of Our Lady of Fatima at San Vittorino, bringing numerous pilgrims with him. In December of 1975, a young woman who came with him was also cured.

While the world, inclined toward atheism; may scoff at this type of cure as merely the result of the sick person overcoming a psychiatric or neurotically-induced illness, and while this could be true of some people, yet, it is worth noting that several doctors have maintained that the corruption of nerve cells in the hands and, to some extent, in the back of Francois should still render him incapable of the totally free activity he continues to enjoy.

The above should suffice as samples of the unexplainable events that happen frequently in the life of Brother Gino. Yet, he does not present himself as a miracle-worker or a healer, like those we sometimes hear about in other contemporary movements. Any credit for what appears to be the supernatural is attributed to the intercessory powers of the Blessed Virgin Mary or to those of the founder of the Oblates, the Venerable Pio Bruno Lanteri.

An example of Brother Gino's anxiousness to attribute physical cures to others is found in the following story which is summarized from an article which appeared in *Il Tempo,* an Italian daily newspaper, written by reporter Alfredo Pasarelli on December 4, 1975. I heard the same account from Brother Gino's secretary. The article describes the cure of a Belgian woman at the Shrine of Our Lady of Fatima in San Vittorino, but I discoverd from Oblate priests some important details not known by the Italian press.

The woman had come from Koersel in Belgium to visit the Sanctuary after learning of the cure of a fellow Belgian that had taken place the previous August 15. (Hereafter this woman will be referred to as S.V. since she did not want her name to be made public.)

S.V. was 38 years old at the time. She had two children. When she was 19 she began to notice strange physical disturbances that eventually were described as multiple sclerosis. Soon she suffered from partial blindness, dizziness, and, eventually, from paralysis of the lower limbs. There is no known cure or sure control of this disease. The only consolation the young woman gained during her years of confinement to a wheelchair was from her steadfast faith and devoted family.

Sometime late in the summer of 1975, she learned of the cure of Francois, also from Belgium, and she was induced to make the same pilgrimage, arriving in Rome on November 30, 1975, accompanied by her husband. When they arrived at San Vittorino, they turned to Brother Gino for his encouragement and prayers. Brother Gino was hoping to see the founder of the Oblates, the Venerable Pio Bruno Lanteri, beatified and canonized. What has been lacking in his cause, however, are the requisite miracles. With this in mind, Brother Gino insisted that the woman turn her prayers to the Venerable Lanteri that she might obtain a cure through his intercession. She did just that.

The novena to the Immaculate Conception had begun at the Shrine and every afternoon around four o'clock the faithful and pilgrims to San Vittorino and the Sanctuary would go to the crypt chapel for the recitation of the Rosary and the novena Mass. S.V. attended these ceremonies, faithfully confiding herself constantly to the care and protection of the Immaculate Mother and Venerable Lanteri.

Finally, on the morning of December 3, after participating in Mass and continuing her prayers in the hope of a cure, she went up to the "barracks" where Brother Gino was receiving the faithful every morning and evening. Suddenly and unexpectedly, S.V. got up out of her wheelchair and began to walk around. For a few moments everyone was oblivious to what was happening until finally the wonder of the cure dawned on those present.

There were several people present at the time, including the rector of the Sanctuary, Father Carmine Saracino, several seminarians, and Brother Gino. Shortly afterwards, the town doctor was called on the scene to examine the woman. He had seen her several times in the days preceding the cure and was shaken by the extraordinary events. It is to be noted that in such incidences we avoid the word "miracle," not wishing to presume on the judgment of the Church. What Brother Gino, the woman, her husband, and other witnesses did was to thank the Blessed Mother and Venerable Lanteri for their intercession and pray that God's glory be manifested through the event as He so wills.

The following account was written by the Reverend Joseph G.

Breault, the Oblate priest who not only served as translator between Brother Gino and myself but also was the interpreter for a man from Canada at the time his grandson was cured, far across the ocean:

"In May, 1976, a very close friend of mine, Andre Gagnon, from near Montreal, Canada, was visiting Europe with his wife and came to see me in Rome. One day, we went to San Vittorino where he wanted to ask Brother Gino to pray for his grandson, Jack Gagnon of Granby, Quebec, who had encephalitis and had a paralyzed arm and leg, and part of whose face was crooked and not responding to the command of the nerves.

"He was just over seven years old and had started to go to school, but could not follow the others; if he could walk, he could never run, and his condition had reached a point where doctors had decided to ask the help of a specialist from Toronto. The final decision was that an operation was necessary, but the success of the intervention was not assured.

"While the grandfather was in Rome, we went to visit Brother Gino and to pray at the Sanctuary of Our Lady of Fatima for that poor little fellow. I interpreted the request of my friend Andre Gagnon and told the story of the little boy to Brother Gino asking him to pray with us for a change and, if it were the will of God, a cure of the paralysis.

"Brother Gino promised his prayers and recommended that we consecrate him to the Madonna. When the grandfather returned home a couple of weeks later, he visisted his son, who told him that in the evening of a particular day at a precise hour, he and his wife noticed that Jack was looking completely different; his face was no longer crooked and he stood up and walked normally as if he had never been sick. That was exactly the day and the hour his grandfather had been asking for prayers at the Sanctuary of San Vittorino. Later, in August, I visited my brother in Granby, and Jack's father came to get me, and I met the family, noticing myself that Jack was in perfect health and running around and going to school, like any other boy his age."

The spirit of atheism, the sign of the times, is still with us. There has even been introduced in the United States a "Dial-an-Atheist" is as follows: "Atheism is a life philosophy which accepts the fact that there are no supernatural forces or entities. There are no gods, devils, angels, souls, heavens or hells."

Although atheism may be a sign of the times, it can never be victorious. In the end, Truth always wins and can never be conquered. Jesus said, "I am the Way, the Truth and the Life...I am with you all days, even until the consummation of the world." God provides His own signs, for all times.

I have personally met persons who witnessed the miracle of the sun at Fatima, Portugal, at noon on October 13, 1917. The present century was into its second decade. The forces of atheism were winning victory in Russia under the leadership of Lenin, who engaged in battle from April to November, when he firmly grasped control of the country, so as to install there a Communist government as the first step to world conquest. In between those months, from May to October, God's Mother, under the title of Our Lady of Fatima, was appearing in central Portugal with a message of faith. She confirmed her presence and message there by a great sign, so as to give faith.

As the miracle of the spinning of the sun came to an end, during which time people feared it was the end of the world and atheists were converted on the spot, people became aware of another miracle. Whereas minutes before they had been standing in rain, mud and pouring rain, soaked to the skin, they now noticed that their clothes were perfectly dry.

The Bishop of Leiria-Fatima wrote a Pastoral letter after long and careful investigations of many who had witnessed the miracle of the sun. In it he wrote: "The children long before set the day and the hour at which it [a miracle, so that all could believe] was to take place...The news spread quickly over the whole of Portugal, and although the day was chilly and pouring rain, many thousands of people gathered...They saw the different manifestations of the sun paying homage to the Queen of Heaven and Earth, who is more radiant than the sun in all its splendor. This phenomenon, which no astronomical observatory registered, was not natural. It was seen by people of all classes, members of the Church and non-Catholics. It was seen by reporters of the principal newspapers and by people many miles away."

That day of the great miracle at Fatima, to name but one case of those instantly converted, there had been a godless man who had spend the morning making fun of the simpletons who came to Fatima. During the minutes that the miracle of the sun lasted and the people fell to their knees in the mud, the non-believer was numbed, his eyes riveted on the sun. He trembled from head to foot. He then raised his hands toward heaven, falling to his knees himself, and cried out, "Our Lady, Our Lady." People were crying and weeping, asking God to forgive them their sins.

When it was over, people ran to the chapels, and soon they were filled. Out of some one hundred thousand of them who had traveled to the top of the mountain, under primitive conditions, it is doubtful that any atheists remained.

Brother Gino, stigmatist, has been given a job to do at San Vittorino, and his influence continues to spread throughout the world. As we approach the end of the century, God has raised up this stigmatist who points to the message of Fatima, the message which controverts all the signs of these our times—the message designed to bring men to faith in Jesus Christ, our Lord, God and Savior.

"When he saw the crowds he went up on the mountainside. After he had sat down, his disciples gathered around him, and he began to teach them:

'How blest are the poor in spirit: the reign of God is theirs.

Blest too are the sorrowing: they shall be consoled.

Blest are the lowly; they shall inherit the land.

Blest are they who hunger and thirst for holiness; they shall have their fill.

Blest are they who show mercy; mercy shall be theirs.

Blest are the single-hearted, for they shall see God.

Blest too the peacemakers; they shall be called sons of God.

Blest are those persecuted for holiness' sake; the reign of God is theirs.

Blest are you when they insult you and persecute you and utter every kind of slander against you because of me.

Be glad and rejoice, for your reward is great in heaven; they persecuted the prophets before you in the very same way.' " (Matthew 5:1-12)

IX. A Conversation with Brother Gino

While the materials of this book have been gathered from many sources and shaped by my own hand in an effort to relate events as accurately as possible, there comes a time when one must simply allow Brother Gino to speak, if one is to fully understand this remarkable instrument of God. One day during the interviews, Brother Gino said to me: "Consecrate yourself well to the Madonna, because when the Madonna becomes the Mistress of you then there is the assurance of being the Tabernacle of Jesus Christ."

At this point I reminded Brother Gino that the day previous I had met and talked with Pope John Paul II, who had placed both his hands on my shoulders. The Holy Father said, "You must make your work in the spirit of the first Sermon on the Mount." Brother Gino replied, "That Sermon on the Mount is a continuation of what we have been saying. There is detachment, acceptance of the will of God: detachment from material things and also acceptance of the will of God as it is said, 'Blessed are those who are persecuted.' There is an acceptance. *This is exactly the true consecration.* This is the way a consecration should be.

"In other words, living the spirit of the Sermon on the Mount is a practical application of the Consecration to the Immaculate Heart," I replied.

Brother Gino: "It reveals to us what a consecration should be. And if we are not making the effort to practice the Sermon on the Beatitudes, the Consecration to the Immaculate Heart of Mary remains a simple reading of a formula on a paper."

Author: "I don't know yet to what point I can live the Consecration, but I am pleased as regards what you are saying about it."

Brother Gino: "And also for me. I don't know if I will ever arrive to that point, but I know that this is it and I want it. I want to arrive there, and I want to struggle to arrive at the full realization of that consecration."

Author: "That gives me courage. Did you feel that by remaining a brother you could fulfill a mission better than as a priest?"

Brother Gino: "I believe that I could approach people with much more simplicity and could be closer to the people by either working in the sacristy or doing some works of charity as my family taught me in the past."

Author: "Do you still think this way today, that a brother has a different way of making contact with the people?"

Brother Gino: "I feel that even today, as was the case of the deacon in the early centuries, I could distribute soup to the people. Usually, it could be from sixty to eighty people. This was more the work of a brother than a priest. The brother acts in more simplicity and is more pleasing to the people. It was in Pisa that I carried food like that to the people. When I would go to the market place, the people knew that I was helping the poor, so they would call me and give me some food, some vegetables, some other articles for the poor, and I tried to leave them with some good spiritual thoughts."

Author: "Brother Gino, it seemed to me that yesterday when you were with the seminarians, the novices, you were the most happy. Would you care to comment on that?"

Brother Gino: "I used to spend recreation with them and give them a few words of encouragement and some good advice. I enjoy helping them, but I am not responsible for their training."

Author: "Do you have great hope for the priests of the future?"

Brother Gino: "I think so. If they hold to the Blessed Mother. It depends on how much they adhere to the Blessed Mother. Otherwise they will not make much change."

Author: "Why do you say 'Blessed Mother,' and not Jesus Christ?"

Brother Gino: "Because Jesus has used the Blessed Mother to draw us to Himself. Without the Blessed Mother we would have nothing."

Author: "Would you give us your concept of the religious life?"

Brother Gino: "First, to live with sincerity the act of consecration that one has made; then to follow with the help of God the evangelical counsels. Also, this consecration is not only for me personally, but to help others to live it. This is what I believe is the essence of religious life, to consecrate ourselves to God and be brothers of all. This is, to me, the idea of dedicating the whole life to the service of God and the benefit of others."

Author: "What do you understand by living one's consecration?"

Brother Gino: "I believe that I must live the vows I have made and therefore live according to the evangelical counsels and according to the Beatitudes. This is what consecration is, and if I do not live that consecration, I am not a good religious and not even consecrated to the Madonna."

Author: "Since St. Louis de Montfort Christians have been emphasizing consecration to Mary, but at the beginning of the Church, that was not the case. How is it that now we are emphasizing consecration to Mary ? Why do we now feel the necessity to consecrate ourselves to Mary?"

Brother Gino: "From baptism we are already consecrated, and it seems that we have to relearn our catechism concerning this first consecration. For us religious, our consecration includes, besides the baptismal consecration, the religious vows. This is the way man should live, and since the Blessed Mother is the Model of our Christian life in imitation of Jesus Christ, we learn from her how to live our baptismal consecration. The first, baptismal consecration did not result in all the fruits intended, so the consecration to the Madonna will give a new importance to our Christian life and make our first consecration more effective."

Author: "I noticed that you stress a great devotion and loyalty to the Pope. What relationship is there between love of Mary and loyalty to the Pope?"

Brother Gino "In all times the popes have been for all people the men to rely on, particularly for the Christian, and still more in our times because he is giving us a word that gives a certain life. In other fields, like in politics, one day they say one thing, the next, another thing, and therefore the world is all confused. Therefore, if we want a secure orientation, we have to look toward Peter. At Fatima, the Madonna showed interest in the person of the Pope because our modern world has gone through a moment of bewilderment and disorientation."

Author: "Do you see any significance in the promised triumph of Mary's Immaculate Heart to the fact that at this particular time we were given Pope John Paul II, who is totally consecrated to Mary? [*Totus tuus ego sum*]. One who is totally Marian?"

Brother Gino: "All popes of the past have had a great love for the Blessed Virgin Mary, but there came a moment when there was some kind of cooling for what concerns the Blessed Mother. Pius XII, John XXIII, and also Paul VI and John Paul I, insisted much on the devotion to the Blessed Mother. Maybe the clergy had neglected or disregarded it, but Peter has never neglected the devotion to the Madonna, and it seems that now the clergy are waking up and are putting more emphasis on the devotion to the Blessed Mother."

Author: "Brother Gino, each one of us is given a vocation from God, a mission to carry out. How do you understand your mission?"

Brother Gino: "I would make two distinctions: First, really to tend to love Our Lord. Second, to make Him loved by all means possible, particularly through the devotion to the Blessed Mother."

Author: "What do you consider to be the work of the Sanctuary?"

Brother Gino: "I think it should *not* be just a work of reinforced cement, *not* just a lifeless monument. It has to be more in order that the Church may be living, even to help man find the right way to the Church, especially for those who have abandoned it."

Author: "Do you see any connection between St. Louis de Montfort and the Venerable Bruno Lanteri?"

Brother Gino: "I think so, because the founder [of the

Oblates] made the Act of Consecration, and therefore I really think that they meet in the devotion to the Blessed Mother.''

Author: ''I know it is true in my own regard that I have never exercised the power of healing the bodies of those physically afflicted, but I have seen some sudden cures after administering the Sacrament of the Anointing of the Sick. Lately, it has occurred to me that perhaps Jesus intended that priest should have this power and that many of us are not exercising many of the powers of the priesthood. And I am wondering if it would be proper to use something, like a relic of the True Cross, or of St. John Vianney, the patron of parish priests—to apply such relics to people and ask them to pray with the priest for the cure of the people as it seems to be needed.''

Brother Gino: ''Certainly, we should use those relics with more faith and do these things when giving a simple blessing to implore the help of the Lord on this particular sick person. *It is the Lord that is acting.* We are simple instruments, and those that will not be cured will receive help to accomplish the will of God. If we don't obtain the cure of the body, we will obtain an increase of grace to accept the will of God.''

Author: ''In some cases, like those of cancer, could they be cured by the priest's intervention, such as a blessing, prayers, and application of a relic?''

Brother Gino: ''That certainly could happen, as it has happened sometimes in the past, and for those for whom it will not happen, there will still be a certain help to accomplish the will of God. This particular way of acting is often no longer used because we all become like machines, and all has to be done fast and superficially. We are born fast and we do everything fast; even God, we think, should do things in a hurry.

''As we are accustomed even to make the Sign of the Cross quickly and do everything in a hurry, we should now learn how to be patient, and the work of God will have time to manifest itself.''

Translator: ''He is referring to the priest, who should administer with reverence and thoughtfulness.''

Author: ''Was it your decision to be ordained a deacon? Was it your own will and decision?''

Brother Gino: ''At the beginning, no. I felt very content the way I was. Then, while I was hearing what was said by diverse sources, like confessors and spiritual directors, that I should go to the Bishop to have my condition regularized to give blessings, I understood it would be good to accept.''

Author: "Now that you have been ordained a deacon, do you experience any more power, more influence of Christ?"

Brother Gino: "I am not ashamed to say that I feel a difference in myself, in the way of talking about the things of God which is different from two years ago (before ordination). I really believe in the Holy Spirit."

Author: "How are you different now?"

Brother Gino: "In a certain internal strength such as someone might feel when his character has changed. He is more resolute and also more illuminated regarding the things of God, the way of expressing and of explaining."

Author: "Do you now experience in your work, as in sacraments like Penance, when you receive it, a special sense from God that the Sacrament will help you to help other people?"

(*The above question was asked because I had learned that on occasions when Brother Gino has some decisions to make, such as helping a special person who comes to him, he wants to be especially purified and close to Jesus, so he asks to go to confession shortly before having to encounter the challenge of the meeting.*)

Brother Gino: "Certainly. It is true that there comes extraordinary strength. They don't sell it in bottles, not even in drugstores. And I feel that it rather comes from the grace of God."

Author: (*Remembering that Brother frequently goes to a spring a couple of miles away where the water is drunk for health purposes, something many Italians hold to, and where I had gone with Brother Gino, receiving from him there the instruction that the best effects are observed when the water is drunk slowly*): "We can't expect it *even* from that mineral water you use so often?"

Brother Gino: "That one does not do anything (laughter). It doesn't add anything. It can act on the exterior or purify the interior physically, but spiritual strength it does *not* give to anyone."

Translator: "Brother Gino at this time also joked that if you want to lift your spirits, you'll have to throw in a little wine."

Author: "Where did the concept of this new order of sisters come from? (*I was here asking about the Oblate Sisters of the Virgin Mary of Fatima, which Brother Gino is credited with founding with the permission of the Bishop. I wished to determine if the brother received any supernatural message to found this group. Interested young women should write to them at 00010 San Vittorino, Rome, Italy.*)

Brother Gino: "Again, I want to jump over the ditch (laughter). You can find something about this in the diary." (*Brother Gino has kept a diary which is available to his superiors. At different times during the lengthy interviews he made reference to the diary when he did not care to reveal certain things except in brief passing comments*).

Author: "What do you think will be the purpose and the mission of these sisters?"

Brother Gino: "Certainly a devotion to the Blessed Mother, a help to the poor and the apostolate of good publications, and all that is included in their constitution. They are also to contribute to the work of the priests as associates."

Author: "Would you tell me why so many other religious are not effective? What are they doing wrong? It seems they must be thinking of themselves. Explain more. What is missing?"

Brother Gino: "There is nothing missing because everthing is at their disposition. God gives everything...(Long pause.) Then everything is missing of self, because to walk uphill is difficult. It makes us tired, and not everybody wants to make the effort. So they are waving from one side to the other side of the road, and, as a consequence, they don't climb very fast. We all quote what the Gospels say, "He who loses his life will find it," but for those religious not affected, they don't want to lose it. They don't lose their lives, and therefore they don't progress much."

Translator: "One moment they are religious and another, secular. They are not constant in their vocation. They want to remain religious, but not to leave the world. This should give you an idea of where the Consecration to Mary does its work and why baptismal consecration and vows are not working—because of attachment to worldliness."

Author: "It must be that they forget the Beatitudes?"

Brother Gino: "Yes. They want the blessings of the world and the blessings of the other part at the same time."

Author: "Brother Gino, you have such an interest in there being holy priests. You encourage priests to be holy, and yet you have not become a priest. Do you care to comment?"

Brother Gino: "For me, personally, I am pleased the way I am. But I see that God has changed my program many times. Now, if He changes again, that will be the will of God, but for me now, I am satisfied the way I am. I am not looking for anything. If

God happens to change His mind, I'll accept whatever He decides."

Author: "Brother Gino, if you were able to have before you all the youth of the entire world, especially those now leaving their teen years and early adulthood, and you could speak to them and they would be listening, what would you like to say to them?"

Brother Gino: "I would like to stir up their devotion to the Blessed Mother. When they are devoted to the Blessed Mother, they understand better the life of the Gospel. If the Blessed Mother is lacking in their spiritual lives, certainly they will be missing much of the life of the Gospels.

"Devotion to the Blessed Mother helps us practice our religion. If they have love for the Blessed Mother, they will have it for the Gospel. Wherever love for the Blessed Mother does not exist, the Gospel is left aside, and I say it out of personal experience, because I have seen some youth of today who are always talking about the 'the Gospel, the Gospel,' and after thirty years of experience, I realize that they are only chattering and gossiping. They talk about the Gospel, but they do not practice it. I notice that these have no Blessed Mother and no Gospel. But the one who holds the Rosary in his hand and prays to the Blessed Mother lives in reality the evangelical life."

Author: "If you were able to do the same thing with priests, to speak to all the priests of the world, what would you say to them, the same, or something additional?"

Brother Gino: "To these I would repeat what I have said many times, 'Hang on to the Madonna,' and then you will exercise well your priesthood, and you can rest assured that the Blessed Mother will never let you neglect the life that comes from the Sacraments, because usually the clergy hear the confessions of others but don't go themselves. The priest who has devotion to the Blessed Mother, I see him kneeling down before the statue of the Blessed Mother and kneeling also in the confessional."

Author: "Brother, at Fatima Our Lady said that God wants devotion to the Immaculate Heart of His Mother spread in the world. What do you understand by 'devotion to the Immaculate Heart of Mary'?"

Brother Gino: "The devotion to the Immaculate Heart of Mary must consist in a change of our lives, so that in time the triumph of the Immaculate Heart of Mary may take place. It is necessary that men, in consecrating themselves to the Heart of

Mary, learn to detach themselves from the current of the world which is not favorable to the Spirit. This current is in contrast to the Spirit.

"As the Gospel of today said, Christ preached to this world, but not all in the world accepted His preaching, and so, if there are not these men who are able to detach themselves from so many things of the world and give themselves totally to God, then the consecration is dead. Because the fruit of the consecration should be this: to transform the heart of man and lead him to a total union with God."

Author: "Brother, what do you understand to be the essence of the Fatima message?"

Brother Gino: "For me, the message of Fatima is a recalling to live the Gospel."

Author: "Do you think the importance of the Fatima message is only now coming to full bloom?"

Brother Gino: "I think so. I think that it is the dawn, so I hope. The day has yet to come."

Author: "Do you look forward to the triumph of the Immaculate Heart of Mary in our own time?"

Brother Gino: "I think so. I think so."

Author: "Do you expect things to get much darker before that triumph comes?"

Brother Gino: "It is my hope that the Madonna obtain from God this miracle: to make many young people feel the need to rediscover the things which are much more important than materialism."

Author: "You mean it will take a miracle?"

Brother Gino: "Our Lady will do it, if all do their part to merit it."

Author: "Do you think the spirituality of Venerable Bruno Lanteri is applicable to these times?"

Brother Gino: "I say that it is urgent to apply it, because I believe that in these times we should return much more to Lanteri. This applies in a special way to fidelity to the Pope. If priests, if the clergy, all of the clergy, including the Oblates, had a fidelity to and used a teaching derived from the Pope in guiding souls, it would be all...Rather, it is, most necessary."

Author: "A diversion here. Brother Gino, you are very good at giving nicknames to the young men, the seminarians. Do you have a nickname for me?"

Brother Gino: "The one you already have, *una volpe per scoprire tutto*, 'a fox who finds out everything.' "

Author: "When the book comes out, you may even discover some things about yourself you did not know."

Brother Gino: "It is better so."

Author: "What place should the Sacrament of Penance have in the lives of Catholics?"

Brother Gino: "I think that it should have the first place, because every day we need to convert ourselves and to purify ourselves and to fortify ourselves. Hence, the first place. Because if I do not remove the obstacle, there is never union with Jesus Christ, and so, Communion is nothing if I do not confess myself well."

Author: "How often do you think the average Catholic should go to confession?"

Brother Gino: "I think that as a maximum every eight days and as a minimum every fifteen days."

Author: "When someone has just gone to confession, can you tell the difference in them?" (*This question was asked because Brother had commented on the whiteness, "like snow," of the soul of a person who had just gone to confession without Brother Gino being told about it.*)

Brother Gino: "Certainly it can be seen. The difference can be seen, the soul is more good, more disposed, more generous toward Christian life. When this is missing, even if the person goes to Communion, he remains cold and the same...When this fruit of Confession is missing, we receive Communion, yes, but Christ can't act within us. He remains paralyzed."

Author: "What place should the Holy Eucharist have in the lives of Catholics? Since, while they are receiving more frequently today, it does not seem to have the effect. Could you comment on this?"

Brother Gino: "This is because this should have a first place and all else should be put in a second place, not first material things and then go and receive Communion. In order that Communion act in man there must be a certain cleanliness from material things and the ability to use them with the equilibrium shown by the light of God."

Author: "Brother, would you mind telling us how long it takes you to say a Rosary of five decades?"

Brother Gino: "A Rosary of five decades: when I am alone, I spend an hour to say it."

Author: "Do you mind telling us how many Rosaries you say a day?"

Brother Gino: "At times ten, at times less. According to the work I have.''

Author: ''That hour it takes you when you are alone, that must mean you take time, not saying the Hail Marys, but just meditating on the mystery?''

Brother Gino: ''In meditation, yes, and also in asking in the ten Hail Marys the help of Our Lady to put into practice the proposal which the mystery points out to me.''

Author: ''Do you prefer praying the Rosary over the Divine Office?''

Brother Gino (*hesitation, then a laugh*): ''I would prefer the Rosary, but I have to say the Breviary, too.''

Author: ''The same here. Why is the Fatima message so important for these times?''

Brother Gino: ''Why? Because in the world there was the great spreading of materialism, and it was just that from Heaven should come a reminder so that men should pay attention and be careful not to fall into the error of materialism, but rather should strengthen themselves in the Christian life. I think the message of Fatima is for all, but certainly also for me, to help me live my life well as a Christian and also as a religious.''

Author: ''What do you make of all the conversions and healings which reportedly are taking place here at San Vittorino?''

Brother Gino: ''I think there is the finger of God and the real presence of Our Lady.''

Author: ''Have Communists ever come to you? And what has been your relationship to the Communists who have come here?''

Brother Gino: ''There has been a conversion, and, also, to many I have given the holy card of the Madonna, telling them, 'You, give me your Communist membersip card, and I will give you my card.' So this man gave me the card of the Communists and I gave him that of the Madonna...This was very easy because they were very surprised that I should know that they had the membership card in their pocket.''

Author: ''How did you know?'' (I asked this question because during all the interviews it was obvious that Brother Gino wished to avoid speaking of supernatural experiences in his life. On this occasion he seemed to slip. When the question was posed, before answering, Brother Gino shrugged his shoulders, looked heavenwards while raising his hands, and then answered.]

Brother Gino: ''God, when He Wants, has no trouble finding ways.''

Author: "Brother, do you know what I am thinking sometimes?"

Brother Gino (*Directing his answer to the translator and correctly reflecting the author's mentality*): "Generally when souls come, these things come, and then it is sufficient to make a quick little telephone call to Heaven, and the reply suited to that particular soul comes. He certainly right now is thinking about how to make a good image with this book and to know as much as possible for it. With this book he has forgotten everything, even his problems. He has forgotten everything. The only thing that interests him is to get material for it. He is doing like the fox (laughter). He always wants to find out where the good chickens are so that he can go get them."

Translator: "As the fox seeks the good chickens, so you seek the interesting details."

Author: "Brother Gino, the other day you told me that you have kept your promise to pray and be a spiritual father in suffering for the Fatima Youth Apostolate, the Blue Army Cadets of Our Lady of Fatima. Do you have a word for these Cadets, which are now going international?"

Brother Gino: "Seek to discover well the message of Fatima in order to discover then the Gospel of Christ and carry this within yourselves."

Author: "Was there any particular reason that you chose 'Mother of Sweetness' for that image you painted for me?"

Brother Gino: "Yes, because we should have a heart that is gentle, full of charity. All of us. For you toward the young, all the young, also between you and the Madonna."

Author: "Do you find your art a therapy, and when do you get time to paint?"

Brother Gino: "It is a way to rest and to meditate, because first I must feel it myself, within me, as if I already see it, and then it is easier, after I have a good meditation interiorly, to reproduce the subject on the canvas. The time. I find a little at a time. Sometimes the inspiration for a picture comes to me while I am walking with the seminarians, as we speak of the Madonna, 'She is this way or that way,...etc.,' and then it is easier to go and put it down on canvas, some day or hour in the evening, perhaps."

Author: "To what do you attribute your perfume?"

Brother Gino: "I think that when a soul lives with Christ, Christ lives in him and in some way will manifest Himself. In some He will manifest Himself by a perfume, in others in another way, in others yet another way. It is Christ Who manifests Himself...In the same way, when we have receptacles, we put in one of them jam, in another sugar, in another milk, in others one or another thing, and each receptacle manifests that which it has within it.''

Author: ''October, 1975, was the first time I met you, Brother, and for the rest of that day, about every hour I experienced the perfume, but always by surprise, never when I was thinking of you would it come to me. Never after that day in October until I came to visit you now did I experience the perfume.''

Brother Gino (*With a laugh directed to the translator*): ''One can see then that he didn't have need of it.''

Author: ''That afternoon in October '75, at two o'clock in the afternoon, I went up to a young man by the Sistine Chapel. I did something I had never done before. I imposed my hands on his head and I said, 'Young man, some day you will be a priest,' and the young man fell apart emotionally, and at that moment I and others around experienced the perfume. What do you make of this?''

Brother Gino: ''Good, because one can see that what you said to the young man was right.''

Author: ''Should I do that again with other young men?''

Brother Gino: ''Go ahead and try'' (laughter).

Author: ''Maybe I will have happen to me what happened to Brother Ron when the young man said, 'But I'm married and have children...' ''

Brother Gino: ''That too is a priesthood [of the laity], as long as it is lived well.''

Author: ''Do you experience sufferings in your wounds throughout the year?''

Brother Gino: ''This always.''

Author: ''Do you remember what happens from Holy Thursday evening until Good Friday afternoon? Do you recall what goes on, especially during the three hours?''

Brother Gino: ''Yes, I remember, but I do not give too much weight to these things. I give weight to doing the will of God and loving Our Lord, and this is enough.''

Author: ''Does the devil bother you physically and visibly at times?''

Brother Gino: ''Sometimes, yes. But I am not afraid because I know him.

Author: ''Has he actually physically beat you?''

Brother Gino: "He tried."

Author: "What does he look like?"

Brother Gino: "Eh! A great monster, a great monster."

Author: "How often does this happen?"

Brother Gino: "A few times a year."

Author: "Do you feel the influence of your Guardian Angel?"

Brother Gino: "Certainly, and also of the Madonna, who comes to give help and also to send the devil away."

Author: "Have you seen your angel or the Madonna at times?"

Translator: "This he does not want to answer."

Author: "You know they are there?"

Brother Gino: "Yes."

Author: "At what age did you formally consecrate yourself to the Blessed Virgin Mary?"

Brother Gino: "This was in 1953...before profession, during novitiate."

Author: "Did a great change immediately begin to take place in your life with that?"

Brother Gino: "A great help."

Author: "Why did you never carve anything more after you carved that Bambino?" (*I was referring to a beautiful, lifelike wooden image of the Baby Jesus carved by Brother Gino, which gives off a perfume and is publicly exposed at Christmastime.*)

Brother Gino: "Because I couldn't work with my hands. To work with brushes is easier than with wood."

Author: "What year did you carve the Bambino?"

Brother Gino: "The winter of 1965."

Author: "Did you have help in doing it?"

Brother Gino: "I think that of the Madonna and of the Most Holy Trinity."

Author: "At present I am making solicitations in the national Catholic press for St. Clement's in Boston [*Motherhouse of the Oblates of the Virgin Mary in America*]. Is there anything in the future I can especially do for you?"

Brother Gino: "For San Vittorino, do the book well and give the money which comes from it toward the final work to be done on the Sanctuary."

Author: "In conclusion, will you give me your blessing so that I may do well in this book and in my work in the priesthood in general?"

Brother Gino: "May the blessing of God, the Father, Son, and Holy Spirit, descend upon you and remain with you forever. Amen."

"And there was a man who came to him and asked, 'Master, what good deed must I do to possess eternal life?' Jesus said to him, 'Why do you ask me about what is good? There is one alone who is good. But if you wish to enter into life, keep the commandments.' He said, 'Which?' 'These,' Jesus replied. 'You must not kill. You must not commit adultery. You must not bring false witness. Honour your father and mother, and you must love your neighbor as yourself.' The young man said to him, 'I have kept all these. What more do I need to do?' Jesus said, 'If you wish to be perfect, go and sell what you own and give the money to the poor, and you will have treasure in heaven; then come, follow me.' " (Matthew 19:16-21)

X. Brother Gino at Fatima: A Call to Youth

"This was doubtlessly the happiest week of the entire past year for Brother Gino," is the way an Oblate priest, close to Brother Gino described that week in August of 1980 when the Stigmatist of San Vittorino came to Fatima, Portugal, and lived for a week amid 150 young men from America. The boys ranged in age from their early teens to early twenties. Another young man represented 1160 Cadets in Nigeria, for he had come from Africa to be present. Brother Gino, spiritual father in prayer and suffering for the international youth apostolate known as the Blue Army Cadets of Our Lady of Fatima, made himself available to these American boys, who represented every part of the United States, from California to New York, from North Dakota to Texas.

I was able to observe Brother Gino at work among youth, with whom he apparently does his best work. He arrived in the late afternoon of August 8th while I was giving one of the many conferences one must give when one is spiritual director for eighteen days at Fatima for such a large group of youth.

Though he was obviously tired, strained from the plane flight and then the bus ride from Lisbon to Fatima, an exhausting experience on the narrow and crowded ninety-mile stretch of Portuguese road, I asked Brother Gino on his arrival if he would at least come briefly to the front of the auditorium to greet the boys. This he did. He was very serious and tense, as one often sees him while greeting adult pilgrims. The boys had been well prepared to greet him. They stood, and with one voice the English-speaking youth loudly proclaimed: *"Ben venuto a Fatima, Fratel Gino. Noi ti amiamo."* (Welcome to Fatima, Brother Gino. We love you.) The brother relaxed a moment, smiled and replied in Italian, "I am happy to know you speak Italian. Now I shall be able to speak Italian to you." Its translation brought laughter to the boys, who had only mastered the greeting with difficulty an hour earlier.

The informal greetings exchanged, Brother Gino retired to his quarters to return that evening at 9 p.m., refreshed, smiling, relaxed. Now he appeared his usual self when among youth. The perfume of his wounds was experienced by many of the young men throughout the auditorium. They listened with obvious awe and frequently commented later that what impressed them most was the obvious humility, the quiet demeanor of a man they considered a "saint." How different from the American scene, where noise, forcefulness, wordiness, flashing lights and rapid changes of atmosphere seem to be needed to gain and hold attention.

The youth had heard stories of the stigmatist's ability to read souls. They were not about to take chances. They had kept me in the confessional until one a m on each of the preceding three evenings. They were not at Fatima out of mere curiosity to see a stigmatist in person. Most every youth was there because he wished to encounter Jesus Christ through the Immaculate Heart of His Mother. Brother Gino would be a further aid to them. Their recognition of the power of Jesus in the Sacrament of Reconciliation continued even after Brother Gino had returned to Rome. Many of the things which were to happen during the week Brother Gino was with the youth could be analyzed only after he had left and in the following weeks. After his departure, the boys would continue to come to confession for grace and spiritual guidance, some desiring help in interpreting what Brother Gino had said to them in private.

The opening conference brought repeated laughter from the youth. If they had any concept that "saints" are sad or have only long faces, it dissipated with the very first conference given by the Stigmatist of San Vittorino. When I introduced him to the young men, telling him how they had kept me up so late for confessions, saying that if they did not get to confession before he arrived they would have to sit in the back, the brother smiled and suggested they come forth. He apologized for seeming so serious at their first brief encounter earlier and expressed his great joy at being in Fatima among these youth, whom he was later to describe in this manner: "These boys are like a mystery, the mysteries of the Rosary." Such was his observation of the intense interest in spirituality of such a large group of boys come together in one place.

The brother expressed that very special graces were available to the youth at Fatima and added that his prayer was that they accept that grace and use it for the best results in their future lives. Then the brother talked about consecration to Our Blessed Mother's Immaculate Heart, as connected with the living of our baptismal vows. By entering into such a life more fully at Fatima, the youth were told, they would then return home more full of grace and with a greater spiritual strength to do the will of God. "When we go before the Capelinha, the little chapel (where God's Mother appeared), so humble, so simple, we must remember that there has come to us a most important message that we must try to understand. The Blessed Mother is asking us to live the Christian life in our daily duty. This will not be too difficult if we continue in our devotion to the Blessed Mother and avail ourselves of the means she has requested, the Sacraments and prayer as often as possible. In this way we will have certitude that the Blessed Mother will form us into new men in Jesus. Only in this way can we have peace and happiness. Otherwise we are sad, since we become slaves of sin rather than living in freedom from sin."

In his opening talk to American youth at Fatima, Brother Gino said further, "The Blessed Mother has insisted upon penance. We should practice penance and sacrifices every day...We must also discover the will of Our Lord for each one of us. The world usually indicates that matrimony is the only way to do God's will. This is a good way of sanctifying ourselves. We must also consider other ways besides matrimony. I mentioned matrimony. Sometimes the world does not even consider marriage necessary, but just for man to have a woman next to him."

The youth listened intently as Brother Gino said, "Even before we were born, God had a plan for each of us. Even before we were born, God in His designs had already assigned some particular work for us. We must discover what that plan of God is. How can I realize it in my life? Even if God is calling us to serve Him totally for Himself, we must not be afraid, because He will take care of us. When the blind man passed by and asked, "Who was that?" and was told it was Jesus of Nazareth, he started to call, "Jesus, son of David, have mercy on me!" When he heard that Jesus had called him to come closer, he sprang to his feet and received the grace of interior light—and also the gift of sight (Mark 10:46-52).

"Do not be like some young men who go to church and say, 'Jesus, I want to pray. I want to receive many graces. But please don't come too close to me. Sanctify me, but please do it my way.' We must come to Jesus with confidence and permit Him to work in us. Pray to Him with confidence and He will help you to know His will, what you are to do..."

After these opening remarks, beginning a week of intensive encounters, Brother Gino proceeded to look over the young men and he recognized by mere appearance that some were brothers of those already at San Vittorino.

Leaving the auditorium, the young men flocked toward Brother Gino like objects drawn to a large magnet. He looked them over and picked out various young men with priestly and religious vocations. "This one...There is a Nazarene...Leave your nets behind and come and follow Christ and fish for men. There is another..." Later, in private interviews, Brother was to point out to others that obviously their vocation was to matrimony.

The next morning, addressing the young men early and discovering that about two-thirds of them had already been to confession since arriving at Fatima, he suggested that those who had already gone encourage the remainder. Then the brother emphasized that, in speaking of the heavenly messages of God's Mother, he was not referring to unauthenticated apparitions, but only to the Church-authenticated visits of Our Lady to this earth, such as at Lourdes and Fatima. "If you consider these authentic apparitions, they all contain within them the teachings of the Gospel. I am going to speak about the two latest important apparitions, Lourdes and Fatima.

"Lourdes was in the last century. At that time materialism and Masonry were spreading throughout Europe, seeking to destroy the faith of the Christian people, especially with regard to the Blessed Mother, the Immaculate Conception, and her virginity, to the point where the Holy Father made it a dogma of faith. Shortly after the Holy Father declared it a dogma of faith, Our Blessed Mother appeared at Lourdes to declare that she is the Immaculate Conception, conceived without sin.

"In 1917, in our century, Our Lady came to deny another materialism which is worse. The first materialism concerned certain aspects of the faith, while this materialism seeks to destroy with atheism. It is a total destruction of the faith. Now we see how Our Lady has asked for the consecration of oneself to the Immaculate Heart of Mary so that these errors of materialism which have spread throughout the world will not enter into our hearts. Our Lady has given us a way so that our hearts will not open up to embrace this materialism.

"*First*, she calls us to prayer and a certain way of prayer: saying the Rosary. If we are attentive in looking around us we see that the modern mentality of materialism and atheism has attacked each one of these ways of salvation which has been given to us. So Our Lady says to pray the Rosary; in our times the Rosary has been attacked. At the same time there has been an insistence on the part of all recent popes for the praying of the Rosary, and if we ask why we should pray the Rosary, we see very clearly that in the Rosary is contained the truths found in Sacred Scripture.

"Every single image we find in meditating on the mysteries of the Rosary should lead us to imitate a certain virtue of that mystery which we must implement in our lives. If we imitate that virtue we will find, then, that our hearts are not open to materialism.

"The *second* way is the call of Our Lady to frequent the Sacraments. Our Lady has asked us to go to confession and receive Holy Communion on the first Saturday of each month for five months, but she means us to continue to do this always. The soul of one who does this becomes very rich with a continuous union with Christ, and thus the soul offers these acts, not only for himself, but for the entire Mystical Body of Christ in the world. Thus, our own souls, through these sacrifices, become continuously more rich and priceless before God. We can see that our hearts will be closed to all this materialism and it will not enter.

"But in our time we see that there are contradictions to this way of life. There are attacks against the Sacraments, confession and the Real Presence of Our Lord in the Blessed Sacrament. These are not just the errors of some theologians but of Christians in general who have interpreted the Sacraments wrongly.

"Our Lady calls us to a certain penance also. Usually, when

we think of penance we think of the unusual saints who have done extraordinary penances. Blessed are they in the great love they gave to Our Lord, but what Our Lady is asking of us is simply to do the things which we must and to do them well. If I do what is good, if I do the will of God, it shows that my heart is not open to materialism.

"Another thing we should look at is that the message of Fatima has not been heeded to its fullest extent, and we can see around us today the effects of this. Materialism has brought us to a great confusion, and we don't know who to follow anymore. We read about how little Jacinta came to the other two children and said that she had seen a vision of the Pope, who was weeping because no one would listen to the message, because their hearts were no longer open. Therefore, we must listen to the secure guide who is the Pope. We must not make the Gospel into a political thing, which today is bringing the world to disaster.

"We must always obey the Pope, the bishops who are united to him, and the priests who are not war-mongers but who obey and are in union with their bishops. In this way we walk with certainty in the light of God and not in the error of man. We must also remember another thing. We must pray every day for those who are behind the Iron Curtain, for the conversion of Russia, for the conversion of sinners who do not believe. Our hearts pray as part of the Mystical Body of Christ. We must pray that every single man, through the intercession of the Blessed Mother, will have the time in which he will be able to hear the call and listen to the message of God.

"I wish to underline one thing: *This materialism is truly an incredible thing. Let the man beware who opens the door of his heart to it. It will kill him. It will bring death into the heart of the man, and it will kill all the life which Christ has brought to him. It has a very cruel goal and that is to bring man lower than an animal. We all must see the need to prevail upon Our Lady to bring about this miracle to destroy the materialism that destroys the commandments of love* [love of God and love of neighbor]. *Man separates them and then does not love any longer. Then he is finished.*"

The American young men, who had listened so intently to the above that one could have heard a pin drop, applauded loudly at the conclusion of the stigmatist's talk. He was then asked to define materialism. "The virtue of Jesus Christ is taken away. When one lives in love, one lives in peace. Why? Because by living in the love of Christ one has all. Materialism destroys. It destroys Christ in man and elevates the animal part. It not only takes away the Christian ideals but makes us worse than animals. Materialism includes pampering the body, wanting excessive property, the best of food, giving in to desires of the flesh. This is a freedom which is *not* a freedom. Actually, you become a slave of all these things, and then you are not even a master of yourself. You become a slave to vice, to carnal vices, the desire to have more than is necessary—one is never content. It is a construction of hell which we create on this earth.''

When asked about meditating on the Rosary so as to grow in virtue, Brother Gino responded that in the Annunciation, for instance, there is enough to meditate on all day and night. He spoke of Mary's faith and trust in the power of God. ''We must draw out from the mystery certain virtues, certain practices. Then one knows his weakness as a man, and it is an act of humility to practice this certain virtue. The ten Hail Marys can be offered to Our Lady to help in the practice of this virtue and to thank her for helping to discover it. If you recite the Rosary like this it is not just a monotonous throwing of rocks over the mountain. Rather, it becomes a chain of love and prayer, and we'll get to the point where we will not be able to sleep unless we have said the Rosary; we will love the Rosary. It is no longer just a repetition of words which tires us and makes us go to sleep.'' The youth applauded Brother Gino's answer. He admitted that it took him at least one hour to say a Rosary.

Asked about guardian angels, Brother Gino replied, ''In our times there has been an attempt to destroy an awareness of our guardian angels. We know that we have had many saints who were greatly devoted to their guardian angels. There was St. Gemma Galgani whose guardian angel was like a mailman, taking letters from her to her spiritual director. Being open to our angel, we seek to do fully the will of God, after all the mistakes we have made. We will then find ourselves in a more perfect state, living supernaturally. An example of this is seen in the Angel who brought the three Fatima children Holy Communion. Through the praying of the Rosary, and also through the reception of the Sacraments, man has an extraordinary power. Almost without effort, we find ourselves transformed. If those children had not had the grace of the Sacraments, they would not have had the courage and the strength to bring with such clarity the message of Our Lady of Fatima to the world and to suffer the trials which they endured. The Sacraments make the life of Christ explode within us like a volcano, and this transforms and renews man."

It makes us better to be near a virtuous person. The youth were experiencing this in being near Brother Gino. In both his first and second conferences he inspired them to come close to their guardian angels, to the Madonna, and thus to Christ. The youths had begun their stay at Fatima by making an act of dedication to their guardian angels; hopefully, it would blossom someday into a consecration to each one's guardian angel, according to the movement known as *Opus Sanctorum Angelorum* (Work of the Holy Angels). God uses the Holy Angels, and especially our guardian angels, to show us the existence of God, Who God is (our Father), how much God loves us (He sends His Son), and how much He wants to be loved, by our responding to the Holy Spirit living within us.

Brother Gino was asked by the boys if he did much scriptural reading, and he responded, "Yes, but I also seek to read what is in my heart—what is there, what is lacking. We must also learn to seek God within us. God is within us by grace. Seek God in Sacred Scripture, but also look within your hearts." He went on to explain that Sacred Scripture should be read with the assistance of the Church, not simply by ourselves.

Asked about handling temptations, Brother responded, "Russia takes God away from man from his head to his belly-button, and America takes God away from man from his belly-button to his feet. Both of them are incredibly evil." Later he gave the youth some very strong words on how to deal with the devil, who is so proud. "Humiliate him when he comes with his temptations. Do as St. Francis of Assisi did; send the devil back to hell with words that humiliate him. He knows well enough, for he *was* a most beautiful angel. The devil will use every occasion to devour you and destroy the good you have been acquiring. You must be strong and persevere in the practices you have been performing here at Fatima. Then you will retain the same joy in the Lord."

The events of just one week of Brother Gino's life with Our Lady at Fatima, surrounded by young men, is related in this final chapter as it typifies his constant work among youth, the great love of his heart for them, and his ongoing search for priestly and religious vocations, while recognizing that those called to Holy Matrimony also have a special calling from God. The week at Fatima was one year after the intensive interviews that formed the original basis for this first book on the life of a contemporary mystic and stigmatist. Readers will have discovered that the life of Brother Gino, whose apostolate to the world is only beginning, is not a repeat performance of other reported mystics and stigmatists of present or preceding centuries. God works uniquely in and through individual souls and personalities, and the Christ-life is revealed in Brother Gino according to his individual talents and personality, which is very human, very warm, direct, practical, full of common sense. Never in his lectures, question periods, informal encounters with youth, private interviews, or participation in the Divine Liturgy or Holy Hour with the Blessed Sacrament exposed, was there anything but a balanced approach of common sense in harmony with the Church. Never was there a seeking for attention or anything sensational.

The young men who gathered with the Stigmatist of San Vittorino at Fatima were not hand-picked by me, although they were there as part of a national apostolate which I direct. If there was any hand-picking, it was done by Our Lady. Two of the young men came without faith in the Holy Eucharist or in the power of Jesus Christ to forgive sin through the Sacrament of Reconciliation. One of them simply had not believed in general that the Catholic Church was the true Church since the age of eight or nine. He was eighteen years old. The other was twenty-two years of age, enrolled to enter a college seminary in the fall, although he believed in neither the Real Presence of Jesus Christ in the Blessed Sacrament nor the power of the priest to forgive sins in Jesus' Name. He substantiated his lack of faith by consistently refusing to go to confession since his graduation from the eighth grade of a Catholic school. One of these young men ended the pilgrimage with deep faith, the other still without faith. Both had direct encounters with Brother Gino and won his serious concern and prayers.

I took the eighteen-year-old lad without faith to Brother Gino to be one of the first to be interviewed privately. I asked him to kiss Brother Gino's had. "Did you smell the perfume?" I asked. "Yes." I hoped it was a sign of forthcoming grace of conversion. Brother spent close to an hour with the young man, much longer than he could give to any of the others. "You need humility...Kneel down..." The lad did. He held that there was nothing wrong with pre-marital sex, that the Catholic Church was merely a human institution, and the like. Admittedly, he was on the pilgrimage under false pretenses, for every youth, before coming on the "Youth for Fatima" pilgrimages, must sign a statement that he is identified with the Catholic Church and not undergoing a faith crisis. There were times when it seemed he would submit to faith, but then the effects would dissipate. After the interview, Brother commented that such a person was very hard to reach. He did not know how to love and indicated there was some barrier with a parent.

Frequently during the eighteen days of the pilgrimage, I met and spoke with the eighteen-year-old man without faith. He was present at all the conferences, all prayer exercises, every Holy Mass. He genuflected to the Blessed Sacrament but said it was done so that he would not offend the faith of others. One day at dinner Brother Gino said, "It is his father. The faith problem of that young man is coming from his father. There is a lack of love between him and his father." I went to the boy and, after casual visiting, asked, "Do you love your father?" He broke into tears and shouted, "I don't know my father." He ran. Reporting to Brother Gino what had happened, I was told, "You must go back to that boy at once. Say to him, 'Behold your father. I am your father.'" This I did. The lad looked up and smiled.

I was to learn later that when he was very small, the boy's father had deserted him and his mother. At eight or nine years of age he looked up at the altar and beheld the priest, whom people call "Father." He thought, "The Catholic Church cannot be true." Fatherhood had come to mean to that young man something that betrays. Brother Gino, doubtlessly from some heavenly illumination, had laid his finger precisely on the problem. It was a real example of the role parents have in communicating the faith to their children. God is abstract to the mind of a child. But love, strength, mercy, understanding, compassion, forgiveness, caring—all are virtues which God possesses infinitely and which are communicated by parents to children. The concept children form of God and the Church of Jesus comes largely from parents. The Fatherhood of God is communicated by the father of the family. At the pilgrimage's end, the young man said, "I am going to do all that I can to promote these pilgrimages for others...As regards faith, if anything happens, I'll let you know."

The twenty-two-year-old man was met by Brother Gino at the Cabeco where the angel gave the three children Holy Communion and held the chalice with the bleeding Host. There the young man, who believed neither in the Real Presence of Jesus Christ in the Holy Eucharist nor in the power of the priest to forgive sins, waved to Brother Gino, who was on an upper level of the steep hillside overlooking Aljustrel, the home village of the Fatima children. Brother Gino waved to the young man and admitted later that at that moment he received an interior illumination at the Cabeco concerning this young man, that he should be a priest and would be an instrument in the salvation of many souls. But the youth had not gone to confession for many years nor come to faith in the power of the Sacraments.

Approximately one hour earlier, the same young man had offered Brother Gino a glass of water at the well behind Lucia's home, the well at which Portugal's angel-guardian had said to the children in 1916, "Pray! Pray a great deal! The Hearts of Jesus and Mary have designs of mercy for you. Offer up prayers and sacrifices to the Most High." Buying a glass from a vendor, the youth obtained water from the well, which Brother Gino graciously accepted. There Brother Gino also led the youth in praying the Rosary. A week after Brother Gino had returned to Rome while the 150 youths remained in Fatima, that glass radiated exquisite perfume, the same as comes from the stigmatist's wounds.

Neither the young man nor I knew anything about Brother Gino's illumination at the Cabeco when I walked back to Fatima from the Cabeco with him, a distance of at least one and a half miles in the hot Portuguese sun. For the first time the youth admitted to me that he had no faith in the Eucharist or the Sacrament of Penance. I opened for him the Sacred Scriptures on both these sacraments, as well as the constant teachings of the Church. Finally, I was convinced of his sincerity when he said, "I believe." He then made his confession under the open skies as we sat on a stone wall, the like of which one sees so frequently in the fields of Portugal.

I asked this young man, after his conversion, to put his story into writing before leaving Fatima. His strong faith, which continued after his return to America, was described as follows:

"As to my experience with Brother Gino: When he first saw me, I sort of ducked in and out of other boys to avoid him. But our eyes met, and up went his hand. The next time was at the Cabeco where the angel appeared. We both exchanged smiles and a wave, and I felt an inner peace about this man. Later he told me he experienced some kind of light or illumination when he saw me there, and he said, 'If there had not been other boys there, I would have come down to talk to you at once. At that moment I wanted to give you my Rosary.'

"Finally, the day came for my personal interview with Brother Gino. As I waited my turn, I pondered something personal to give him. I wanted to give him something that was very close to me. The only item I loved which meant much to me was something I brought from America, my Pittsburgh Steeler hat. I had wanted one for a long time and had finally obtained one just before the trip. So, this being my most dear possession in Portugal, I decided to hand it over.

"When I entered the room where Brother Gino met the boys privately, I was very nervous, and you know that the first words spoken were of my hat. He really liked it. Well, I then informed him of the custom of giving something you love to a special friend. I abandoned my hat into his hands. He accepted it very graciously and said that he would wear it for recreation at San Vittorino. He also said he would wear it for the first Mass I celebrated.

"During our talk I felt a peace of mind, one which I had never felt before. Also, it was the only time I did not experience his rose perfume. It was very hard to retain what he said, due to the excitement and the translation...But what I do retain is this: My *true* happiness would lie in heaven, where many souls that I had been instrumental in saving would gather around me before God. 'A savior of many souls,' he called me. He also said that he felt I have had a great love for Mary and that Mary has a greater love for me. Even though I've sinned many times in the past, God still calls me. He said this after touching my heart with his hand. He went on to say that married life was not for me but that I was to be a Father among many. He warned me to beware of those who would discourage me from entering the seminary. The devil works among people."

Brother Gino warned the young man in more detail that his family, relatives and friends would discourage him from entering the religious order of the Oblates of the Virgin Mary. In the weeks and months that followed, I kept in contact with him and discovered that, not only did all these people offer opposition, but even his pastor. The following year, when I shared the difficulties the young man had in entering the Oblate seminary, Brother Gino advised that the young man *should* seek entrance in another seminary."

Another young man, almost twenty-two years of age, described his experiences with Brother Gino at Fatima as follows:

"Before the pilgrimage I knew very little about Brother Gino, only that he was a stigmatist and had on different occasions bilocated. I had heard different stories about the perfume his wounds give off and his ability to look into souls. The latter bothered me slightly, even though I had been to confession. I also did not know how I would conduct myself around a man who had been given the crucifixion wounds of Christ Our Savior. But after seeing and talking with him, I realized that he is human also.

"When he arrived in the conference room August 8, I was taken by his humility. I have seen very, very few people of his humility. It was during the conference that I experienced his perfume. I thought it smelled like roses; however, a few others disagreed. From that day on I have experienced Brother's perfume even when he wasn't in the area. A friend and I were walking back from Aljustrel. We were about one mile from Fatima when he turned to me and said, "Did you..." Before he finished, I knew what he meant. We had just experienced the perfume, which seemed to come in the wind.

"On August 9th, Brother was talking to the boys in the lobby. I was standing against the wall when I noticed he was looking at me. His eyes seemed to look into me. Slightly smiling, he approached me and said, 'You will be a fisher of men, not of fish.' My reaction was one of slight uneasiness. But later on it seemed to make sense. While with friends, several times before my private interview, Brother pointed to me and said, 'This one.'

"On August 10th, I went for the interview with Brother. When I opened the door, Brother smiled broadly and said, 'This one is ready to come to San Vittorino.' I stepped forward and sat beside him, with Brother Ben as interpreter. He told me many things pertaining to calls to the vocation which I cannot remember sufficiently to quote...I learned that during the interview, when Brother was certain a boy had a religious vocation, he would pass one rosary bead through his fingers as the boy entered the room. August 10th was a very special day for me, and Brother said during my interview, 'You will always remember this day.' It was this same day that my friend and I experienced the perfume coming back from Aljustrel. And it was also that same evening at the Castle program at Ourem, when halfway through the dinner, that Brother called me to his table. I went up and gave him a hug. He then said, 'I want to give you a gift.' At this point I didn't know what to expect. He unbuttoned his cassock a bit. Brother Gino gave me his professional cross. He said, 'You bring this to San Vittorino when you come. I will be happy then and greet you with open arms...We must lay down all of our material things and take on our crosses to follow Our Lord.

This cross represents the crosses which you must carry before and after you become a priest.' The cross has a relic of the True Cross on it which makes it very dear to me.

"On the night of August 13th, Brother was to leave right after the Holy Hour. I was standing right by the door when he came out. I had on the cross he gave me. When he got to me, he touched the cross and said, 'Keep this close to your heart and have courage.' After Brother told me to have courage, I really felt peace. He told me that he would help me to become a saint when I go to San Vittorino."

A considerable number of the young men asked Brother Gino in their private interviews about their grandparents who had died. "Are they in heaven?" They were told: "Yes, because of their prayers, you are here on this pilgrimage at Fatima."

This extraordinary vision of Brother Gino naturally endeared him to the youth, but on the afternoon of the 13th they beheld an added quality of humanity in Brother Gino that they had not anticipated. They gathered under the trees of a recreation field at Fatima. There Brother sang for them, imitated Mussolini, Pius XII, John XXIII and Paul VI He told them jokes and stories of his childhood; then he invited the young Americans to reciprocate with songs and jokes of their own. Gathered around Brother Gino, who sat on the only chair available, the older boys commented that the sight of the Stigmatist of San Vittorino seated in their center under the open skies with many youth gathered around him for a couple of hours, reminded them of Christ in the Gospels, who gathered children unto Himself.

In the evening hours of August 13th, his last night at Fatima, the stigmatist conducted a Holy Hour. As a deacon he could expose the Most Blessed Sacrament and give the blessing. The slow pace, the deliberateness with which he raised the sacred monstrance aloft, tracing with it the sign of the cross over the young men kneeling devoutly in adoration before the altar, was a sight those present will never forget. Brother's eyes were fixed on the Sacred Host in the monstrance as the distinct shape of a large cross was slowly traced. He had led the Holy Rosary in Italian, and the boys had answered in English. His meditations were profound; between each decade he had introduced the mystery with thoughts which attracted the complete attention of all and challenged them to grow in virtue as they meditated on the mysteries.

"First Sorrowful Mystery: We contemplate Jesus' Agony in the Garden. Here we are at Fatima. We look to the three children of Fatima for help in contemplating how we are to accept sufferings, as Our Lord Himself accepted them. The spirit is willing, the flesh is weak. We must not forget that Our Blessed Lord Jesus said, 'If it be possible, take this chalice of suffering away,' but then He said, 'Father, may your will be done.' During this mystery of the Rosary we must ask from the Divine Heart of Jesus the grace to know how to accept our sufferings when this is the Holy Will of Our Lord, because all is for our good. Hail Mary...

"Second Sorrowful Mystery: The Scourging of Jesus at the Pillar. Before our eyes we see Our Blessed Lord scourged. He accepts His sufferings for love of us. We ask Our Lady during this mystery for perseverance in the good proposals that we have made these days [at Fatima]. Only in this way can we continue in the love of Our Lord, that is, if we are strong in our resolutions. Behold Jesus! This is the exchange we offer you. Those scourgings were accepted by Our Lord in reparation for acts of impurity. Through Our Lady, as we meditate on this mystery, let us ask Our Blessed Lord to forgive us. We have sinned in some way. Ask pardon also for the sins our brothers commit, for those who do not realize the sins they commit in offending Our Blessed Lord. Let us obtain for them, too, in this mystery, His pardon and mercy and the grace to conquer sin.

"Third Sorrowful Mystery: Our Lord is Crowned with Thorns. We, too, have sometimes placed this crown of thorns on the Sacred Head of Our Lord. Like the soldiers, we, too, have driven the thorns deeper into His head by beating Him over the head. Our Lord accepted this for love of us in order to obtain pardon for all the times we should have thought about Him when our minds were occupied with impure thoughts and bad desires, for all that is in us that is not clean. How many times have we failed to guard our eyes so that bad thoughts sprang up in our minds and so that we committed sins which have caused the crown of thorns. We must ask pardon in this mystery for that in us which caused the crown of thorns on Our Lord. Let us also ask forgiveness for the many poor sinners who keep their hearts and minds constantly submersed in sin. Through Our Lady, let us today beg for mercy.

"Fourth Sorrowful Mystery: Our Lord Carries the Cross. Our Lady calls us to embrace our cross. What is our cross? It is that which we must do well in our daily Christian duty in the observance of the Holy Laws of God. This must be our cross. Cost what it may, we must not commit sin, because sins destroy that which is most beautiful, the grace which Jesus has placed in our hearts. We must always be on guard so that this ugly cancer will never enter within us. Therefore, let us embrace our cross. There will never be a time but that the devil is prepared to destroy within us all those beautiful resolutions we have made these days. This war we must embrace. With the aid of Our Lady, we shall be victors. When one fights in this war, there is always some suffering. Let us accept that, too, for the love of God. We must not ask only for ourselves, but let us ask for all our brothers who don't wage war against the devil and who accept no cross. We must ask the Immaculate Mother to obtain help for us but also to obtain help for those poor sons of hers who have great need of the help of God.

"Fifth Sorrowful Mystery: The Crucifixion and Death of Our Lord Jesus. The crucifix must be our way of life each day. Generally, when we stop along the Way of the Cross and we see the nailed hands of Our Blessed Lord, we think more of the person who raises the hammer than we do of ourselves. Rather, we must think how many times we have recrucified Our Lord. How many times have we failed to hear his voice but have listened to a voice that was not His. How many times have we gone the way of the perverse world rather than go the way of His love. Such behavior kills the mind and the heart. It makes us like poor dead men. But let us thank God, for Mary will give us the strength to come forth and regain within ourselves the divine life, because at the foot of the Cross *she* stood. She does such beautiful things for us. She consented to be our Mother, and this meant becoming Mother to all those who crucified her Son. We all had a part. We should now be among those who take Him down from the Cross, and not those who continue to nail Him there. We must ask Our Lady to bring Our Lord to those who continue to crucify Him with deeds, acting as if sin were a beautiful thing. They excuse themselves instead of accusing themselves. Let us ask through Our Lady's intercession that these souls now in darkness finally come to light."

As the Stigmatist of San Vittorino led these meditations on the Rosary, those who listened intently were well aware that this man bore the marks of the crucifixion in his own body. His meditations revealed his keen understanding of youthful temptations. Their devout participation revealed their own desire to be pure, and their own resolutions to do so were strengthened by a man who was in their midst for a week at Fatima and who bore the wounds of Jesus, which were made by their sins.

The Holy Hour completed, Brother Gino moved to the rear of the chapel, where the youth gathered around him to present him with a spiritual bouquet and a statue of Jacinta of Fatima. As he walked to the car in the darkness of the August night, the youth spontaneously formed an honor guard on two sides down the steps to the car door, clapping loudly as he walked between them, cradling the Jacinta statue in his arms. He said, "It is a sin I do not speak English." But language had been no barrier that week. Even without interpreters, the meeting of eyes, the penetrating of souls, the manly embraces, the kissing of hands, the waves of perfume, the serious glances, the joyful smiles, would have been sufficient.

Brother Gino had met privately with me in a side reception room after the Holy Hour, embraced me the Italian way on both sides of the face, telling me we were "blood brothers in Christ." Now, as I stood back and watched the departure, amidst loud applause and youth running beside the car until it disappeared in the evening darkness, I finally turned to re-enter our resident building and asked myself, "Have I been dreaming this past week? Have I actually seen youth so warm and tender but manly around this man from San Vittorino? What is it about him? What has been happening?" The answer came to me, "We have just seen Christ, as it were, walking in our midst for the past week. It was, indeed, no dream."

In the week that remained at Fatima, the youth would come to me to ask for help in interpreting what Brother Gino had said to them, just as some were to write for guidance in the months ahead. Some days after his departure and return to San Vittorino, the youth still at Fatima had another Holy Hour with the Most Blessed Sacrament exposed. Immediately afterwards we were to go to the Cova da Iria and its *Capelinha*. There a sixteen-year-old lad approached me with great emotion because of something that had happened at the Holy Hour. "I am so nervous, Father. While you were preaching on the Holy Eucharist as Sacrifice, your voice faded to a whisper. I was looking at the Sacred Host in the monstrance. I heard the voice around me, within me, 'If you want to see this often, become a priest.' " Thinking the youth had permitted his imagination to work overtime, I respected his sincerity, and calmed his nerves.

Later that night, he approached me again in the chapel. His heart was beating so hard I could hear it. His shirt, over his heart, visibly moved up and down rapidly. I took him in my arms to comfort him. Then he told me, "When I went to Brother Gino, I was asked if I had any questions. 'I have only one question. I would like to know if God has a special vocation or calling for me?' By 'special' I meant the priesthood or religious life. Brother Gino answered, 'All have a special calling. It is just a manner of hearing it and carrying it out.' 'How will I hear my call?' 'When you hear your call, you will hear it loud and clear.' 'How will I know it is my calling?' 'Talk to your spiritual director. He will help you to know.' 'I don't have one.' 'What is your priest at home like?' 'We had a priest who went kind of liberal, so we moved away from him and started going to a different parish.' 'Why not ask Father Fox? He is good.' 'He is kind of far away.' 'That is all right. Why not write to him? St. Gemma Galgani used to write letters to her spiritual director, and her guardian angel delivered the letters. Talk to Father Fox.' 'Thank you.' "

The young man looked up at me in the chapel that night and asked, "Father, what is a spiritual director?" As we discussed matters, still thinking his imagination had played tricks, I experienced a strong perfume, as of Brother Gino. Ignoring it, I continued the counseling. Again the perfume came strongly. "Do you have a rose rosary in your pocket?" "No, I have a wooden rosary." "Where did you get it?" "I bought it here at Fatima for about a dollar." "Let me see it." He placed it in my hand. The perfume that came from it was overwhelming. I asked the lad to smell the rosary. All he could smell was the steel from the chain. "May I keep this until tomorrow?" "Yes."

It was after midnight when I finished counseling that young man. Holding the rosary tightly as I left the chapel, I noticed the light on in the room with three counselors still up. To one about to be ordained I said, "Smell this." He took the rosary and was overwhelmed also with its perfume. "I've never seen anything like this." To another, older seminarian I extended the rosary. He, too, experienced the same. Finally, to the third, who said, "Oh! This is not a rose rosary. This is the perfume of Brother Gino."

The thought was beginning to develop seriously in my mind that the sixteen-year-old had not imagined what he heard in the chapel before the Most Blessed Sacrament, exposed: "If you want to see this often, become a priest." The next day I asked if I might keep his rosary and present to him my own as a gift, one I had obtained in 1974 at Lourdes and carried throughout the world, some days praying as much as fifteen decades on it. Humbly, the youth accepted my rosary. The next day, while praying the rosary on what had been my beads, it too broke out in perfume, something I had never experienced in the years I prayed on it. This time the boy himself was the first to experience it. One day later the perfume had changed, to something more bitter.

Before leaving Fatima for America I was to discover that the youth had never told me the full story of what had happend in the chapel the night of the Holy Hour. He had been afraid to tell all lest I think he were crazy. I assured him of my conviction that he was telling the truth and that, after the incidents of the rosaries, I knew he had not imagined things. The the full story came out. He told me only under obedience. He wrote down the account as follows:

"When you were talking about the Mass as Sacrifice, which was the first part of your two-part sermon, I stopped listening and started talking to Jesus in the Blessed Sacrament. Then your voice was like a whisper in the background and the room became all hazy. I knew you and the boys were there but covered with the haze. That was when I saw the light. It kept going around the top of the monstrance, back and forth, and it did this for about a minute. It was ten or so inches long, circular, and rotated about the monstrance. Then it went down around the stem of the monstrance where you pick it up. Then it went back up and kept circling. After that the strip of light turned into a ball at the top of the monstrance and grew little arm-type things from its sides and wrapped them around the monstrance. That is when I heard the voice. It was a calm but loud voice and seemed to just echo throughout my head. It said, '[Using the boy's first name], if you want to see this often, become a priest.' Then the arms were pulled into the circle and the light started circling the monstrance again."

Such was the beginning of spiritual direction for a young man. It was another example of the charismata which surround Brother Gino and the influence he has as God's instrument in the lives of others, involving others in the care of souls. One young man, after being in direct contact with Brother Gino for six years, remarked that hundreds of times he had witnessed incidents for which there was no known natural explanation.

To a newly ordained priest, preaching at his first Mass on June 15, 1980, Brother Gino turned and said, "We are so many times poor and limited here on this earth, but a priest is a man, I can say, raised to the infinite. He cannot be replaced by anyone, not the president of the republic, nor the governor; no one can take your place in the world. Only you have the authority to call Jesus down that He may sacrifice Himself for the good of man, for those who believe and for those who do not, for the salvation of all. Only you, Father Daniel, can do this. No other man receives the command, 'Do this in memory of Me.' Only the priest.

"Your lips, from the moment of the first word of Consecration, become like the open side of Christ: Christ is sacrificed through the open words from your lips. And your lips are as the side of Christ when you confess people who through many things have been separated from Christ. You, and only you, will be able to pardon their sins with the words, 'I absolve you in the Name of the Father and of the Son and of the Holy Spirit,' and when you raise your hand to forgive their sins, you reunite them to God...

"To be a good Father means to be always a Father to all. And today he [the newly ordained] must understand well that his heart has become the heart of Christ. He must think that his heart is as bread in time of war when there is starvation. Everyone depends on him for a piece of bread. And, Father Daniel, if you continue this way, you will be a good priest and will be this bread. You will always be looked for by souls starving for God. How many times will you absolve sins! And so I say, thanks be to God for your beautiful vocation as a priest.

"I said you are as a piece of bread. Yes! For when you have worked the whole day long you will be tired, and at the last hour of the evening you will have to run to your brother who has the need to be reconciled with God. Blessed are you when you go into your room at night exhausted, for if you are tired at the end of the day, you will know that your life has been dedicated to God and to your brothers and that you have not wasted your time. And you will be happy. So you see, blessed are you. You are bread. And leave yourself to be eaten by others. You told me yesterday that you wanted to be the Heart of Christ. He, let us remember, lets Himself be consumed every hour of the day.

"I remind you of your great love for Our Blessed Mother. It is true; on your knees you will save your priesthood. Continue in your spirit of prayer and sacrifice. Your satisfaction will be in the saving of many souls."

Expressing his reasons for coming to Fatima, other than to be among young men, Brother Gino said, "I came to Fatima for three purposes: 1) I wanted to build a sanctuary to Our Lady of Fatima. Now there is such a sanctuary at San Vittorino. 2) I wanted to found an order of nuns in honor of Our Lady of Fatima. Now there is such an order. 3) I wanted to fill the seminary at San Vittorino. Now it is filled.'' The Stigmatist of San Vittorino had come to Fatima to thank the Mother of the Church, the Mother of God, under the title of Our Lady of Fatima, for these three favors. In thanking God's Mother in the very land, in the Cova, where she appeared with her message for the world, he also helped many young men recognize their vocations in life.

What is the message of Brother Gino, who suffers in his wounds ''always''? What is the message of the Stigmatist of San Vittorino who, from all medical points of view, dies each Good Friday, only, as it were, to rise again? The message is that Christ suffers yet in His Mystical Body, the Church. As Mary once stood beneath the Cross as Mother of the Mystical Christ when the Church came forth from His open side, so Mary reminds us, through Brother Gino, that the Church must still carry a daily cross in each one of us performing the sacrifice of living our daily duty. We must live our daily lives in harmony with the Magisterium, the official teaching Church, and, above all, listen and obey the voice of the Holy Father, the Pope.

Thus, God has placed Brother Gino in the world today, at the end of the twentieth century, to remind us that each one of us has a special call of Heaven, and that, as Mary said at Fatima, ''In the end, my Immaculate Heart will triumph.''

Appendices

"Indeed, as the sufferings of Christ overflow to us, so, through Christ, does our consolation overflow. When we are made to suffer, it is for your consolation and salvation. When, instead, we are comforted, this should be a consolation to you, supporting you in patiently bearing the same sufferings as we bear. And our hope for you is confident, since we know that, sharing our sufferings, you will also share our consolations." (2 Corinthians 1:5-7)

1. The Testimony of Brother Gino's Doctors

There follows an interview I had with Dr. Alfonso Bernardo, personal physician to Brother Gino, on August 5, 1981. Dr. Bernardo is a surgeon at the Sanitary Station at San Vittorino, Commune of Rome. The interview also involved Dr. Bernardo's wife, Dr. Fiorella Maria Mato, who is also a surgeon and analyst at a Roman hospital.

Dr. Bernardo and his wife have known Brother Gino since October 4, 1972. The wife heard of Brother Gino in an operating room in the hospital where she worked. The sisters in the hospital told her that there was a patient in the hospital who no longer had cancer. The surgeon, opening the patient, did not find any of the cancer. She decided to go to San Vittorino when she discovered that the cure was associated with Brother Gino. Being a doctor, she wanted to know the truth about the cure. Together with the sisters, Dr. F. Maria Mato made an appointment to see Brother Gino and also introduced Dr. Bernardo to him. The most important thing they found is reported by the doctor-couple as follows: "Brother Gino helped us out, gave us a new vision, helped us spiritualize our union." Previously they had not been living in the good graces of the Church within the Sacrament of Matrimony.

Since that time, however, both of these doctors have treated Brother Gino medically. Before they came into the picture, according to Dr. Bernardo and Dr. Mato, other doctors had already made a thorough study of the stigmata. Brother Gino's previous personal doctor, Dr. Bianco, who had made a thorough study of Brother Gino, died in 1980. Dr. Bernardo and his wife came to know Brother Gino already stigmatized. Their detailed observations of Brother Gino follow:

Concerning the Hands:

"On the dorsal side of the hand, corresponding to the pulse, a centimeter from the pulse, a circular wound exists, a diameter of one centimeter and one-half, sometimes bloody, covered with a scab, like a wound that is healing. On the palm side of the hand is a red mark, no hole there. On the dorsal side, the hole is near the articulation of the pulse. If you like, you can get the precise description from Father Piazzi [superior of Brother Gino at San Vittorino]. I made a precise description on Easter of 1981. It is very detailed, very complete. There also exist preceding descriptions."

Concerning the Side:

"I examined the wound in Brother Gino's side. It opens and bleeds some days before Easter. It is located [here Dr. Bernardo used precise Italian medical terms which the interviewers could not catch]...on the left side, two centimeters below the breast..."

"The side wound is between the fifth and the sixth ribs, the same as on the [Holy] Shroud." Dr. Bernardo then left his chair, walked to a large, almost life-size painting of the dead Christ in the arms of His Mother, and indicated that the artist had placed the wound in the left side correctly, almost the exact length, which seemed to be about an inch and a half. He said, "Brother Gino's side wound is placed as on this picture, the same size. The heart cannot be seen in the wound in Brother Gino's side; it does not reach to that depth. The wound appears on the surface, but on Good Friday it becomes bigger. Some weeks before Holy Week, it begins to bleed, about ten days before Easter; the times when this happens vary.

"Last Lent, it was either Palm Sunday or the Thursday or Friday before Palm Sunday in 1981 (can't remembert for certain the exact day), I visited Brother Gino because of a fever he had. Listening to his lungs, the chest area, I noticed that the wound in his side was closed, as a wound healed. There was the scar."

Both Dr. Bernardo and Dr. Mato indicated that they have seen the wound in Brother Gino's side five or seven years before my own interview with them in August of 1981. Both Dr.

Bernardo and Dr. Mato have witnessed the Passion of Holy
Week, with religious novices also assisting. Dr. Bernardo added:
"I have assisted at every passion since 1974. On the Thursdays
and Fridays preceding Passion week, the wound in Brother
Gino's side has been closed. I've witnessed this with two other
doctors, but on Holy Thursday it has been open and has bled. On
Good Friday, beginning between Holy Thursday evening and
Good Friday, the wound in the side has enlargened. Precise
information which I've written down indicated 2-1/2 to 3
centimeters long, 1/2 centimeter wide, 2 or 3 millimeters deep.
This wound is more bloody."

Concerning the Feet:

"The feet have the same thing during Holy Week. The
wound is very light, on the dorsal part, the beginning of a
wound. There is nothing on the feet during the year, only
tiredness and pain. During Holy Week, the stigmata appears on
the feet."

On Blood and Infection:

"The passion becomes more intense every year. The hands,
side, etc., bleed. The side begins to bleed about ten days before
the triduum [the last three days of Holy Week] and then closes.
The amount of blood that comes out cannot be stated for certain
since the bandages soak it up.

"An infection has never been seen on the wound.
Disinfectants and penicillin have never been administered." Dr.
Bernardo and his wife, Dr. F. Maria Mato, then stated
emphatically, speaking only for themselves, "Certainly *we* have
never administered anything like that for infection."

When I asked for the medical explanation for the wounds
which have continued in the hands and side, and which reappear
during Holy Week in the feet, both Dr. Bernardo and Dr. Mato
stated: "There is *no explanation* of the continuous wounds with
no infection."

"The pain is not treated," both doctors agreed. Dr. Mato
analyzed the blood, a procedure for which she is medically
trained. She stated, "In the blood analysis, an infection
would have shown up, but there was none. The white corpuscles
would have to increase and their velocity be greater. This would
have to be the case of a wound or infection of long duration. But

there was no increase. In a laboratory analysis, the data is normal. There was indicated that which does not take place in a normal subject. Even without infection, an open simple wound has to cause increase of white corpuscles and velocity. This does not take place in Brother Gino. Velocity means an increase and deposit of white corpuscles, indicative of a wound, like a rise in temperature indicates a fever. There is no velocity in Brother Gino's wound. No velocity takes place if there is no wound. Velocity is called 'hetero sedimentation.' (Velocity does not refer to the heart). A toothache, headache, sore throat, etc. are enough to cause a velocity. But never is this seen in Brother Gino's wounds.

"This 'hetero sedimentation' of a substance in water explains the velocity process and rise of an infection. This is *not* seen in Brother Gino's blood."

Concerning the Perfume:

Dr. Bernardo: "The perfume was present before I knew Brother Gino. It was always present. Father Dino tells the story of one of the three doctors who didn't believe in the perfume. The perfume then became so intense that the unbeliever got on his knees and begged for forgiveness. All three were then on their knees.

"On October 5, 1972, I was studying medicine in Bologna and I happened that day to be in Rome, 20 kilometers away from San Vittorino, after having met Brother Gino. I was visiting my aunt, telling myself that roses don't bloom in October, yet, I could experience that same perfume for two consecutive hours that October 5, 1972, 20 kilometers away.

"My aunt, who did not know Brother Gino, came to perceive the same perfume. We went into the garden, still smelling the same perfume. My aunt, who knew Padre Pio and had smelled this intense perfume, although I had never before mentioned Brother Gino to her, said, "This is the perfume of sanctity." [There were no roses in bloom in the garden.] Dr. Bernardo remained there in silence, "so important was that event to me."

"Two months later, around Christmas, I went to thank Brother Gino, because my exams had gone well. My aunt came with me to meet Brother Gino and then recognized the same perfume we had experienced two months previously."

Dr. Bernardo told the story of a certain Father Filippo of Rho who came to Rome and said, "I believe in all except the perfume." He went to Assisi and, during the celebration of the Mass, at the Sanctus, was enveloped by this same perfume unexpectedly. He came back to Rome and said, "Brother Gino, you shouldn't have played this joke on me." Brother Gino replied, "Why didn't you believe?"

"The perfume comes from the stigmata but not only the stigmata. It comes from the entire body of Brother Gino. It comes from the blood," stated Dr. Bernardo. It comes, too, from the Christ-statue in his room, a crucifix. During Holy Week three or four years ago there was a *"sciva"* or sweat that oozed from the side of this crucifix.

Dr. F. Maria Mato stated that on Good Friday at the Holy Stairs in Rome, together with five or six persons, she smelled the perfume of rose from the feet of the stone statue of Christ. They were making the Holy Stairs for Brother Gino. Upon kissing the feet, they smelled the perfume.

"There is no natural explanation for the perfume. The perfume remains a long while on his handkerchief, even though there is no blood on the handkerchief. The perfume is not smelled by all simultaneously," Dr. Bernardo and Dr. Mato explained. "A body can't produce the perfume. The aroma can't be analyzed. It is not a chemical reaction. Blood does not give a perfume."

Dr. F. Maria Mato explained, "The blood never gave the perfume when I was analyzing it." Both doctors agreed that the perfume comes especially from the wounds but not always.

Concerning the Passion:

"For a few variable seconds (varies from year to year), 7 or 8 seconds, the pulse stops and is not heard." While both agreed that Brother Gino biologically dies, appears to be a whitened, lifeless corpse, they have never used a cardiograph. They have not wanted to cause embarrassment by asking for that procedure. They stated, "The heart seems to stop. In a few seconds, the body seems to be a corpse. After some seconds, respiration begins again (Brother Gino had stopped breathing). Brother Gino continues to suffer much after the passion. He has often said that he felt tired after having suffered so much. He talks about what he has had to offer to Jesus. By Easter Sunday, Brother Gino begins to get better. His hands and feet are cold during the time of the Agony in the Garden on Thursday."

At this point Dr. Bernardo explained the repeated loss of consciousness which Brother Gino experiences during the passion of Holy Thursday and Good Friday. The body becomes rigid, and the hands and feet, cold. Beginning about 7:30 p.m. on Thursday evening, the loss of consciousness may last from fifteen minutes to as long as forty minutes at a time. The loss of consciousness also occurs during the three hours of Good Friday that Christ hung on the Cross. Dr. Bernardo emphasized again, "Every year the passion becomes more severe."

When I asked for the natural explanation for all this phenomena in Brother Gino and what effect they have had on their own lives, Dr. Bernardo and Dr. Mato responded as follows:

"It is a supernatural thing. It is not scientifically explainable. It has changed our lives. It has given us a new life, a new dimension." Dr. Mato added, "When I see people suffering in the hospital, I tell them to offer it up. I now understand that suffering has a place in Christianity. I see the presence of the Lord in people's sufferings. I see suffering as a great method of expiation...I see Christian suffering as a beautiful thing to take on. Sometimes, when I have seen an atheist suffering, I have become very moved. Then some other sick person would be moved, also, because of my reaction and, understanding my deep feelings, ask, 'What can I do for you?' "

Recalling a special occasion when this happened, Dr. F. Maria Mato said, "I gave him a rosary and said, 'Pray for him,' and he did. The principal thing is love. Love is at the bottom of suffering. 'God is love.' "

"Take yourselves, for instance, brothers, at the time when you were called: How many of you were wise in the ordinary sense of the word, how many were influential people, or came from noble families? No, it was to shame the wise that God chose what is foolish by human reckoning; those whom the world thinks common and contemptible are the ones that God has chosen—those who are nothing at all to show up those who are everything. The human race has nothing to boast about to God, but you God has made members of Christ Jesus, and by God's doing he has become our wisdom, and our virtue, and our holiness, and our freedom. As scripture says: if anyone wants to boast, let him boast about the Lord." (I Corinthians 1:26-31)

2. The Testimony of Brother Gino's Secretary

The spirit of Brother Gino and of San Vittorino can be captured by sharing the insights of those who have had long and intimate association with both. It is the burden of this appendix to touch on a variety of aspects of Brother Gino's life which are not part of the principal narrative. For this, I rely principally, but not entirely, on one special man, Brother Ronald Warren, from Ireland, secretary to Brother Gino for four years until late summer, 1979. He had first come to San Vittorino in 1972. In addition to serving as secretary, he frequently served as interpreter for many pilgrims from America, Canada, Ireland, and Australia, and for those from South America who speak English.

Reading Souls

One of Brother Warren's favorite stories concerns two young men who came to San Vittorino and were in the Communion line. Brother Gino lifted the Sacred Host from the ciborium and told the two young men in succession, quietly so as not draw attention, that they should go to confession before receiving Our Divine Lord in Holy Communion. The two young men complained bitterly afterwards that they *had* been to confession but that Brother Gino had refused them Holy Communion. They insisted on finding out why he had done this. Brother Gino said that they had not been sincere in their confessions. They waited all day to speak to Brother Gino, and he continued to insist that they had been insincere.

Brother Warren points out that Brother Gino does not read every soul that comes to him for Holy Communion or at any other time, but only when God gives him the light. It is a grace to be told that there is need of repentance.

Perfume

Brother Warren also told of the many times he was challenged about the perfume that comes from Brother Gino's wounds: "This perfume we experience as coming from Brother Gino, does it not come from a bottle?" In four years of experience he learned to respond, "Look, there is no sin in believing that. If you believe that, there is only one challenge I give you. Go into the world and find that bottle." He added, "No one has returned with the bottle to prove that this is a substance that has come from manufactured perfume out in the world. I have always asked the groups who have come here, 'Did everyone smell the perfume?' There is always one or two that did not."

The fact that not everyone experiences the perfume is in itself a sign of authenticity when those who do not experience it otherwise have a normal sense of smell. Others, hearing that some did not smell the perfume, respond, "It is impossible that you didn't receive it, it was so strong."

Brother Ronald Warren admitted that he himself had long periods of not smelling the perfume, up to two or three months while working close to Brother Gino. He inquired of Brother Gino why this was and was told, "It is not of importance. Have courage and continue." Even with the response, Brother Ronald felt downcast and that he was not in God's favor, even though he was not conscious of anything particular to repent of and to confess.

The same day that he had asked this, in the afternoon, he walked into the sacristy. "It was as if months of the perfume were all in that room for me. It came whacking me on the face, like a wind blowing in my face with the most beautiful perfume.

It was like three months of the perfume all wrapped up for me, supplying for that period of time when I had not smelled it. I still experience the perfume now and then. I must confess that when people get the perfume very strong, I don't get it. Other days, I get it when other people say to me that they don't receive it."

All of this points out that it is supernatural, not natural, or all with normal olfactory functions should be able to smell it alike. The very same charge was made about Padre Pio regarding the perfume that came from his stigmata. He was ever accused of having bottles under his bed. But it was never proven.

The Wounds

As regards changing Brother Gino's bandages, if there are students at San Vittorino who have studied medicine or have worked in hospitals, they are chosen to assist during Passion Week. Brother Gino otherwise normally changes the bandages himself. Brother Warren admitted to having seen the wounds three or four times and describes the incidents as follows:

"I was here in 1973, in 1974 and in 1975, and I never saw any wounds. In 1975 I received my habit. I was then given the responsibility as Brother Gino's helper with the pilgrims. During this period of time I had terrible doubts as regards his wounds due to the fact that I hadn't seen them. Second Thomas. I went through a very, very hard tribulation on this to the extent that I was almost going to leave. I prayed to Our Blessed Mother to give me strength to believe. I asked for a sign. I must see these wounds.

"Finally, the temptation came to such a degree that I could not mentally take any more. I went into the church one night, into our small chapel here. I said to Our Lady, 'Take these away from me. I don't want these doubts. As long as I stay here, I *never want* to see the wounds.'

"The following morning I was coming down the stairs. It was the custom of the Mother to bring up a small flask of tea at that time, early in morning, for Brother. On going up the stairs, the Mother twisted her ankle and she could not continue her passage upwards three flights. She gave me the flask and said, 'Take this to Brother Gino.' I hadn't an idea of where his room was. I knew the corridor, so I asked, in my limited amount of Italian at that time, 'Where is his room?' She described it. I went up and along the corridor, not thinking anything of wounds, but just that it was a privilege to bring him the tea. I knocked at the door, and he responded, 'I am coming.'

"I waited a few moments and the door opened. He opened the door with both of his hands bare up to his elbow. I saw the wounds and they were bleeding. Both sides of the wrist were bleeding. There was a trickle of blood to the right and to the left, depending on how he held his hand. It was not Holy Week. I experienced the perfume then, extremely strong.

"I wuld say that the wounds bleed when he changes his bandages. That was my first occasion to help bandage his wounds. We put a wad of cotton first on both sides of his wrists, on the palm side and on the back of the palm, then, on top of that, a white bandage. Then a white mitten on top of that, with a black mitten afterwards. And I feel that this is pressurized, this material is then pressurizing on the wound, that for the period of time that it is bandaged it forms in clots or it congeals and a scab for the wound forms on it.

"Well, you can imagine, like any ordinary person who has a wound, when removing the bandage, it has to be done very slowly. I think the slower you do it, the more scab you rip off. If you do it quickly, once again, the scab may come off. I feel that is what happened that particular morning...I think he changes the bandages once a week on Friday, because I've seen him with new mittens on Friday."

Brother Gino told me, when I inquired about the perfume which the stigmatist admitted he does *not* experience himself, that the night before he had washed out his mittens in disinfectant (not to disinfect the wounds, as they never become infected), thinking that people the next morning would then not be able to smell any perfume. The first person who came, however, said, "Oh, what a strong perfume!"

The wounds in Brother Gino's feet, which his former secretary observed during Easter Week, reportedly appeared "on the top of his feet, very, very red. A round red mark, very red. I have seen that in Holy Week." Describing this in August of 1979, he said, "For the past two years the skin has been broken and the blood has come to the surface with no sore or no wound." These comments had reference to the fact that the foot wounds, which have been the last of the stigmata to appear visibly, seem gradually to become more pronounced.

Of his wounds and suffering, Brother Gino has said, "Isn't it really a mystery? You know I never asked for these. I only prayed to her, as the Mother, and to Him, as Baby Jesus...Anyone who would ask for the stigmata would have to be crazy.''

Harassment by the Devil

Regarding the interferences of the devil physically and visibly in Brother Gino's life, his secretary had this to say, ''I have never seen anything with regard to any marks upon his face or on his person. I do remember once when he came down in the morning that he had a small tape around his finger. I asked him what happened. He said that his finger was cut in an accident. I asked him how it was that it happened. He said that he was shaving, and the shaving mechanism, which was an ordinary blade, not electric, flew out of his hand—was taken out of his hand or flew out of his hand, he didn't know which, but it flew—and it cut the top of his finger...Needless to say, it was an unusual experience.''

The Passion of Brother Gino

About the three hours of Good Friday, when Brother Gino apparently dies:

''Yes, I have seen him during that period of time for the last four years, more so in the last two years, because of my position as his secretary. I have been permitted to stay in the room...He is laid on his bed. His hands are still bandaged. Before I go in, his wounds are attended to by one or two doctors. When he goes into his passion, he has tremors from head to toe. He calls on Our Blessed Mother, 'Mamma...Good Mother...' Continuously he says these words.

''I remember once hearing, 'What a great darkness,' or 'What darkness.' 'Jesu, Jesu! Help me!' And many ejaculations.

''We don't see any blood because the bandages are on his hands. There are no mittens at the time, but the bandages are doubtlessly very thick...Around the time of two-fifteen to two-thirty, it varies, Brother Gino dies, in my experience of seeing many people die. I have seen four or five people as they took their last breath. It is what I call 'the last gasp.' He continues to breathe heavily until the last gasp, which takes all the air out of his body. Then he is silent, with no movement of his body. His mouth is slightly open when he stops breathing. His pulse stops and his heart stops.

''There are usually about two doctors present at that

particular time. The doctors go over him, feel his pulse and his heartbeat; there is none. They wait for a period of time. It varies. No medical treatment is applied whatsoever as regards cardiac arrest, etc., no pumping the heart or putting an injection in. Nothing is done. We pray. The first signs I have seen of his returning is a slight trembling of his eyelids. His eyes are closed when he dies. A slight tremor of the nervous system in the upper eyelid and then his breathing comes back, just like a baby, very, very slowly."

As to how long it takes for him to come back to normal, his secretary answered, "It varies. I remember the first years it took longer. He was very weak. Now he seems to be recuperating much more quickly."

About the crucifix in the stigmatist's room which reportedly bleeds at times, his secretary answered, "Bleed? I don't know. But I do know that a certain liquid comes from the side of it which has perfume as well."

Holiness

"I look at Brother Gino as an obvious example of his own words. This is the most important thing to me about Brother Gino. Certainly, when I first came here I was interested in the wounds, etc. Now I've seen them. I am content. They're there. The perfume is there, and I don't worry about it very much. I can be upset by many pilgrims coming, telling me that they're false and they say this without any of the slightest bit of proof. These are persons who have made a judgment rashly. I think these people leave here not believing. They are persons also who consider him very, very harsh, particularly the women who say, 'Who is he to tell me that this is immodest? I have a complaint...I shall wear a light dress...'

"He responds like this: 'Do you realize that the sun is beating down more on you? I don't want to judge for the doctor, but as far as I can see, the better the clothing, the better you are protecting yourself from this intense heat? On one occasion, Brother Gino used a different tactic when a lady approached him scantily dressed. 'Have you ever eaten an apple?' 'Oh, yes, Brother Gino, I have eaten many apples.' 'I'm surprised. Eve ate only one apple, and she had sense enough to put on some clothes. You have eaten many apples and you dress like this?' The lady good-naturedly promised to dress modestly in the future."

When Brother Gino is around the young men, the seminarians and people who are close to him, he seems so much more relaxed. When the pilgrims line up to kiss his hand and are wont to ask him questions, he seems rigid and almost like a different man. Brother Ronald Warren reacted as follows:

"I can understand this from my own experience. I am beside him all the time. I've got to have a break, too, and I've asked for a break, due to the fact that all eyes are watching. This gets into your nervous system. They should not be looking at him. He is an exceptional person, and I think this causes a certain amount of interior feeling, so that he can become nervous, distracted... People afterwards come up and say to me, 'Oh, how blessed you are to be near him!' I don't want to listen to that. I want them all to go into the church and to look at the Eucharist. That is what Brother Gino wants, too. The tabernacle deserves attention, and people should be attentive to the Mass. The other attention causes a strain."

An example of things about particular pilgrims which can test his patience most is seen in the pilgrim that came and said, "Brother Gino, can you help me? I want to buy an apartment...I have four floors to select from, which one should I select?" "Well, my dear woman, if you select the one at the top, and if there is, God forbid, an earthquake, you will fall all the more." Brother Gino is indirectly telling such a person that she has just asked a very stupid question and should have used her brain to think the matter out herself.

Brother is not indifferent to people's needs, even when they are not directly spiritual. If the person is in financial difficulty, certainly he will help if he can. If an unfortunate woman, for example, has three or four children to support, and if he sees that the Good Lord is testing her, he will shed enlightenment. If he has knowledge of why her shop may not be doing well, and it is not the woman's fault, he will help.

There are times when Brother Gino would like to escape it all and be as an ordinary man. Those closest to him admire his patience. While there are only two periods of time each day when he receives, yet the line of pilgrims wanting exceptions is always growing. "We didn't know the program...We have come a long way...We are desperate...have only two months to live..." There is always a good response from Brother, but if he were to receive all in one day, as they would like, there would be no time for him to do his religious duties, even to pray. Brother Warren has said, "Just think, a stream of persons is coming to you, and they all want to see Brother. *Every* solitary thing they say to him is a problem. They are dying. Their parents are dying. Their sons and daughters are away from the sacraments. Another has no house. Their husbands have left them. Their wives have left them. Nothing but problems...Then you say, 'Well, Good Lord, is there nothing but problems? Is nothing in the world going right?' And that's not just one day, but day after day after day. Therefore, I am just waiting for someone to come in and say, 'You know, I feel great today.' I haven't heard it in a long time."

It was a great privilege for me to have Brother Gino request me to assist him in his role as deacon at a Mass to be offered at San Vittorino. Since Brother Ronald had for some years assisted the stigmatist, including being present in the pews beside him at Mass, the next comment of the secretary concerned the trembling that Brother Gino obviously endures at the two-fold consecration at Mass. Does it have anything to do with the crucifixion of Jesus Christ? Anything to do with the dogma of faith that the Sacrifice of the Mass perpetuates the Sacrifice of the Cross?

Brother Ronald replies, "I did ask him about that. I hope I remember the words he spoke. He can experience Christ's suffering for us. He experiences that suffering of Christ in a mystical way, probably, I don't know, or in a physical way. But he said he can experience it. Also, he wishes to get out of his body and go to Him. The soul longs to be united with Jesus. Now, why the shivering? Whether it is the force of his body holding back the soul, I don't know. Maybe one day he will take off. I don't know. He seems tense at that period of time, a tightening up of his body and his senses. He moves back and forth, twists his shoulders. It seems that if it were not a thing that was controlled by him, he would certainly shiver the more. There is more of this when he is kneeling than when he is standing at the altar. When one stands behind him, one can see his feet actually tapping on the floor. If you are close, you can feel his trembling. I never look at him, because I would have to look to the side...When he is deacon, he is at a distance from me. It seems that he suffers the more on his knees...I feel the trembling on the pedestal he is kneeling on. If I am behind him, at times I see his feet, his soles, moving up and down, sandals tapping on the floor...Mystically or physically, I don't know. He told me that he feels Christ's suffering, experiences Christ's suffering...There are certain priests who celebrate Mass more reverently than others. Brother Gino experiences the suffering regardless...I have found that he doesn't shiver any more or less...I have never actually come across any Mass when there was not a reaction.''

Brother Gino's Impact

My final question: "And if Brother Gino died tomorrow?"

Brother Warren's reply: "Brother Gino's death would be a very difficult thing to look at. Would they come to visit his tomb? It depends. Once again, after his death, if the miracles or the graces were received through his intercession, through his prayers, certainly they would come...It would be in God's hands. Brother Gino has said, when asked why people come here, 'Because of the good work, because the helping hand was available.' And this is what he wants. He wants priests, some brothers and our new nuns, even though they are a different sex, he wants all of them to be open, helping and kind. Yes, to be other Christs.

"I have seen in the young men that we have had here these same virtues. I use the word virtue, speaking of patience, kindness, charity. If they didn't have them before their entry, they've got them now. I ask, where did they get them from? By their prayers. I would believe also by Brother's example. The sisters' as well.

"Brother founded this new order of sisters with the permission of the Bishop of Tivoli. They were started on the thirteenth of May, 1978. They have the convent, now, which is attached to our Sanctuary. When young women come here and see the sisters vested well, this gives a good example. They, too, want to enter the order. There are many stories about how God works with His grace. There is in the life of one saint [a story]that he was attracted by the buttons on the cassock of a priest. He joined that particular community of priests due to the fact that God worked simply by the use of little buttons on the cassock...God can work through these things as sacramentals.

"We have vocations to the priesthood, and I'm not going to be a stop to that. We need priests! But we also need brothers! Because the brothers' job is to help the priests, to help them so they have time to hear confessions, communicate with people, to celebrate Mass, to baptize. Brothers give time to priests so they can perform these functions while the brothers do such things as clean the rooms, do sacristan work, wash plates, pray. These things all have to be done. We have many students here for the priesthood. If we have no brothers, who's going to do it?''

"May God our Father himself, and our Lord Jesus Christ, make it easy for us to come to you. May the Lord be generous in increasing your love and make you love one another and the whole human race as much as we love you. And may he so confirm your hearts in holiness that you may be blameless in the sight of our God and Father when our Lord Jesus Christ comes with all his saints." (1 Thessalonians 3:11-13)

3. Brother Gino, Director of Souls

While Brother Gino is neither the superior of the seminarians at San Vittorino nor responsible for their spiritual formation, he does take an interest in them and has an effect on them. This appendix can well conclude with an actual sample meditation which he gave the students, not in the manner of a formal presentation, but as they surrounded him for informal conversation, such as at the time of recreation. It consists of his own reflections on a particular subject that was of interest to the students as he detected their temptations to discouragement.

If you can picture yourself, on the sidelines, watching Brother Gino, with the young men who aspire to the Holy Priesthood surrounding him during recreation period, the meditation below is what you would have heard on a particular day:

"1. We must be on our guard against discouragement, the demon's great method of deceit. In an instant, he can show us our life of :

a. Yesterday...making it seem even worse than it was, and putting in our minds the doubt that we have been forgiven by God.

b. Today...suggesting that we've done little, that we could have done more, and that, in fact, we are going backwards in virtue.

c. Tomorrow...as a catastrophe, ruin for ourselves and others.

"To really please God in these moments, throw yourself into

God's arms, abandon yourself to Him, letting Him sanctify you as He wills, even with that defect you don't want to have, if it can serve to give you humility. God wants us all to be saints...but His way, not ours.

"2. God sometimes tests us by letting us feel so much internal pain and desolation that no other person living can understand if he has not experienced it for himself. In these moments, the passions awaken more vigorously than ever, especially anger and lust, and, like a runaway horse, want to drag us wherever they wish to go. Also here, stand firm in the hands of God; He sees you and will give you strength until it ends...whenever He wishes. This is sanctity.

"Many times God lets us climb a mountain, only to slide down again on our behinds. But why wish to go underground? Let us get up and start again. Becoming a saint requires time and a lot of patience, so if we should slip into an old defect, let us not become discouraged. If I fall but then arise telling God I'm really sorry, it's more pleasing to Him than His disappointment was in my falling. In fact, God may allow us a fall to show us just how weak we are. We must never become discouraged, for once discouraged, we won't even listen to our confessor, but will remain fixed in this discouragement, and then an extraordinary grace is necessary."

To those who respond well in love to the King's love for us are revealed more of the secrets of His Heart. And, of course, our all-good Heavenly Mother, the Queen of Heaven and Earth, is fond of sharing those secrets with her spiritual children as well. She works well to share the secrets of the King's Heart so we can *know* Him better and thus be motivated to respond in our wills with love to the King's love. Love for love. *It is the way of the Mother of Love.* While we often do not match our own ambitions, our own desires to grow in union with God in Jesus Christ, yet we can desire. To desire what is good, especially the Good God, is already an act of the will. Below is another reflection given the students by Brother Gino. We name it simply *DESIRE*.

1. I desire to make my Holy Communion well.
2. I desire to make a good confession.
3. I desire to pray the ROSARY well.
4. I desire to hear Holy Mass well.
5. I desire to recollect myself well when I pray.

6. *I desire to conduct myself well in church.*

7. *I desire to live well through chastity.*

8. *I desire to dress myself always modestly.*

9. *I desire to mortify my eyes.*

10. *I desire to mortify my tongue.*

11. *I desire to mortify my curiosity.*

12. *I desire to deny comforts to my body.*

13. *I desire to mortify my own will.*

14. *I desire to be patient with everyone in all things.*

15. *I desire to treat everyone as Jesus Himself.*

16. *I desire to send away the temptations without looking at them.*

17. *I desire to mortify my musical appetite.*

18. *I desire to avoid the proximate occasions of sin.*

19. *I desire to mortify my use of alcohol.*

20. *I desire to mortify my laziness.*

21. *I desire to act in such a way as not to disturb others.*

22. *I desire to do each action of the day as an act of love.*

23. *I desire to maintain myself in the presence of God.*

24. *I desire to be punctual in following my schedule.*

25. *I desire to develop a true devotion to the Sacred Heart of Jesus and to the Immaculate Heart of Mary.*

26. *I desire to control my character.*

27. *I desire to speak of others with charity.*

28. *I desire to give a good example always.*

29. *I desire to remain joyful always.*

30. *I desire to inspire confidence in others.*

31. *I desire to become holy following always the will of God.*

32. *I desire to maintain the cleanness of my body and my room.*

33. *I desire to distract myself from the things of the world.*

34. *I desire to be meek and humble in all things.*

"DO THIS AND YOU WILL BE FOLLOWING IN THE FOOTSTEPS OF SAINTS."

ACT OF CONSECRATION TO OUR LADY

By Brother Gino Burresi, O.M.V.

O Mary, my most lovable Mother,
I, your son, today offer myself to you,
and I consecrate FOREVER
to your Immaculate Heart
all that remains to me of life,
my BODY with all its miseries,
my SOUL with all its weaknesses,
my HEART with all its affections and desires,
all my prayers, toils, loves, sufferances and fights,
and, in a special way, my death,
along with all that will accompany it,
my extreme sorrows and my last agony.

All this, my Mother, I unite
ALWAYS AND IRREVOCABLY
to your LOVE
to your TEARS
to your SUFFERINGS,

O my most sweet MOTHER,
remember this your son, and the CONSECRATION.

If I, overcome by discouragement and sadness,
by disturbances and anguish, might go so far sometime
as to forget about you, O then, my Mother,
I ask you and I beg you
—instantaneously—
by the Love that you carry for Jesus,
by HIS WOUNDS,
by HIS BLOOD
to protect me as your son and NOT TO ABANDON ME
until I may be with you in the Glory of Heaven.

Amen.

"Now as they were eating, Jesus took some bread, and, when he
had said the blessing, he broke it and gave it to the disciples.
'Take it and eat,' he said, 'this is my body.' Then he took a cup,
and when he had returned thanks he gave it to them. 'Drink all of
you from this,' he said, 'for this is my blood, the blood of the
covenant, which is to be poured out for many for the forgiveness
of sins.' " (Matthew 26:26-28)

4. Brother Gino on the Eucharist

*This appendix contains a sermon given by Brother Gino,
deacon, in the Sanctuary of the Sacred Particles at Siena in
September, 1980.*

BREAD OF LIFE

I want to share something with you, even though
somewhat personal.

Every time that I kneel down before a crucifix, the wound of
Jesus which strikes me most and attracts me is that of the side,
because there, above all, I read the word "love"!

Even though it is a fact that men have become evil (but they
have always more or less been that way), God does not destroy
them, and He cannot destroy them, because the eye of the
Father also reads in the opening of that wound the same word,
"love"!

Christ loves us. He loves us to the point of becoming for us in
the Holy Eucharist daily nourishment for life and for eternal life.
Look at those enamored of the Holy Eucharist. Look at our saints.
What lively hearts they had. All was alive in them with Jesus
Christ.

Consider the many slaves of materialism who no longer
nourish themselves with that Bread of Life. Even if they walk and
run about the streets of our own land, Italy, or throughout the
world, they are among the dead, the poor dead. Their actions

speak each day only of death.

Blessed Jesus, however, who loves us so much, wishes to resurrect Himself in these dead hearts. He asks us all to give Him a hand by way of sacrifice and prayer in accomplishing their resurrection. First of all, He asks us to be alive ourselves in His divine life and in perfect harmony with His Heart, without fears of any kind.

Frequently, however, we are afraid of Jesus. Have you not said to Him sometimes, "Jesus, I wish to be close to You. I want you to make me a saint. I want You to free me from an ugly vice." Then, miserable souls that we are, we later add, "Don't come too close...I am afraid that you will ask too much of me." Perhaps only five minutes before we had prayed in church, "I want...," and, barely out the door, add, "Don't come too close"! Why is there so much fear of the greatest friend we have?

You, then, O people of Siena, right here in the Basilica, even if you were as incredulous as Thomas, you always have it within reach, on the invitation of Jesus Himself, present in the Most Blessed Sacrament, to touch Jesus through the species of this Bread that challenges the centuries and proclaims His love.

Begin here in the presence of the infinite love poured forth from the side of Jesus to prostrate yourselves in adoration. Repeat with St. Thomas, who became a believer because he saw and touched, *"My Lord and my God."*

My dear friends, do not believe that Jesus asks too much of us or that he might hurt us. It is the world that asks too much of us, and too often we follow its call. The world does not place a cross with Jesus on our shoulders. Rather, a worldly mentality forces a huge cross of great worldly burdens on us, and without Jesus it is not easy to carry. And it comes to the point of placing the blame on Our Lord for the cross that we ourselves have constructed with our own hands. We then complain to Him, "Jesus, what are you doing?" "Jesus, where are you?"

Our Blessed Lord draws near. He lifts the heavy cross of the world from us and gives us His own, which is light. Jesus does this as a true friend and a true brother, because He has the biggest and most loving heart in the world. In that heart we will find all things: goodness, charity, mercy, meekness, patience and generosity. That heart will always open to us, no matter what hour of the day or night we knock. Jesus never rejects anyone and never makes anyone wait. He receives everyone immediately, giving goodness and comfort to all.

Jesus desires to achieve total union with us in giving each one the possibility of receiving Him in Holy Communion. In fact, Jesus made it a command: "Take it and eat...This is My Body...Drink all of you from this...For this is My Blood..." And when we feed ourselves on that Bread, something truly great happens within us. Our poor hearts, miserable creatures that we are, beat in unison with His and we become one with the heart of the Creator. It's stupendous!

We would commit, however, the most enormous sacrilege if, with the death of sin in the soul, we ate the white Bread which is Christ. It would be like crucifying Jesus again, making the living Host ineffective and powerless to achieve union within us.

It is true that today we see endless lines of persons who go to Communion, but no longer do we see the lines around the confessionals. Could it be that by some touch of a magic wand we have all become saints? The saints confessed often and some of them every day. The saints were afraid of even the least sin. They were not afraid of sinners.

When the pastor of little Francisco of Fatima was to bring Holy Communion to this child who was to die shortly, as the Madonna had foretold, the boy called for his cousin Lucia. "Lucia," he said, "tomorrow I must go to confession and then receive the Hidden Jesus." "Hidden Jesus" was his name for the Holy eucharist. "Tell me, have you seen me commit any sin which may have offended Jesus?" Lucia answered: "Sometimes I saw you throw stones...Be at peace, Francisco. Our Lady said that she will come to take you to heaven..."

Do you hear? A child afraid of sin! The adults today are not afraid of sin. They go arm in arm with sin.

If we want our heart to become the heart of Jesus, the first thing to do is to go to confession with the will to spit out the death we have inside. Christ is alive. He carries divine life and does not want to hide it in a sepulcher. Let us not neglect that great gift of God which is the Sacrament of God's pardon.

When we make a good confession, the soul is purified, fortified, and rendered more beautiful in the eyes of God. It then becomes worthy to receive the Lord.

After a good confession we are made ready to eat that "Bread come down from heaven" which gives us everlasting life. We will then be one heart with Jesus and one heart with our neighbor, capable of smiling at everyone, of being close to the one who suffers, and of saying a good word to all, while living to the full the commandment of love.

About Christendom

Christendom Publications is a division of the Christendom Educational Corporation, which also runs Christendom College. For information on Christendom Educational Corporation and Christendom College, see page 205 A list of Christendom Publications' offerings appears beginning on page 201.

Christendom Publications

Christendom Publications consists of periodicals and books under two imprints, all designed to directly advance Catholic Truth. All materials are available by mail from Christendom Publications, Route 3, Box 87, Front Royal, Virginia 22630. Please add 90 cents postage for books.

PERIODICALS:

Common Faith: monthly bulletin of Catholic commentary, edited by J. A. Mirus (Christendom Publications), William H. Marshner (Theology, Christendom College) and Charles E. Rice (Notre Dame Law School). *Common Faith* seeks to reach all Catholics of good will with fast-paced, tart news commentaries featuring family, educational, political and Church problems; careful apologetical reflections on the faith by the editors; Fr. Robert J. Fox's column offering spiritual counsel; a saint's life in each issue; guest features on vital aspects of Catholicism. Title taken from Romans 1:12. *Price: $10 per year; $25 subscription aids press.*

Faith & Reason: quarterly academic journal edited by J.A. Mirus, Ph.D. and RV. Young, Ph.D. (N.C. State University). Features 352 pages each year including: articles by Catholic scholars in fields such as theology, philosophy, politics, literature, history and philosophy of science; reviews of significant books of Catholic interest. Assists in developing informed faith. *Price: $15 per year; $30 subscription aids press.*

CROSSROADS BOOKS:

Annulment or Divorce?, by William H. Marshner: a ringing defense of matrimony, attack on current tribunal practice and critique of the proposed revisions of canon law. Treats theological and legal aspects of the problem of easy annulment. *96 pp., 1978, paper, $2.95.*

Call of Heaven: Bro. Gino, Stigmatist, by Rev. Robert J. Fox. The biography of a living stigmatist, Bro. Gino Burresi, O.V.M., of San Vittorino, who bears the wounds of Christ and suffers the Passion each Holy Week. Bro. Gino's charisms are presented as signs of God's call to men, making this a rare, inspirational book. *216 pp., 1982, paper, $3.45.*

1917: Red Banners, White Mantle, by Warren H. Carroll. This dramatic account of the year 1917 weaves revolution in Russia together with the apparitions at Fatima. It is a story both natural and supernatural: malignant Lenin vs. innocent Charles of Austria; diabolical Rasputin vs. Our Lady. *168 pp., 1981, paper, $4.95.*

CHRISTENDOM COLLEGE PRESS:

Bioethics and the Limits of Science, by Sean O'Reilly, M.D. A masterful treatment of the ultimate scientific, philosophical and theological issues underlying such current bioethical horrors as abortion and euthanasia. A special appendix on *in vitro* fertilization offers a paradigm for bioethical decisions. Author is post graduate neurobiology research training director at George Washington University Medical School. *176 pp., 1980, paper, $5.95.*

The Consciousness of Christ, by Rev. William G. Most. One of the few orthodox scripture scholars of our day proves from Scripture, the Fathers, the Magisterium and speculative theology that Our Lord really did know who He was, even before the Resurrection. Meets an important challenge to Christ's Divinity. A major appendix critiques Biblical form criticism. *232 pp., 1980, paper, $5.95.*

Reasons for Hope, ed. J.A. Mirus; authors W.H. Carroll, K.P. Burns, W.H. Marshner, J.A. Mirus. This book by faculty at Christendom College is a complete work of apologetics for the general reader or undergraduate. Ten chapters defend Catholic teaching on God, the Soul, Revelation, Scripture, Christ, Church, Papacy, Dogma and Doctrine. *204 pp., 1978, paper, $5.95.*

OTHER TITLES:

Newman: A Bibliography of Secondary Studies, by John R. Griffin, professor of humanities at the University of Southern Colorado. 2500 entries. *156 pp., 1980, paper, $12.00.*

The Oxford Movement: A Revision, by John R. Griffin of the University of Southern Colorado. Limited edition, reprinted from a series of four articles in *Faith & Reason*. A fresh look at this Anglican movement. *104 pp., 1980, paper, $2.50.*

Christendom College

Christendom College is a four year, coeducational liberal arts college dedicated to full Catholic truth in higher education. Licensed by the State of Virginia to grant degrees and approved by the Bishop of Arlington, Christendom is located on the banks of the Shenandoah River in the Blue Ridge Mountains. The College emphasizes training for the lay apostolate with a rigorous curriculum in English, History, Political Science, Philosophy, Theology and foreign languages. Mathematics is offered but not required. Required of all students are such courses as Catholic Doctrine, Apologetics, New Testament, Metaphysics and Social Teachings of the Church. The College was founded in 1977 by Dr. Warren H. Carroll. Donations to Christendom College are tax deductible. Information is available from Christendom College, Route 3, Box 87, Front Royal, Virginia 22630.

Christendom Educational Corporation

Christendom Educational Corporation is a non-profit tax exempt organization dedicated to the promotion of Catholic values as taught by Jesus Christ and preserved by the Roman Catholic Church under the magisterium of the Papacy. It provides a unique funding program for its twin apostolates, Christendom College and Christendom Publications, by allowing a broad range of orthodox Catholics to participate as members in the Corporation.

Membership in Christendom can be obtained by donating or investing $1000 or more. Investments are in interest bearing promissory notes which are redeemable on demand at competitive rates. The Corporate holdings are used as backing for capital investments which protect the membership fund, chiefly buldings for the expansion of Christendom College. Persons interested in membership should write to Christendom Educational Corporation, Rt. 3, Box 87, Front Royal, VA 22630.